D1098647

Judith Samson,
Jason Byars,
Dallas Releford

SAMS
Teach Yourself
Red Hat® Linux®
in 24 Hours

SAMS

201 West ... *RTC Limerick* ... *A*

3 9002 00038819 0

Sams Teach Yourself Red Hat Linux in 24 Hours

Copyright © 2001 by Sams Publishing

International Standard Book Number:0-672-31845-8

Library of Congress Catalog Card Number: 99-066705

Printed in the United States of America

First Printing: December 2000

03   02   01   00   4   3   2   1

Trademarks

All terms mentioned in this book that are known to be trademarks or service marks have been appropriately capitalized. Sams Publishing cannot attest to the accuracy of this information. Use of a term in this book should not be regarded as affecting the validity of any trademark or service mark.

Red Hat is a registered trademark of Red Hat, Inc. Linux is a registered trademark of Linus Torvalds.

Warning and Disclaimer

Every effort has been made to make this book as complete and as accurate as possible, but no warranty or fitness is implied. The information provided is on an "as is" basis. The authors and the publisher shall have neither liability nor responsibility to any person or entity with respect to any loss or damages arising from the information contained in this book or from the use of the CDs or programs accompanying them.

ACQUISITIONS EDITORS
Betsy Brown
Laura N. Williams

DEVELOPMENT EDITOR
Laura N. Williams

MANAGING EDITOR
Charlotte Clapp

PROJECT EDITOR
Carol Bowers

COPY EDITORS
Kim Cofer
Barbara Hacha

INDEXER
Erika Millen

PROOFREADER
Daniel Ponder

TECHNICAL EDITORS
Jason Byars
Dallas Releford

TEAM COORDINATOR
Amy Patton

MEDIA DEVELOPER
Dan Scherf

INTERIOR DESIGNER
Gary Adair

COVER DESIGNER
Aren Howell

PRODUCTION
Gloria Schurick

Contents at a Glance

Contents

About the Authors

Judith Samson is a writer and graduate student in math and computer science at Eastern Michigan University. She has written three books and numerous articles on Linux, and contributes to the GNOME Project. She is the author *of Sams Teach Yourself GNOME in 24 Hours* and *Sams Teach Yourself WordPerfect Office 2000 for Linux in 24 Hours.*

Jason Byars (`mailto:darth@purdue.edu`) is a graduate student at Purdue University. He has a Bachelor of Science degree in computer engineering and enjoys both the hardware and software aspects of the field. His interests draw him to robotics, 3D graphics, software development, and IT work. He has been a fan of Linux since going to Purdue in the fall of 1996.

Dallas Releford has worked as a writer, technical editor, reviewer, consultant, and just about everything else in the publishing field. At present, he has worked on more than 60 books on computers for such companies as Macmillan, Sybex, and many smaller companies. He has published more than 30 full-length articles on everything from computers to how to set up a solar-powered house suitable for the year 2000.

Dedication

To Mom and Dad—Judith Samson

Acknowledgments

Thanks to Dallas and Jason for contributing their expertise and talents to this book. I definitely couldn't have done anything without you! Thanks to my agent, Christian Crumlish, for all your support and encouragement. Thanks to Betsy Brown, acquisitions editor, for putting up with me and keeping me honest, and to Laura Williams, development editor, for all your great work and for giving me this opportunity. Thanks also to Amy Patton, Carol Bowers, Kim Cofer, and Barbara Hacha. Finally, thanks to Bram Moolenaar, Jack Wallen, and John Fleck for your advice and help, and to Alain, for everything.

   —Judith Samson

I would like to thank everyone at Macmillan for helping me through this project. Shelley and Heather, thank you for giving me the opportunity. Laura and Betsy, thank you for being so patient and supportive during this hectic semester. Dallas, thank you for double-checking all the little details that bothered me. Finally, I would like to thank my friends and my parents for their support and their efforts to keep me sane while working on this book.

   —Jason Byars

I would like to extend my everlasting gratitude to Betsy Brown and Laura Williams, the development editor at Macmillan who worked with me during this time. Thanks also to Carol Bowers, Kim Cofer, and Barbara Hacha. I also would like to thank my coauthors Judith Samson and Jason Byars. My special thanks to Jason for his assistance and help. Of course, I would like to extend my thanks to all those people who work behind the scenes to make this book and all other books possible. Without them, writers wouldn't get very far.

I should also thank my next door neighbor, Ron Baker, who did most of the work on my new office while I was buried in getting my work on the book completed. And last of all, but not least, I want to thank my wonderful wife Sharon, who really made this possible because she did all the work that I would normally do.

   —Dallas Releford

Tell Us What You Think!

As the reader of this book, *you* are our most important critic and commentator. We value your opinion and want to know what we're doing right, what we could do better, what areas you'd like to see us publish in, and any other words of wisdom you're willing to pass our way.

You can email or write me directly to let me know what you did or didn't like about this book—as well as what we can do to make our books stronger.

Please note that I cannot help you with technical problems related to the topic of this book, and that due to the high volume of mail I receive, I might not be able to reply to every message.

When you write, please be sure to include this book's title and author as well as your name and phone or fax number. I will carefully review your comments and share them with the author and editors who worked on the book.

Email: `webdev_sams@mcp.com`

Mail: Mark Taber
Associate Publisher
Sams Publishing
201 West 103rd Street
Indianapolis, IN 46290 USA

Introduction

Welcome to the wild world of Linux! Linux is a UNIX-like operating system that can be run on many different kinds of computer platforms, most often on personal computers that contain an Intel processor. Linux is also a true creation of the Internet—a vast project involving thousands of volunteers who communicate via email, Internet Relay Chat, and Usenet newsgroups. Linux is a community of people who care passionately about the art and craft of creating well-written and useful software programs. It is also a community of people who care passionately about the freedom to share their creations freely with everyone. Linux is also a lot of fun, as well as being an ideal tool for learning about how computers work and how to make computers do wonderful things.

We hope that as you read this book you get as excited about Linux as we are, and that you have as much fun reading this book as we have had writing it.

Why Teach Yourself Linux?

Linux offers a true alternative to the monopolistic hold that Microsoft has had on personal computing for the past ten or so years. If you are tired of being forced into using rigid, poorly designed, overpriced and unstable, bloated software, consider Linux as a low-cost and superior alternative.

The bywords of Linux are freedom and adaptability. You can do anything you want with Linux. You can change it any way you want, you can adapt it to almost any kind of hardware, and you can make it work easily with your other operating systems. Linux was designed to be used in a network environment and to have multiple users, but you can also use it by itself as the only user. It is as simple or as complex as you need it to be.

Should You Read this Book?

If you have no experience with Linux or any other flavor of UNIX, this book is for you. However, this book is not designed to give you just general, diluted ideas, nor are the topics dumbed-down to the point where you learn almost nothing about a lot of subjects. We have carefully chosen the topics that we feel are most important for a beginner to know, and we go into quite a lot of detailed explanation. Our aim is to teach you a few things very thoroughly, and to provide you with as many references as possible to continue your study of Linux.

If you want to learn Linux painlessly and relatively quickly, but you want more than just a brief glimpse, this book is for you.

What You'll Learn in 24 Hours

At the beginning, this book delves right into the operating system. We assume no prior knowledge, but we also don't skimp on the details of how and why things work. You will learn how an operating system interacts with the hardware of your computer to make a working system that enables you to do useful things. We'll talk about what exactly is going on when you boot your Linux system, how the whole system of files and directories is organized, and how to communicate via commands.

You will learn how to feel comfortable entering text commands on the command line, and how to use graphical desktop environments to point and click, just like in Windows or Macintosh. You will learn how to perform the most important administration tasks, how to keep your system secure, and how to use scripts to automate boring, repetitive tasks.

We'll discuss how to use Linux on the Internet, useful applications to get work done, and of course, how to have fun with games and other amusements.

You will also learn where to go to expand your knowledge, get help, learn about more advanced topics like programming and advanced system administration, and get more applications.

By the end of this book, you will have a thorough introduction to the most important aspects of running a Linux system. You will feel comfortable with performing, or learning how to perform, any task. You will also understand how things work and why Linux works the way it does.

Helpful Learning Tools

Included in the discussions for each hour are additional elements that provide you with more information on how to work with the Linux operating system. These elements are designed to offer extra knowledge without encumbering your progress.

Find Additional Information

Notes are used to clarify a topic or to provide additional information that might be of use to you. Notes aren't necessary to the discussion; they're just tidbits of information that you might find interesting.

Work More Efficiently

> Tips tell you about shorter, more efficient methods you can use to accomplish a task. Tips are designed to help you make your job easier and give hints to solutions that might work for you.

Avoid Potential Problems

> Cautions point out potential problem areas with the Linux operating system. You'll want to step carefully when you see the Caution icon to avoid performing actions or making decisions that could cause adverse consequences. You don't want to hurt your system.

Practice Your Skills

Tasks lead you on a step-by-step tour of the information covered in each hour. By following along with the tasks, you can practice real-world implementations of concepts, commands, programs, and scripts.

Special Fonts

Many elements are presented in a font that is different from the rest of the text. Here's what they mean and how to treat them:

- Words that appear in *italics* are technical terms that are explained the first time they are used in the book.
- The commands, utility programs, lines of code, statements, and script names are displayed in a plain `monospace` font. In other words, any terms used as code or are used in the process of creating or using code uses this special font. You'll also find that any featured Web sites appear in the plain monospace font.
- Any input that you need to type to perform the tasks described or to follow along with the lessons appears in a **`bold monospace`** font.
- The `italic monospace` font designates placeholders in a command. Placeholders must be replaced by an actual filename or command option.

Chapter Wrap Up

After reading a chapter, you might have a few questions, need help clarifying tasks, or want to learn more about a topic. A Q&A section provides a list of frequently asked questions about the topics covered during the hour. It answers specific questions and helps you review the material presented in the chapter. The "Workshop" section contains a quiz that tests your knowledge of the subject matter and exercises that help you practice what you've learned. You might even find that you learn new things by working the exercises.

We hope that you enjoy yourself as you explore the Linux operating system while working through these 24 hours, and that you find the information covered in each hour to be valuable. We also hope that you continue to learn, and that you find using Linux as fun and rewarding as we do.

PART I

Installing and Learning About Your System

Hour

HOUR 1

Getting Started with Red Hat Linux 7.0

There are probably few computer-using people left in the world who have not heard of Linux. Articles about Linux appear almost daily in the newspaper, as well as on the Internet, TV, and radio. Although Linux has been getting quite a lot of publicity for the past two years, many of the fundamental ideas behind Linux are not mentioned in the mainstream media. Before we get our hands dirty in Hour 2, "Installing Red Hat Linux 7.0," we will try to introduce some of the most important concepts behind Red Hat Linux. If you have heard of Linux but have not seen or used it before, this chapter is particularly for you.

In this hour you will

- Learn what an operating system does
- Discover what makes Linux special, and how it was created and continues to be developed and maintained
- Learn about the history of Red Hat, and how Red Hat fits into the Linux community

What Is an Operating System?

Because Windows has been the overwhelmingly dominant OS for personal computers, many ordinary home computer users never think of the operating system. When you have the choice between Linux and Windows, or if you use both Linux and Windows on the same computer, the operating system becomes less transparent. To help you understand the difference between Linux, Windows, Macintosh, and other operating systems, it is worth a quick look at exactly what an operating system does and how it works with the hardware of your computer.

A computer consists of three main parts: the processor, or CPU, the memory, and the input/output devices that get data into and out of the computer. The processor gives instructions to all the other parts of the computer so that it can do useful work. The memory stores the instructions along with relevant data. The input/output devices, including the keyboard, mouse, monitor, and disk drives, are used to send instructions and data to the memory so that the processor can carry out the instructions on the data.

The operating system coordinates and oversees all the hardware devices on your computer so that you can run programs to do useful work. As a simple example, when you copy a file from the hard disk to a floppy disk, the operating system locates the file on the hard drive, keeps track of the filename, size, and creation date, locates a free place on the floppy, and then correctly names the new file on the floppy disk.

The operating system also contains a filesystem for storing and accessing files, user interfaces so the user can interact with the operating system, and a collection of special programs, such as the cp (copy) program, that make it possible to perform basic tasks, such as copying a file.

Different operating systems contain different programs and different ways to communicate with the processor, memory, and input/output devices. As you can see, the operating system is fundamental. Without it, your computer would just be a collection of plastic and metal parts. So how is Linux different from Windows or other operating systems? The rest of this book indirectly answers this question, but following are some basic facts that should help give you a preliminary idea:

- Linux can run on many different platforms, including Intel, Alpha, Sparc, PPC, and some others.
- Linux is free software, distributed under the GNU General Public License (GPL), which guarantees that Linux users will always enjoy the basic freedoms that we will discuss later in the chapter.
- You can easily obtain the source code for Linux without restriction or cost and study it, customize it, or improve it in any way you want. This makes Linux arguably the most flexible and fastest-improving operating system in existence.

1

- The development of Linux continues to be dominated by people who have no commercial interest in Linux, but who do it out of sheer love. This means that many of the applications and tools are carefully designed and crafted works of art. Linux has a large, worldwide community of passionately dedicated users, developers, testers, and documentors who are linked by email, IRC, friendship, and a fundamental commitment to making Linux the best and freest operating system and collection of applications on the planet.

The Free Software and Open Source Movements

Why does Linux have these attributes that proprietary software does not? How can something so inexpensive (some Linux distributions cost under $30) be any good? To understand the Linux phenomenon, we must delve a little into the history of two parallel and often complementary movements in the programming world: the Free Software Foundation and the Open Source movement.

 For Richard Stallman's history of the GNU Project, including his reasons for starting the project, go to http://www.gnu.org/gnu/thegnuproject.html.

Much of Linux came into existence because of a desire for free software. It is worth looking at exactly what the term "free software" means. The GNU Project's definition of free software is fourfold:

- The freedom to use the program for any purpose that you want
- The freedom to examine and study the source code of the program and to change it to suit your needs
- The freedom to distribute as many copies of the program as you want, to whomever you want
- The freedom to make improvements to the program, and to make those improvements public

Free software does not necessarily mean software that doesn't cost anything, a point that Stallman frequently emphasizes. The fundamental argument of the GNU Project and the Free Software Foundation is that software should be freely available to anybody who wants it, and that users of the software should be completely free to use, study, modify, and give away the software without restriction. The GNU General Public License is a copyright that ensures the preceding freedoms for all GNU software. This copyright is referred to as "copyleft," since its aim is to free use of the software, rather than restrict it.

Free software differs in a fundamental way from open source software, although the terms are often used interchangeably. Open source was a term that was coined when it became apparent in the free software world that there was business interest in the software that was being developed in open communities, and that open source could be a winning business model. The open source community is much more practical in its stance on free software. The philosophy isn't nearly as important as the usefulness and developmental superiority of the open-source development model.

Eric Raymond wrote a series of essays on the open-source model, which he eventually published as a book, titled *The Cathedral and the Bazaar*, O'Reilly, October 1999. You can read the essays online at http://tuxedo.org/~esr/writings/cathedral-bazaar.

You may notice that this book, although about free software, is not copylefted itself. There is quite a lot of disagreement in the publishing and software worlds about how to copyright documentation. See Richard Stallman's essay at http://www.fsf.org/philosophy/free-doc.html and Tim O'Reilly's response at http://www.oreilly.com/ask_tim/orabooks_os.html for differing opinions on how computer documentation and publications should be copyrighted.

A Brief History of Red Hat

Red Hat was founded in 1994, three years after Linus Torvalds posted his first kernel code to the Usenet. Red Hat Linux is quickly emerging as the dominant Linux distribution for individual and enterprise users. Red Hat also holds a special place in the free software community because of the company's commitment to the philosophy of free software and the value it places on the people who develop it.

Red Hat provides support to many free software projects, including hiring developers full-time to work on projects. Red Hat has repeatedly pledged that only free software will ever be part of a Red Hat Linux distribution. Red Hat also holds 68% of the U.S. Linux market share (according to International Data Corp. (IDC) research), demonstrating that the values of the free software movement and financial success are not incompatible.

1

Red Hat licenses all of its software under the GNU General Public License (GPL) and other similar licenses, which means that the entire distribution is available to the open source/free software community. Most of the packages in Red Hat 7.0 are "copylefted" with the GNU GPL and the GNU Lesser General Public License (LGPL). These licenses are a way of copyrighting that guarantees that Red Hat 7.0 will always be freely distributable. Not only Red Hat 7.0 is copylefted, but any software that is made using Red Hat tools or based on Red Hat software is also freely distributable—in fact, it *must* be freely distributable, or the copyright is infringed upon.

What Is a Linux Distribution?

You have probably seen that there are several *distributions* of Linux available, such as Red Hat, Mandrake, Caldera, Corel, SuSE, Debian, and Slackware. A Linux distribution is the Linux kernel, combined with all the utilities, commands, applications, environments, and other programs that are included in an operating system. Different distributions are geared toward different users or different kinds of computer hardware. Some distributions, such as Corel and Mandrake, are geared toward beginners who prefer ease of use over configurability and control. Other distributions, such as SuSE and Slackware, are favored by advanced users and experts for their maximum flexibility and challenge. Debian is a popular distribution with those who insist on purely free software for philosophical reasons. Red Hat has the advantage of providing both maximum flexibility and configurability with ease of installation and use.

You can get a Linux distribution by downloading it off the Web, with the CD-ROM that comes with this book, or by buying a shrink-wrapped software boxed set. You can also buy a computer system that has Linux preinstalled on it from companies such as Dell, Gateway, and IBM. Most importantly, you can get a Linux distribution from a friend, or you can copy your CD-ROM and give it to all your friends.

Visit http://www.redhat.com, http://www.linuxmall.com, and http://www.cheapbytes.com for Red Hat and other Linux software.

Although Linux itself is copylefted, not all applications that are included with some distributions are copylefted. Be careful that you understand any licensing restrictions that may apply to different packages.

Once you install a distribution, you aren't limited to the programs you find on the CD-ROM. You can download individual packages from the Web, install individual packages from the CD-ROMs of other distributions, or compile and install the source code for Linux programs that you get from friends. After you become more familiar with Linux, you can even tinker with the source code on your computer to customize your programs to do anything you want them to do. In short, don't think of your distribution as the final version of your Linux system, but as a jumping-off point. After you've installed your distribution, the universe is the limit...

Summary

In this hour, you learned the basics of how the operating system and your hardware work together to create a usable computing system. You learned about some of the advantages of using Linux, including how the General Public License makes free software free. You also learned about Red Hat and other Linux distributions.

Workshop

The Workshop contains quiz questions and exercises to help reinforce what you've learned in this hour.

Q&A

Q Is it possible to download Red Hat Linux without paying for it?

A Absolutely. You can download Red Hat Linux 7.0 from the Red Hat Web site at `http://www.redhat.com`. In fact, even if you install Red Hat Linux 7.0 from the CD-ROMs that come with this book, you should periodically check the Red Hat Web site for patches, updates, and new software.

Q Must applications that are created with copylefted software tools also be free software?

A No. There is a growing number of applications that have proprietary licenses attached, even though they were developed specifically for Linux. An example is Corel's WordPerfect Office 2000 for Linux. This isn't necessarily bad, as some people would argue that such applications draw more attention and resources to Linux, although Richard Stallman probably would not agree with this notion.

1

Quiz

1. Name the three main parts of any computer.
2. True/False: You can obtain a copy of the Linux source code if you send $50 to Linus Torvalds.
3. What does "GNU" stand for?
4. True/False: UNIX was invented at Red Hat in 1990.
5. What are the differences between the different Linux distributions?

Quiz Answers

1. Name the three main parts of any computer.

   Processor, memory, input/output devices.

2. True/False: You can obtain a copy of the Linux source code if you send $50 to Linus Torvalds.

   False. You can download the source code for Linux from the Web for free. It is also usually included in Linux distributions on a separate CD-ROM.

3. What does "GNU" stand for?

   GNU's Not UNIX

4. True/False: UNIX was invented at Red Hat in 1990.

   False. Dennis Ritchie and Ken Thompson invented Unix in the 1970s.

5. What are the differences between the different Linux distributions?

   There are differences in applications that are included, installation tools and other utilities, but the basic Linux operating system is the same.

Exercises

1. Visit the GNU Web site at http://www.gnu.org. How are the four software freedoms numbered?
2. Visit the Red Hat Web site at http://www.redhat.com.

Exercise Answers

1. Visit the GNU Web site at http://www.gnu.org. How are the four software freedoms numbered?

   Number 0 through 3.

2. Visit the Red Hat Web site at http://www.redhat.com.

   No answer.

HOUR 2

Installing Red Hat Linux 7.0

Installing Linux used to be one of the greatest challenges a new Linux user would face. Most steps had to be done manually, and there was a lot to learn before you could even begin installing. There were few scripts to help you edit files, and there were no graphical installation programs; everything was text-based. With the release of Red Hat 6.0, installation became *much* easier, with autodetect utilities that detected much of your hardware for you, and online help at every screen. Red Hat 7.0 makes installation even easier, with a smoother installation interface, more probe utilities, and automatic sound configuration. Even with all these improvements, there is a bit more to do than to insert the CD and click Next. A lot of concepts are introduced in this hour with just enough information to get you through the installation. Don't worry if you feel a bit confused (or a lot confused). The aim of this hour is to get a working Linux system up and going. You will understand more as you continue through the book. The Red Hat installation process is virtually the same as for any other Linux distribution. Some of the steps require you to enter information, and other steps are automatic (unless you perform an expert installation).

In this hour you will

- Plan the installation and gather the necessary information about your hardware
- Partition the hard drive
- Configure a boot loader
- Create root password and user accounts
- Install Red Hat software packages
- Configure X (the graphical windowing system for Linux)

Getting More Information

Red Hat comes with excellent documentation for installing and using Red Hat Linux. In most cases the information in this hour should be sufficient to get you through the installation, but it does not go into very great detail. If you run into any problems or if you want more background information, be sure to read the Red Hat installation and reference guides. The Red Hat documentation is available in HTML format in the /doc directory on the CD-ROM. If you prefer printed versions of the manuals, you can order them from Red Hat. See http://www.redhat.com for information.

Other documents are available at the Linux Documentation Project Web site at http://www.linuxdoc.org. The *Installation and Getting Started Guide* and the Installation HOWTO are particularly useful.

Red Hat Linux 7.0 Hardware Support

Unlike Windows or Macintosh, you have to get to know your hardware quite intimately before installing Linux.

> Linux 2.4, which will be the next major release of the Linux kernel, will natively support Plug and Play. This support will make a Linux installation almost as easy as a Windows installation.

The first step is to ensure that Red Hat Linux 7.0 supports your hardware. Unless your hardware is more than two years old or your computer is custom-built, it will most likely be supported. To be sure, visit http://www.redhat.com/hardware for a list of supported hardware.

Red Hat Linux has several utilities that automatically choose the right drivers for your hardware, but it is still a good idea to have information about your hardware prepared. That way, if your hardware can't be probed you'll be ready. You can also be confident that the probe detected your hardware correctly. Table 2.1 lists the basic information you should gather about your hardware before you start the installation. If you don't understand some of the items, read on and then come back to the table.

If you already have Windows installed on the computer, you should be able to gather most of this information from the System Properties. Click Control Panel, System, Device Manager for a list of all your hardware information. You can also gather invaluable information from your hardware manuals. If you don't have printed manuals for your hardware, visit the manufacturer's Web site. Most hardware manufacturers have their manuals online. Some may even have FAQs or other information about running their products on Linux. If all else fails, try the installation program to see if it autodetects your hardware. If things seem to work, you will probably be okay.

TABLE 2.1 Hardware Information You Should Have Before Installing

Hardware	Information
Hard disk drive type	IDE/EIDE or SCSI
SCSI Controller (if applicable)	Make and Model
Hard disk	Size
Other OS Partitions	Number and Size
Linux Partition(s)	Size Available/Size to Make
Mouse	Manufacturer
Mouse	Type: Serial or PS/2
Serial Mouse	Serial port number (COM1, COM2, and so on)
CD-ROM	IDE/ATAPI or SCSI or Other
Video Card	Make and Model
Video Card	Amount of RAM
Monitor	Make and Model
Monitor	Horizontal Scan and Vertical Scan rate
Modem	Manufacturer and Model
Network Card (NIC)	Manufacturer and Model
Sound Card	Manufacturer and Model
Printer	Manufacturer and Model

Some MMX/ATX "integrated" motherboards have components that are not
supported by Linux. Because the components are integrated into the board,
you can't just swap out the component for one that is supported. If you
have an integrated motherboard and are having problems getting sound or
X to work, contact the manufacturer of the motherboard to see if there is a
Linux driver available. Also, you can conduct a Web or newsgroup search to
see if someone in the Linux community might have written a driver.

If you have a SCSI hard drive, the install script probes for a SCSI controller. If the SCSI
controller is hardwired into the motherboard, the probe might display a different model
number than that of your controller. If the installation continues to run, then the driver
should be okay. Check your motherboard and controller documentation to be sure.

Your CD-ROM will be autodetected if it's an IDE/ATAPI. If it is a SCSI, the probe
should be able to find the right SCSI driver. If you have an older CD-ROM that's
attached to a sound card, you might need to enter the make and model.

Creating Space for Linux

After you have collected information about your hardware, the next step is to make sure
that you have enough space on your hard drive for Linux. To install all the packages for
everything covered in this book, you need about 700MB of space. To install everything
on the CD-ROMs you need at least 1.7GB of space. You will also need extra space for
your files and any other applications you install later.

If you don't have enough space on your hard drive, one solution is to add another hard
drive to your computer. Adding another hard drive to your computer also makes creating
a dual-boot computer (a computer that runs two different operating systems) much easier.

If you can't add another hard drive, but you have sufficient free space on your current
hard drive, you can repartition your current hard drive to hold both Linux and another
operating system such as Windows.

A *partition* is a section of the hard disk drive that is used for an operating system. With
Windows, you usually have just one partition, or perhaps a couple of logical partitions. If
you want to use Windows and Linux on the same computer, you must partition the hard
drive so that Windows can use one part and Linux can use another part. Partitioning is
like dividing the hard drive into parts, so that each part can be used for different purposes.

If you must repartition and you are currently running Windows, you have two options.
You can back up your entire system, repartition the hard drive to make room for Linux,

and then reinstall Windows. Alternatively, you can use a repartitioning utility such as FIPS to repartition the hard drive without destroying any of the data that is currently on it.

FIPS is provided on the first Red Hat CD-ROM in the dosutils folder. If you use FIPS to repartition your hard drive, *back up all your important data before you use it*. Also, read all the documentation that comes with FIPS, and read the section on FIPS in the Red Hat Reference Guide.

> Be sure to run ScanDisk and Disk Defragmenter in Windows before running FIPS. Although it can take a long time and you might be tempted to skip it, please DO NOT skip the Disk Defragmenter step! Disk Defragmenter makes sure that the used space on your hard disk is as compact as possible, so that space is allocated efficiently. If you try to create a Linux partition on a disk that has not been defragmented, you might find yourself with a very small Linux partition, or you might inadvertently destroy Windows files that were written to the end of the hard disk space.

Preparing to Install

If you already have another operating system installed or files from an earlier version of Linux that you want to keep, the first step is to back up all your important files somewhere other than your hard drive. If you don't have a tape drive or FTP site, simply back up to a floppy or zip drive. In most cases, you can safely repartition your hard drive or upgrade your Linux distribution without losing files, but if you have files that you don't want to risk losing, don't take the chance.

Make sure that your BIOS is set to boot from a floppy disk or CD-ROM before the hard drive boots (this is normally the case). If your computer can boot from CD-ROM, then you should be able to just insert the first Red Hat 7.0 installation CD-ROM and reboot your computer to start the installation. If your computer will not boot from CD-ROM (if your computer is older than 1997 it might not have this capability), then you must boot from a boot disk. If you do not have a boot disk, you can make one from the boot image file that is on CD-ROM number 1.

If you're not sure how your computer boots, check your BIOS. You can check your BIOS by pressing a certain key right after your computer starts up (usually F2, F4, or Delete). Check your computer manual for instructions on how to open the BIOS and change the boot sequence. Usually, there will be instructions on the screen on how to enter the BIOS (it might also be called "Setup" or something similar). In the boot sequence, ensure that the floppy drive is listed first, then the CD-ROM, then the hard drive. (If you have a SCSI computer, the sequence choices might be different; check your BIOS manual.) Insert the first Red Hat installation CD-ROM or the boot disk into the computer, and restart.

It doesn't matter whether you boot from CD-ROM or floppy disk; the installation is exactly the same.

Installing RedHat 7.0: It's Automatic!

After you restart your computer, the Red Hat Welcome screen appears with a list of installation modes.

The Rescue mode is not meant for installation at all, but for recovering a system in an emergency.

Expert mode provides maximum flexibility in configuration. In Expert mode, the installation script does not automatically probe for devices on your computer. Instead, you manually enter the configuration information during the installation. Also, you can enter custom values in Expert mode. We will not cover Expert mode in this book, but for more information, consult the Red Hat reference manual.

The dd mode is for users who want to provide device drivers for their hardware via floppy disk, rather than use the drivers provided on the Red Hat installation CD-ROM.

The text-based installation performs the same procedure as the graphical installation, but it uses a text interface rather than a graphical interface. Press F1 to access help from the text installation. If you can't run the graphical X installation on your display, you can use the text installation. See *Red Hat Linux 7.0: The Official Red Hat Linux Reference Guide* on the third CD-ROM for instructions on installing via text mode.

When you run the default graphical installation, Red Hat configures a generic X configuration file for you, so that you can use a graphical interface before you've actually configured X. Detailed help appears in a pane on the left as you go through the installation steps.

If you're installing Red Hat 7.0 to a laptop, you might have problems with the graphical installation, particularly if your LCD is an XGA. If you don't want to use the text installation, turn off your computer, attach an external monitor to your laptop, restart the computer, and perform the graphical installation. Later, you can alter XF86Config (the X configuration file) to get X to work with your display.

2

To perform the default installation, press Enter at the boot: prompt.

After you press Enter, a miniscule Linux kernel installs from the CD-ROM and detects your hardware. If you booted from a boot floppy, the small Linux system is loaded from the floppy, recognizes the CD-ROM, and continues the installation from CD-ROM.

If you don't enter anything at the boot: prompt, the default graphical installation starts after 30 seconds.

Answering Questions About Your Hardware During Installation

During the first part of the installation you answer some basic questions about your hardware. (Even if you are just upgrading, you must answer the preliminary questions.) If you have all your hardware information ready from the last section, this part is easy.

The first step is to choose a language. If you are running the ordinary graphical installation script, the language you choose to install will also be the default language for the system.

Your Keyboard and Mouse

If your keyboard make is included in the list of keyboards, select your keyboard. Otherwise, select Generic, with the correct number of keys (most English language keyboards are 101 keys). If you want to be able to create characters such as ñ, ç, or Â, check Enable Dead Keys. Select a language layout (U.S. English is the default for an English installation). After you have made your selections, type a string of characters into the test selection field. If the characters appear the way they should, then your keyboard choice should work.

If you choose to enable dead keys, you will have to type certain characters, such as the tilde, semicolon, and quotation marks, twice to make them appear. If you plan to do a lot of programming or word processing, this could become annoying.

Next, select your mouse. If your mouse model does not appear as a choice in the menu, select PS/2 or Serial Generic Mouse, with either three or two buttons. If you have a two-button mouse, be sure to check Emulate 3 Buttons.

Unix mice have three buttons, whereas PC and Macintosh mice usually have only two. When your mouse emulates three buttons, you can click both mouse buttons together to emulate a third button. This can be an invaluable tool, particularly in X.

If you have a serial mouse, enter the serial port location and device name. Serial ports are named differently in Windows than in Linux, so the equivalent Windows name for the serial ports is listed next to the Linux name. For example, COM1 is equivalent to /dev/ttyS0.

After you have finished configuring your basic hardware, the system installation begins. At this point you have changed nothing on your system, but have provided the installation script with information.

Running the System Installer

The first thing the system installer asks you is the kind of installation you want to perform, as shown in Figure 2.1. There are four choices:

- **Workstation Installation.** The Workstation installation deletes all existing Linux partitions and automatically allocates all disk space not being used by another operating system. If you have a partition running another OS, such as Windows, the Workstation installation will not touch it.

- **Server Installation.** The Server installation deletes *all* partitions on the hard drive and automatically sets the partitions for a Linux-only computer.

- **Custom Installation**. For most users, we recommend the Custom installation because it provides the most flexibility within the graphical installation process, without being very difficult to use.

- **Upgrade.** If you already have a Red Hat or Mandrake distribution running on your computer, and you just want to upgrade your packages, you can select Upgrade.

FIGURE 2.1

We recommend the Custom installation, because it enables you to learn more about how your system is set up.

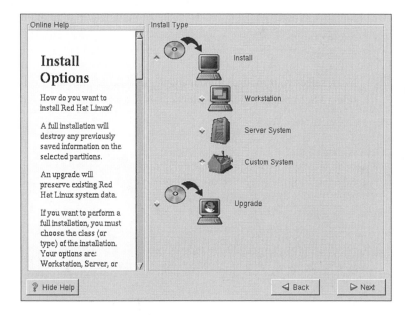

This chapter assumes that you are performing a Custom installation. If you perform a Workstation installation, you can skip much of the material.

We don't recommend the Workstation or Server installation, because you lose control over the size and nature of your partitions. Also, if you're not paying attention, you can inadvertently destroy data and partitions if you select Workstation or Server installation. The Red Hat Installation Guide does not recommend the Custom class installation for new users, but we disagree. Even from the beginning, it is important that you see what is happening on your system, even if you don't understand everything yet. Of course, if you get hopelessly stuck, do select the Workstation installation. At least you will get a working Linux system going.

Partitioning the Hard Drive

Partitioning the hard drive can be a scary experience or it can be a happy experience. The difference is in the preparation. You must have an extra hard drive or a free partition on your hard drive ready before you complete this step.

Red Hat 7.0 comes with two utilities for creating partitions on your hard drive: Disk
Druid and fdisk. Fdisk has more configuration options and is faster for experienced
users, but Disk Druid is sufficient for most users. Disk Druid is graphical, so it is easier
to use. If you use fdisk to create your partitions, you must use Disk Druid to assign
mount points. We will assume that you are using Disk Druid in this chapter. Disk Druid
is shown in Figure 2.2.

FIGURE 2.2

*Disk Druid is easier
than it looks. Be sure
to read the online help
carefully in addition to
this section.*

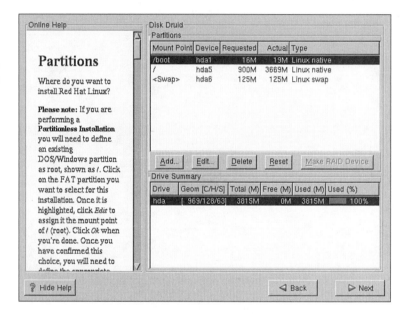

<table>
<tr><td colspan="5">Online Help</td><td colspan="2">Disk Druid</td></tr>
</table>

Partitions

Where do you want to
install Red Hat Linux?

Please note: If you are
performing a
Partitionless Installation
you will need to define
an existing
DOS/Windows partition
as root, shown as /. Click
on the FAT partition you
want to select for this
installation. Once it is
highlighted, click *Edit* to
assign it the mount point
of / (root). Click *Ok* when
you're done. Once you
have confirmed this
choice, you will need to

Mount Point	Device	Requested	Actual	Type
/boot	hda1	16M	19M	Linux native
/	hda5	900M	3669M	Linux native
<Swap>	hda6	125M	125M	Linux swap

Add... | Edit... | Delete | Reset | Make RAID Device

Drive Summary

Drive	Geom [C/H/S]	Total (M)	Free (M)	Used (M)	Used (%)
hda	969/128/63	3815M	0M	3815M	100%

? Hide Help   ◁ Back   ▷ Next

> If you try to resize your Windows partition using Disk Druid or fdisk, you will
> no longer be able to access the data on the Windows partition. You must
> use FIPS or another resizing utility to create an empty partition before con-
> tinuing.

Disk Druid displays all the current partitions on all your hard drives, including those of
any other operating systems. In Windows, each partition or hard drive in your computer
is given a letter name, such as C: or D:. Linux has a different naming scheme for partitions and drives. In Linux, each hard drive is named by letter, such as /dev/hda,
/dev/hdb, /dev/hdc, and so on. /dev/hda is the equivalent of C: in Windows/DOS.

When you partition a hard drive, each partition is given a number. For example, if you
have a hard drive divided into one Windows partition and four Linux partitions, the partitions might be named like this:

/dev/hda1	Windows
/dev/hda5	/boot
/dev/hda6	/
/dev/hda7	/swap
/dev/hda8	/home

> If you have SCSI hard drives, the naming scheme is slightly different: /dev/sda, /dev/sdb, and so on.

Notice that hda2 through hda4 are missing. Disk numbers hda1 through hda4 (or sda1 through sda4) are reserved for primary partitions. In the preceding example there are five partitions, so Disk Druid created an extended partition to hold the logical partitions hda5 through hda8. If you specify more than four partitions on a hard drive, Disk Druid will automatically create an extended partition for you and put logical partitions in it. You won't see the extended partition unless you look at your partition information using fdisk, but it's there.

Now that you understand a little more about partitions, you can use Disk Druid to create your Linux partitions. Each of your hard drives are listed in the Disk Druid drive summary, with a percentage of space already used in the Used (%) column. This tells you how much space you have to create your Linux partitions.

Creating the Linux Partitions

As you will learn in Hour 3, "Linux Basics," and Hour 4, "Exploring the Red Hat Linux Filesystem," a Linux system contains a standard directory structure in which the same kinds of files are stored. There are several major directories, including /, (the root filesystem), /etc, /boot, /home, /usr, and so on. If you click on Mount Point in Disk Druid, you will see a drop-down menu of each of the basic filesystems in Linux. You can create a separate partition for each of these filesystems, or you can create one partition for the root filesystem, and the other directories will reside on the root partition.

Without getting into too much detail, it is generally not a good idea to put your entire Linux system into one root partition. It makes it more difficult to install a new system later (in later chapters we will discuss re-installing versus upgrading). Also, if something goes wrong with one of the partitions, it makes it harder to recover data from the other partitions, particularly the home directory. On the other hand, we don't want to get too complicated in our partitions, because there is so much more to learn.

For beginners, a good all-purpose setup consists of four partitions: /boot, /swap, /, and /home. (You could also install a /usr or /usr/local partition if you plan on installing applications in addition to those on the Red Hat CD-ROM.)

/boot should be about 30MB; /swap should be twice the size of your physical memory, and if you plan on running lots of graphical applications, at least 64MB. Divide the remaining space between / and /home. If you include /usr, then /usr should contain the most space because all the applications, libraries, graphics, and so on reside there. If you don't include /usr, then be sure to make / the largest partition. /home contains all the files that users create (/home is somewhat like the Linux counterpart to My Documents in Windows).

Table 2.2 shows a sample partition scheme for dual-boot computer with a 4GB hard drive.

TABLE 2.2   Sample Partition Table

Partition/Mount Point	Name	Size
Win95 FAT32	hda1	2000MB
/boot	hda5	30MB
/swap	hda6	64MB
/	hda7	1200MB
/home	hda8	700MB

To create a partition, select the hard drive in the Drive Summary where the partition should go. Click Add. Select the Mount Point from the drop-down menu. Specify a size in MB. Except for the swap partition, the Partition Type should be Linux Native by default.

> You can create Linux RAID partitions in Disk Druid, but that is beyond the scope of this book. See the Red Hat Reference Guide.

If you make a mistake, click Reset and the partitions will return to their original state. You can experiment with different sizes and continue to click Reset until you click Next.

Formatting the Partitions

After you create the partitions, they must be formatted. By default, the installation program will list only Linux partitions to be formatted, but double-check to make sure. If you have a /home or a /usr/local partition from a previous Linux installation, make sure it is unchecked.

LILO Configuration

After you format the hard drive, the LILO Configuration screen appears. LILO stands for LInux LOader. You can configure LILO to boot all your operating systems at startup, or you can boot Linux with a floppy disk and keep your other boot loader untouched. The LILO Configuration screen is shown in Figure 2.3.

The advantage to using a boot disk instead of LILO is that you don't have to rewrite your Master Boot Record (MBR). Your operating systems partitions will be completely separate, and the original operating system will always automatically boot from the hard drive when you restart your computer. The disadvantage to using a boot disk is that if you lose the disk, you will no longer be able to boot into Linux (we'll cover what to do in such an emergency later in the book).

If you are running Windows 95/98 on another partition, you can safely install LILO in the Master Boot Record. At startup, you will be able to select which operating system to boot. If you are running Windows NT, do not install LILO in the MBR—either do not install LILO at all or install LILO on your Linux /boot partition.

If you are running only Linux, install LILO at the Master Boot Record.

FIGURE 2.3

You can start Linux either with LILO or with a boot disk.

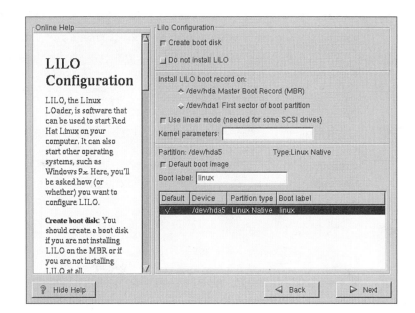

> Regardless of whether you choose to boot Linux with a boot disk or LILO, be sure to check Create Boot Disk. It can be invaluable if something goes wrong with your /boot partition or the Master Boot Record. To learn how to make your own custom boot disk, see the Boot Disk HOWTO at http://www.linuxdocs.org.

If you have kernel parameters that you want to have run whenever you boot into Linux, enter them in the Kernel Parameters field. Most users do not need special kernel parameters.

Finally, if you have a dual-boot system and will use LILO, choose the operating system that should boot by default. For example, if you want Windows to boot by default, highlight the DOS partition and check Default Boot Image. A checkmark will appear by the DOS partition. Follow the same procedure if you want Linux to boot by default. Whichever default you choose, you will be able to boot into the other operating system by selecting dos or linux from the LILO menu when you reboot.

Creating the Root and User Accounts

You must create a root account at the very least. Enter a password for root that is easy for you to remember, but would be difficult for others to figure out. If your computer will be connected to a network (this includes the Internet), selecting a secure root password is particularly important. The most secure password is a random collection of uppercase and lowercase letters and numbers.

Unfortunately, random passwords tend to also be the easiest to forget, so a good compromise is an acronym. For example, a good root password would be mUFloR66. This is an acronym for My Uncle Frank lives on Route 66. *Never* choose a dictionary word or proper name for your password, or you will be asking for a cracker to break into your system.

> Do not forget your root password. It will be extremely difficult, if not impossible, to log in to your system if you forget your root password. Write it down and keep it in a safe place (on paper, not in a file on a computer).

In addition to the root account, you should also create at least one user account to use for everyday work, and you can create as many accounts as you want during installation. As you complete the information for a user account, click Add. The fields are cleared for the next user account. When you have finished adding your user accounts, click Next.

Selecting Security Tools

You can select various security tools on the Authentication configuration screen. For most home users who connect to a network using a dial-up modem, MD5 passwords and shadow passwords are sufficient. For information about security, consult the Red Hat Reference Guide.

After security, select your physical location to set a time zone for your system.

Installing the Software Packages

After you have selected a time zone, the fun part begins—selecting software to include on your new Linux system. To make it easier to install, the packages are organized into groups. If you're not sure whether to select a package group, it's better not to select it. You can always run the Upgrade program or install packages individually later. The Package Group Selection screen is shown in Figure 2.4.

FIGURE 2.4

Package Group Selection saves you from wading through hundreds of individual packages.

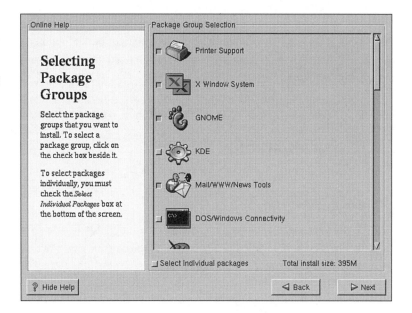

If you have installed Linux before, you can have more control by checking Select Individual Packages.

As you select packages or package groups, the Total Install Size displays how much space the selected packages will take. Make sure that the install size remains smaller than your / (or /usr) partition size.

Be sure to install the GNOME Desktop package group for Hour 7, "Using the GNOME Desktop Environment."

Task: Configuring X

X is the windowed desktop system for UNIX and Linux. Red Hat 7.0 includes XFree86 4.0, which supports just about every monitor and video card.

1. The installation program probes your monitor and video card and selects a driver for you. Verify that the probe was correct.

2. Click the checkbox next to the proper amount of memory for your video card.

3. Test the configuration using the Test button.

4. You would check Graphical Login to start X automatically at boot time. Your X desktop would then always appear immediately after login. We recommend that you do not select the graphical login, because it is important that you learn to feel comfortable with the shell (the command line) before using a graphical interface. Don't worry—you will learn how to configure a graphical login manually later in the book.

5. If the X configuration doesn't work, we will go into great detail on how to configure X in Hour 6, "XFree86—The Linux Window System." If it works—great!

Congratulations!

Congratulations! You have now passed the first major hurdle on the long road to becoming a Linux guru. As you can see, getting Linux installed properly on your computer is a major accomplishment.

If you were unable to install correctly or if the partitioning confused you, try performing the Workstation installation. Throughout this book we encourage you to do a task in a way that will help you to learn the most, rather than the fastest or easiest way (although we'll also teach you the easier way). Still, the most important accomplishment of this chapter is to get a Linux system running, so do whatever it takes to accomplish that.

If you still have problems, skip ahead to Hour 22, "Troubleshooting and Getting Help," for information on where to go for help.

Summary

In this hour you planned your Red Hat Linux 7.0 installation. You gathered information about your hardware, prepared a space on your hard drive for Linux, and selected an installation method. You ran a custom installation of Linux, used Disk Druid to create Linux partitions, configured LILO or a boot disk, created the root and user accounts, installed the Red Hat software packages, and configured the X window system.

Workshop

The Workshop contains quiz questions and exercises to help reinforce what you've learned in this hour.

Q&A

Q My computer won't boot from CD-ROM. How do I make a boot disk?

A Regardless of whether you are using the Red Hat CD-ROM set that comes with this book, you bought Red Hat Linux 7.0 from a third-party vendor, such as CheapBytes, or if you are downloading your installation from the Web, you can make the boot disk the same way. Every Red Hat CD-ROM has a file called a boot image that you can copy to disk using MS-DOS, or another Linux/UNIX-like operating system. See the Red Hat Installation Guide on CD-ROM number 3 in the rh-docs folder for detailed instructions.

Q The instructions in this chapter are for installing from CD-ROM, but I'm installing directly from the Web (or over a network). How much of this chapter is applicable?

A The basics are pretty much the same, regardless of your installation method. See the Red Hat Reference Guide for detailed instructions about each installation method. For a more advanced discussion of installation, an excellent resource is *Linux Unleashed*, by Bill Ball, et al. Sams, 1999.

Quiz

1. Name two ways to create space for a Linux installation.
2. What will happen if you use Disk Druid to resize your Windows partition instead of a resizing utility like FIPS?
3. In what order should your boot order be set in the BIOS before you install Red Hat Linux?
4. Which type of Red Hat installation completely wipes out *all* data on your hard drive before installing? Which type only formats existing Linux partitions?

5. True/False: LILO can boot both Windows 95/98 and Linux operating systems.

6. How many user accounts can you create during installation?

7. What is the minimum number of accounts you should create for a one-user system?

Quiz Answers

1. Name two ways to create space for a Linux installation.

   Add another hard drive or resize the partition on your current hard drive to make room for Linux partitions.

2. What will happen if you use Disk Druid to resize your Windows partition instead of a resizing utility like FIPS?

   You will no longer be able to access your Windows partition, and data could be destroyed.

3. In what order should your boot order be set in the BIOS before you install Red Hat Linux?

   Floppy, CD-ROM, hard drive

4. Which type of Red Hat installation completely wipes out *all* data on your hard drive before installing? Which type only formats existing Linux partitions?

   The Server installation completely formats all hard drives on your computer. The Workstation installation formats only Linux partitions.

5. True/False: LILO can boot both Windows 95/98 and Linux operating systems.

   True. If you have Windows NT, however, you should not install LILO in the Master Boot Record (MBR).

6. How many user accounts can you create during installation?

   You can create as many user accounts as you like.

7. What is the minimum number of accounts you should create for a one-user system?

   Two—the root account and a user account.

Exercises

1. Fill in Table 2.1 for your computer.

2. Create a partitioning plan for your Linux system, including number of partitions and size of each partition.

3. Install Red Hat Linux 7.0 on your computer.

Exercise Answers

1. Fill in Table 2.1 for your computer.

   Answer varies according to the reader.

2. Create a partitioning plan for your Linux system, including number of partitions and size of each partition.

   Answer varies according to the reader.

3. Install Red Hat Linux 7.0 on your computer.

   Answer varies according to the reader.

2

Hour 3

Linux Basics

Now that you've installed Red Hat Linux, you might wonder what to do next. Whether you're the kind of person who learns by jumping right in and starting to play or if you prefer to have some structure when exploring a new subject, after this hour you will have some of the most basic knowledge you need to get around your new Linux system. This chapter assumes no knowledge of Linux, so if you are already familiar with Linux or UNIX, feel free to go on to Hour 4, "Exploring the Red Hat Linux Filesystem."

In this hour you will

- Make a paradigm shift into the Linux way of thinking
- Learn what happens when you start Linux
- Log in to Linux using runlevel 3 or runlevel 5, and learn why you should not log in as root to do ordinary work
- Study the structure of the Unix command and learn some of the most basic Unix commands

- Get help with the man and info pages
- Shut down Linux properly

 Most topics explored this hour pertain to all flavors of Unix-like operating systems, including Linux and BSD. When that is the case we refer to the system as "Unix" (Title case), to encompass all flavors of *nix.

The Paradigm Shift

Many people are scared away from Linux because they think it's difficult to use. Linux is only difficult if you don't understand that with Linux comes power and freedom. You have more power to do things the way *you* want to, and you have more freedom to do tasks in different ways. With power and freedom comes responsibility to learn a little bit more about the reasons why you do things. In the end, a whole universe can open up to you, and using your computer will be a lot more fun and hassle-free than when you were forced to use only Windows.

When you use Linux, you communicate with your computer in a different way from when you use Windows or Macintosh. In Windows, 99% or more of the commands you give and the messages you receive are done via graphical user interface, or GUI. You point on a button with your mouse, click it, and something happens. It is possible to open an MS-DOS prompt and give commands the good old-fashioned way in DOS, but you are strictly limited in what you can accomplish. For almost every task in Windows, you must use the graphical interface.

In Linux, this simply is not the case. There is a graphical user interface in Linux called X, and it looks a lot like Windows. You point your mouse to a button or menu item and click to give a command. An example of X running the GNOME desktop environment is shown in Figure 3.1.

The difference with Linux is that for every task you perform with a mouse within X, *there is a direct and usually more powerful way to do the same task by typing a command on the keyboard*. When you type a command on the keyboard, you are usually in a *shell environment* (or *shell*, for short), and the place where you type the command is called the *command line*. The shell environment is pictured in Figure 3.2.

FIGURE **3.1**

The X interface works on top of the operating system. It is not integrated into the operating system, like the interface is in Windows.

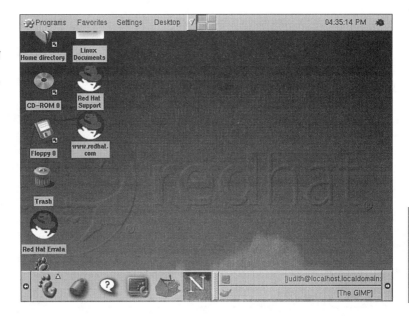

FIGURE **3.2**

Don't be afraid of the shell! It doesn't look as friendly as X, but it's not hard to learn.

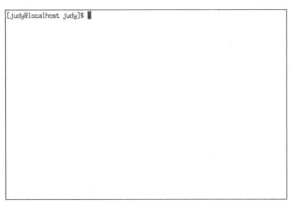

You can use Linux quite successfully without ever using the shell, but it is difficult, if not impossible, to advance beyond basic proficiency if you only use the graphical interface. To explore the true power of Linux, you must know how to use the command line. For this reason, we will start our exploration of Linux in a shell, as if X didn't even exist.

If this prospect makes you a bit nervous, maybe this analogy will help. Imagine that you are carrying on a conversation with a friend, but the only way you can communicate is by holding up little pictures to each other. Your conversation would be quite limited, wouldn't it? Now imagine that you and your friend were having a conversation using spoken language (or sign language!). Think of how much more you can communicate with words than with a limited set of pictures. This analogy is kind of rough, but giving commands to your Linux computer using the command line is much like carrying on a conversation. There are different words you can use to communicate the same command, and there are different options you can attach to your command that mean different things, much like the tone and inflection of your voice communicates different ideas when you say the same word.

Starting Up

When you start Linux, it immediately looks different from when you start Windows. When you start Windows, a picture of a blue sky appears with the Windows logo on it. The logo stays there for a few seconds, and then suddenly the blue sky disappears and the Windows desktop appears. You have no idea what's happening behind that blue sky. For all you know, a little man could be running around collecting bytes and putting them in boxes to start Windows. If the blue sky suddenly disappears and is replaced by the Blue Screen of Death, how do you know what went wrong? How do you fix it? Well, you reboot. What happens if you can't fix the problem? Well, you reinstall Windows. What a frustrating way to use your computer!

When you start Linux, an entirely different thing happens. Words and phrases appear on the screen. Linux tells you exactly what it is doing, and whether the particular process it was loading was successful or not. At first, all those messages might tell you about as much as the Windows picture of the blue sky. Eventually, however, you will be able to understand and use those messages to help you track down and solve problems, or to make your system run faster and more efficiently.

A Quick and Dirty Explanation of the Boot Sequence

When you boot your system in Linux, this is what happens:

Every computer has a chip called the BIOS (for Basic Input and Output). When you turn on your computer, the BIOS wakes up and looks for a program called the boot loader. As you recall from Hour 2, LILO is the Linux boot loader. The boot loader is copied into memory, and then it starts the operating system. The LILO boot loader is special because it can boot not just Linux, but also other operating systems that are installed on your computer.

If you specified that you would start Linux from a boot disk when you installed, then the original (Windows) boot loader is not changed. If your BIOS is set up the way we recommended in Hour 2, it has instructions to look for a boot loader first on floppy, then on CD-ROM, and finally on the hard drive. With a boot disk, the BIOS will load the boot loader from the boot disk into memory, and Linux is started. If no floppy disks or CD-ROMs are found, the normal boot loader on the hard drive is loaded into memory.

After the boot loader is started, it looks for the kernel of the operating system. Once the kernel is found, it is loaded into memory. The kernel's first job is to find all your hardware and to prepare it for use. It then starts the system processes, such as logging, administration services, email, and network services. Finally, the kernel starts the login program (called getty) so that you can log in and use your system.

The entire boot process is logged in the `/var/log/boot.log` file. Just skimming this file can help you get an idea of what happens during startup (also called system initialization).

Logging In

Before you can use Linux, you must enter a user name and password to log in, even if you are the only user. The reason for this is that Linux (like other Unices), is designed to be a multiuser system. Windows/MS-DOS was designed to be a single-user system (except for Windows NT).

A simple analogy to explain the difference between single-user and multiuser systems is the difference between an apartment building and a single-family house. In the house there is usually one front door, and one family lives in the building. In Windows you turn on the computer and start using it, just as to enter a house you unlock the front door and walk inside. In Linux there can be many users, just as in an apartment building there are many people living in the same building. There is a front door that you walk through, but there is also the door to your individual apartment, to which only you have access. The individual apartments are like different user accounts on a Linux system.

There are two ways to start the login screen in Linux. One way, called runlevel 5, starts the X graphical interface automatically when you start up Linux. A graphical login box appears in a window on the screen (just like in Windows NT). When you enter your username and password, the desktop appears, just like in Windows or Macintosh.

When you installed Red Hat 7.0, you were asked if you wanted X to start automatically whenever you booted your computer. If you answered Yes, then your Linux system starts in runlevel 5.

Another way to start Linux is the non-graphical way called runlevel 3. At runlevel 3, when startup is complete, the login: line appears on a blank screen (some distributions display a simple text-based graphic as well). After you enter your user name and password, a new line appears with nothing but your username, the name of your computer, and a $ sign, like this:

```
judith@localhost$
```

Rather than being in a graphical environment, you are in a shell environment. The $ sign is called the shell prompt, or sometimes the command line. There are different shell environments, such as bash, csh, ksh, sh, and zsh, but Red Hat Linux uses bash by default. In fact, most Linux users use bash.

You can start a graphical environment from the command line, but we won't talk about that until Hour 6, "XFree86—The Linux Window System."

For the rest of this hour and for Hours 4 and 5, we will assume that you are in a shell environment. If your Linux system starts at runlevel 5 (in a graphical environment), there are two ways to drop into a shell:

- You can press Ctrl+Alt+F2 (or any other function key, except for F7) to open a virtual terminal.
- You can open an xterm, which is a shell environment within the X environment. To open an xterm, click the computer icon on the panel, as shown in Figure 3.3, or (assuming you're in GNOME), click Main Menu, System, GNOME terminal.

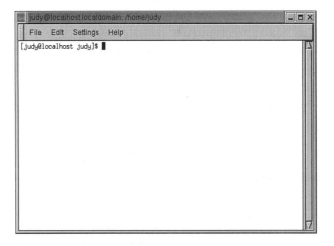

FIGURE 3.3

It would be better not to use X until you've learned the shell, but if you must use X, you can open a virtual shell inside X.

A virtual terminal is one of the niftier tools you can use with Unix. Unix is not only multi-user in the sense that multiple users can use the same computer, it is multi-user in the sense that multiple users can use the same computer at the same time. You can hook up multiple terminals to the computer, or you can use virtual terminals. To use a virtual terminal, press Alt+F[1-12], which means press the Alt key plus any of the function keys (you can go up to as many virtual terminals as your system supports). You are presented with a completely new login screen and you log in as a new user. You can log in as yourself multiple times, or you can log in as a completely different user—it doesn't matter. If you are in X, you can open a new virtual terminal by pressing Ctrl+Alt+F*x*. To return to X, press Alt+F7. (If you are running an X session, F7 is reserved for X.) Virtual terminals are particularly useful if you want to run several processes at one time in the foreground (we'll talk about running processes in the foreground and the background later).

Why You Should Not Log in As Root

Now that you know about multiple logins and virtual terminals, it is time for the advice that every new Unix user gets. *The root account is intended for administrative use only. Do not login as root unless you must do so to perform an administrative task.*

Some new users get into the bad habit of using root for everything. This is bad for several reasons: You can inadvertently destroy important files. You can do irreparable damage to your filesystem or wreak havoc with system processes. Also, if you are connected to a network, being logged in as root is a potential security hole for a cracker to get into your system.

If you log in as root all the time, you increase your chances of making a simple error that can cost you hours of recovery time. If you are the administrator of your system, there is a simple command called su, which enables you to assume the identity of root or any other user (if you know the password). It is much better to log in as an ordinary user, then use the su command to give yourself administrative privileges to perform a task. This is also called becoming the "superuser." If you simply type

```
$ su
```

followed by the root password, you will assume the root identity. If you type

```
$ su other_username
```

followed by other user's password, you will assume that user's identity.

When you become the superuser, look twice at every command you enter to make sure that it is what you intended. When you are finished with the administrative task, type

```
# exit
```

You will re-assume your ordinary user identity.

Do not log in as root, unless you must do so to administer the system. Instead, use the su command to assume root status. Then, carefully review each command you type before pressing Enter. Carelessness can cause a lot of damage!

The Unix Command

Now we are ready to explore our environment by issuing commands to the shell. Unix has thousands of commands, which you can string together to make more complex commands. You can also create new commands in Unix. All this flexibility makes Unix an extremely powerful operating system.

The reason you have all this power is that commands are treated like any other executable file. When you type a command such as ls, you run the ls executable file, which is located in /bin/ls. When you create a new command, you simply add it to the /bin directory, then use it like any other Unix command. (If that doesn't make sense, you will understand by the end of the hour.)

Unix commands come with switches and options, which can extend or slightly change the action that the command performs. Switches are composed of a dash followed by a letter or series of letters that alter or enhance the command's output. Options consist of two dashes, followed by a word, that perform the same way as switches. In many cases, there is a switch and an option to perform the same task. A switch looks like this:

```
$ ls -a
```

An option looks like this:

```
$ ls --all
```

Some Basic Unix Commands

After you have logged in for the first time (using your user account, not root!), you should get to know your surroundings. Directories in Linux are based on a tree structure, just like in DOS and Windows. The very base of the directory tree is called the root directory. Below the root directory are more directories, called subdirectories, and below the subdirectories are the files.

Directories and subdirectories are the same thing as folders in Windows.

Getting Your Bearings with the `pwd` Command

If you lose track of the directory you're in, you can type the `pwd` command to show you the full pathname of your current location in the filesystem:

```
$ pwd
/home/judith
```

pwd stands for *present working directory*. pwd prints the full pathname of your current directory, starting from the root directory and ending at your current directory.

Notice that the slashes that separate directories in Unix are forward slashes (/), not backward slashes (\). Backward slashes also have a meaning in Unix, which we will discuss later.

The root directory is the very lowest level in the directory tree. You might remember the root directory from Hour 2, when you had to assign a mount point to /. Every other directory in your filesystem is a subdirectory of /.

If you enter pwd immediately after logging in, you should see something like /home/ *username* print to the screen (where *username* is your user name). When you first log in

to Linux, you enter the filesystem at your *home directory*. Your home directory is where
you keep all your work, as well as your personal configuration and other system files.

Listing Directory Contents with the ls Command

So now you know where you are. The next step is to find out what's in your home directory. To list the contents of any directory in Linux, type the following command:

$ls

If you're a new user, there probably won't be anything in your directory, unless your system administrator added files. There actually are files in your directory; you just need to
add a switch to the ls command to see them:

$ls -a
```
.  ..  .bash_logout  .bash_profile  .bashrc  .emacs  .screenrc
```

The -a switch to the ls command means "all." That means to show all the files, including the hidden files that are displayed above. Hidden files are usually configuration files
that are used by programs, but anyone can make a hidden file. Notice that no information
is given about the files. The ls -a command doesn't tell you if an item is a file or directory, who owns it, who has permission to use it, when it was created, or anything. To get
more detailed information about the contents of a directory, you need yet another switch:

```
$ ls -la
total 28
drwx------   2 judith   users      4096 Jul 18 14:29 .
drwxr-xr-x  10 root     root       4096 Jul 18 14:29 ..
-rw-r--r--   1 judith   users        24 Jul 18 14:29 .bash_logout
-rw-r--r--   1 judith   users       230 Jul 18 14:29 .bash_profile
-rw-r--r--   1 judith   users       124 Jul 18 14:29 .bashrc
-rw-rw-r--   1 judith   users       688 Jul 18 14:29 .emacs
-rw-r--r--   1 judith   users      3394 Jul 18 14:29 .screenrc
```

First, ls -la tells you the total size of your directory in blocks (1024 bytes) on the hard
disk, which is 28 in our example. Each file and directory is listed with a lot of information.

Notice the first two entries in the ls -la output after the total size are simply a dot and a
double-dot. If you are familiar with DOS, you have probably seen these before. The .
stands for the current directory. The .. stands for the next-highest directory closer to
root. Notice that both the . and the .. directories have a d at the beginning of the first
string in the output. The d stands for directory. On some systems, that might be your only
way of determining whether an item in a directory listing is a file or a subdirectory.

In Unix, commands are space and case-sensitive. If you forget the space between the command and the argument, or if you capitalize a file that should be lowercase, the command will not work the way you intended. For example, if you enter cd.., you will get an error message.

If you have a color monitor, directories appear in blue in the output of an ls command on a default Red Hat 7.0 system. This behavior is arbitrary, however, and is easily changed.

The letters and dashes that come after the d list the permissions for the directory (and for the files, as well). Permissions specify who has access to the file, as well as what kind of access each kind of user has. The name judith means that the user judith owns the file or directory (notice that root owns the .. directory, which is /home). The date and time, July 18, 14:29, is the date and time that the file was last modified. Finally, the name of the file appears at the far right.

Since you haven't created any files yet, your home directory is kind of boring. Let's use another command to explore the system a bit further.

Changing Directories with the cd Command

The command to change directories is cd. At the shell prompt, type cd followed by the pathname of the directory where you want to go. For example, if you type

```
$ cd /
```

you will go to the root directory. If we type ls in this new directory, we see a new set of directories:

```
$ cd /
bin   dev  home  lost+found  opt   root  tmp  var
boot  etc  lib   mnt         proc  sbin  usr
```

If we type **pwd**, we see:

```
$ pwd
/
```

That way, we know for sure that we are in the root directory. The symbol for the root directory is /. No matter where you are in the directory tree, you can always return to the root directory by typing cd / and then pressing Enter.

Copying Files with the cp Command

Now we are at the second highest level in the directory tree. You will learn about all these directories in Hour 4, but for now let's just explore a bit to help you learn some more commands. Enter the following commands:

```
$cd /usr/X11R6/lib
$ls
```

The output of the ls command is shown in Figure 3.4. We are going to copy the XF86Config.eg file from this directory to our home directory.

FIGURE 3.4

The /usr/X11R6/lib/ X11 contains files needed to run X. We're just using a convenient sample configuration file from this directory as an example.

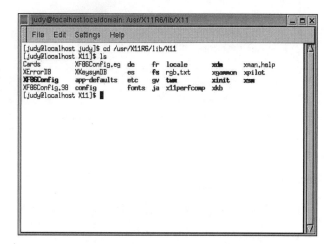

If you are not the administrator of your Linux system, you might not have access to any directories besides your home directory. If you don't have access, ask your system administrator for some sample files to play with.

The command to copy a file in Linux is cp. To copy a file, enter cp *filename desired_location*. For example:

```
$ cp XF86Config.eg /home/judith/
```

This tells the system to copy the file XF86Config.eg from the current directory to the /home/judith directory.

You don't have to be in a directory to copy a file from it. We could have stayed in /home/judith and written the following command instead:

```
$ cp /usr/X11R6/lib/X11/XF86Config.eg /home/judith/
```

or simply:

```
$ cp /usr/X11R6/lib/X11/XF86Config.eg .
```

As you may recall, the . at the end of the last command stands for "the current directory."

Now let's see what that file we just copied looks like. To return to our home directory from anywhere in the directory tree, we can simply type a tilde (~) at the shell prompt. Type cd ~, then pwd and see what happens:

```
$ cd ~
$pwd
/home/judith
```

Now type **ls** and verify that the file is there:

```
$ls
XF86Config.eg
```

Reading Output with the cat and more Commands and Using Ctrl+C

To view the contents of the file, we can use the cat command. Cat is short for concatenate, because you can also use it to combine the contents of two or more files.

```
$cat XF86Config.eg
```

This is a big file! This file is so big that it streams by too fast for you to read it. To slow down the cat command so that you can read one screenful of a long file at a time, you can pipe the cat command to the more command:

```
$cat XF86Config.eg | more
```

When you *pipe* a command in Unix, that means to execute one command, then apply the results of the first command to the second command. In this way, you can build some pretty powerful commands using smaller commands strung, or piped, together. The more command simply means display the output one screenful at a time. To scroll to the next screenful of text, press the spacebar. Continue pressing the spacebar until you reach the end of the file.

If you get tired of reading this very long file before you reach the end, you can issue the abort command, Ctrl+C.

> Ctrl+C means to press Ctrl, then press C while holding down Ctrl. In this particular case, the shell isn't case sensitive, so pressing Ctrl+c is the same as pressing Ctrl+C.

Ctrl+C stops the currently running command and displays a shell prompt, ready for the next command.

Deleting Files with the `rm` Command

After you have finished using the `XF86Config.eg` file, you should delete it from your home directory, since it doesn't really belong there. To remove a file or directory, use the `rm` command:

```
$ rm /home/judith/XF86Config.eg
remove file 'XF86Config.eg'? y/n
y
```

Red Hat Linux gives you a prompt to make sure that you really want to delete the file. Other Unices and Linux distributions might simply delete the file with no warning.

> There is no Undo button in Unix! Once you have deleted a file, it's gone.

The commands you have learned so far are shown in Table 3.1, along with a few new commands that you can experiment with on your own.

TABLE 3.1 A (Very) Few Common Unix Commands

Command	Description
pwd	Displays the present working directory
ls	Lists the contents of a directory
cd *directory*	Changes to *directory*
cp *file new_location*	Copies *file* to a new location or filename
cat *file*	Views *file*
more	Displays the output one screenful at a time
Ctrl+C	Aborts the command (only works while the command is still running)
rm *file*	Removes (deletes) *file*
mv *file new_location*	Moves a file to a new location, also used to rename a file
mkdir *dir_name*	Creates a new directory
rmdir *dir_name*	Removes an empty directory
rm -r *dir_name*	Removes a directory and all its contents

> You can display the last few commands you entered by repeatedly pressing the up and down arrows. This way, you can avoid typing in long commands or filenames over again. You can edit the command on the command line, then press Enter to issue it again.

Getting Help with the man and info Pages

As you explore Linux, you will see many commands, system files, library functions, and other special files that you don't understand. Your best and first reference when learning a new aspect of Linux is the set of *man pages* (short for manual pages). The man pages are the best way of discovering every possible variation and option that you can use with a command. They tend to be long and complicated, because they serve as a complete reference. However, even beginners can benefit greatly from them. Usually, if you read the first couple of paragraphs of the description, you can get a good idea of the topic.

Another reference is the *info pages*, which are somewhat newer than the man pages. Info pages also tend to provide more description and explanation than do the man pages.

3

Task: Look Up Information on a Topic

1. To look up info on a topic, type info *topic*, for example:

    $ info ls

2. To invoke a man page about a command or system file, type man *command* at the shell prompt. For example, to get help on the command ls, type

    $ man ls

    The manual page for that command opens, as shown in Figure 3.5. The first line of the man page is the name of the command, a synopsis of all the different switches and parameters that you can attach to the command, and a detailed description of the command usage.

3. To scroll through the man page, use the arrow down and arrow up buttons.

4. To quit the man page, enter **q**.

In addition to the man and info pages, many commands come with an option that prints out a description of the command, such as *command* --help. Also, all the documentation that comes with application packages that you install is stored in /usr/doc. Many of the files are simple README files or other notes, but you can sometimes find a wealth of information (the X documents are an example).

FIGURE 3.5

As a beginner, you can usually get the information you need by reading the first few paragraphs of a man page.

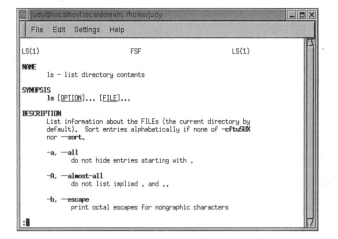

Shutting Down

Unlike Windows systems, it is unnecessary and usually undesirable to continually shut down and reboot, unless you have a dual-boot computer. You can run your Linux system for as long as you like. Even after you install new software, there is no need to reboot.

If you do want to reboot, *never* just turn off your computer or hit the reset button. This can cause data corruption. If you are forced to turn off the computer or you lose power, you might have to run a program called fsck to restore your filesystem. You will learn more about fsck in Hour 16, "Administering the System."

- To shut down and power down the computer, enter the following command:

  `# halt`
- To shutdown and reboot, enter:

  `# shutdown -r now`
- In Red Hat Linux, you can also press the Ctrl+Alt+Del combination, which invokes the `shutdown -r now` command.

By default in Red Hat Linux 7.0, you do not have to be root to shut down. There are steps you can take, however, to prevent ordinary users from shutting down (see Hour 16).

Summary

In this hour, you learned how to start thinking like a Linux user. You learned how the Linux boots and initializes, and how to log in. You learned the basics of the Unix command, and you used the `ls`, `pwd`, `cd`, `cp`, `cat`, `more`, and `rm` commands. You also learned how to use a pipe to link commands and how to use Ctrl+C to abort a command. You discovered the man and info pages and how to safely shut down a Linux system.

Workshop

The Workshop contains quiz questions and exercises to help reinforce what you've learned in this hour.

Q&A

Q I'm still really confused. Where can I get more information about Linux basics?

A Learning how to use Linux takes more than one hour of study. Here are some resources for you to continue studying the basics:

`http://www.geek-girl.com/Unixhelp/` for basic Unix commands

UNIX Made Easy: The Basics and Beyond!, John Muster, McGraw-Hill 1996. An excellent tutorial for learning Unix.

`http://www.linuxnewbie.org` for general help for Linux newbies.

Q I don't see my floppy drive or CD-ROM drive in the root directory. Where are they?

A Linux treats different drives and other devices differently than MS-DOS or Windows. Other drive devices, including floppy drives, ZIP drives, tape drives, and CD-ROMs are usually found in the `/mnt` directory. You will learn more in the next hour.

Quiz

1. What is X?
2. In which environment do you use the command line?
3. What is the first thing that happens when you turn on your computer?
4. What is the login program called, and what starts it?
5. Which login sequence is runlevel 3, and which is runlevel 5?
6. What is a virtual terminal?

7. When is it okay to log in as root?

8. How do you leave superuser status?

Quiz Answers

1. What is X?

   The Linux (actually also the Unix) graphical interface.

2. In which environment do you use the command line?

   The shell environment.

3. What is the first thing that happens when you turn on your computer?

   The BIOS copies the boot loader into memory.

4. What is the login program called, and what starts it?

   The kernel starts the getty program, which makes it possible to login.

5. Which login sequence is runlevel 3, and which is runlevel 5?

   Runlevel 3 starts the text login, and runlevel 5 starts the graphical login.

6. What is a virtual terminal?

   A virtual terminal is like another monitor attached to your system. It enables you to start a completely different session with a new login.

7. When is it okay to log in as root?

   You should log in as root only when you need to, in order to perform an administrative task.

8. How do you leave superuser status?

   Type **exit** at the command prompt.

Exercises

1. Log into your Linux system using the account you created during installation.

2. Enter the command pwd. What is the output?

3. If you know the root password, assume superuser status and then exit.

4. Type **ls** **/etc**. What command would you use to display only one screenful of information at a time?

5. Type **pwd** again. What directory are you in? How would you go to the /etc directory?

6. Copy the termcap file from the /etc directory to your home directory.

7. Make a new directory in your home directory called "play." Put the termcap file in the play directory.

8. Rename the `termcap` file to `this_file`. Hint: use the `mv` command.

9. Delete `this_file`. Remove the play directory.

Exercise Answers

1. Log into your Linux system using the account you created during installation.

   Enter your user name and press Enter, then enter your password and press Enter.

2. Enter the command `pwd`. What is the output?

   Normally, you log in to your home directory. The output should be something like `/home/your_user_name`.

3. If you know the root password, assume superuser status and then exit.

   Type **su**, then enter the root password at the prompt. Type **exit** to exit back to your own user identity.

4. Type **ls** `/etc`. What command would you use to display only one screenful of information at a time?

   The `/etc` directory is probably too long for the entire output to appear in one screen. Type **ls** `/etc` **| more** to display one screenful of output at a time.

5. Type **pwd** again. What directory are you in? How would you go to the `/etc` directory?

   You are still in your home directory. To go to the `/etc` directory, type **cd** `/etc`.

6. Copy the `termcap` file from the `/etc` directory to your home directory.

   `cp /etc/termcap /home/username`

7. Make a new directory in your home directory called "play." Put the `termcap` file in the play directory.

   `mkdir play`

   `cp termcap play`

8. Rename the `termcap` file to `this_file`. Hint: use the `mv` command.

   `cd play`

   `mv termcap this_file`

9. Delete `this_file`. Remove the play directory.

   `rm this_file`

   `cd ..`

   `rmdir play`

HOUR 4

Exploring the Red Hat Linux Filesystem

As you saw in the last hour, the Linux filesystem consists of hundreds of files and directories. But what do they all mean? How do you use them? Now that you know a few Linux commands, you have enough knowledge to explore your environment. This hour you will become better acquainted with the Linux directory structure while learning more Linux basics.

In this hour you will

- Explore the Linux filesystem and learn how the filesystem is set up for use
- Learn about the different subdirectories of the root directory, and how they are used
- Move around the filesystem using cd, and the . and .. directories
- Create hard links and symbolic links
- Understand how permissions work for files and directories

The Linux Filesystem

If you go to your root directory and then list the contents, you will see something like the listing shown in Figure 4.1.

FIGURE **4.1**

The root directory holds the major subdirectories of the system, but no files.

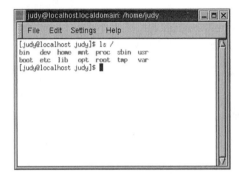

```
judy@localhost.localdomain: /home/judy

 File   Edit   Settings   Help

[judy@localhost judy]$ ls /
bin   dev  home  mnt  proc  sbin  usr
boot  etc  lib   opt  root  tmp   var
[judy@localhost judy]$ ▮
```

As you learned in Hour 3, "Linux Basics," every file and directory can trace its origins on a tree back to the root directory. The directory structure enables you to map the location of every file on your system by its *pathname*. The file pathname lists every directory and subdirectory from the root directory to the subdirectory that holds your file.

The filesystem is usually spread out across several partitions (like those you made when you installed Red Hat), but it's not necessary. You can have your filesystem on one big partition, or on different physical hard disks, or even on a separate computer that you access via a network. In Linux, it doesn't matter—when you use the filesystem, it looks as if every file is in one directory tree on one computer. This is because every partition on every separate hard drive in your filesystem is *mounted* onto a directory in the root partition. After the filesystems are mounted, the system acts as if every separate partition, disk, and remote filesystem is just a subdirectory of the root directory.

> To *mount* a filesystem just means to make it available for access. In Linux, all you need is a *mount point*, which is the directory where the filesystem is added to the root filesystem. Because every mounted filesystem just looks like a subdirectory of /, it all acts like it is one big filesystem.

The root (/) partition holds the root directory of the filesystem. The root filesystem is mounted onto the root directory at startup. After the root directory is mounted, the other partitions are mounted onto a subdirectory in the root partition via mount points. The mount points tell the kernel where to mount each separate partition or filesystem so that it becomes part of the root filesystem. For example, the directory /usr is a mount point for the /usr partition. If your /usr directory is not a separate partition, then it is just another directory in the root partition. If your /usr directory is located on another computer, it is attached to your filesystem by the mount point and then acts like any other directory that is physically in your hard drive.

If you have other operating systems or devices such as a CD-ROM or floppy drive, you must mount them onto the Linux filesystem before you can access the files. For example, when you want to use your CD-ROM, you mount it using its mount point, which in Red Hat is /mnt/cdrom by default. The same applies for /mnt/floppy (or /mnt/fd0), and if you want access to other operating systems, /mnt/DOS or anything else.

> You don't have to use /mnt/cdrom; you can use any directory you want, as long as it's defined in the etc/fstab directory. By convention, however, the names for different mount points have evolved into a generally recognized set of standards that most people follow. The Linux Filesystem Standard (FSSTND) sets the standard upon which the Red Hat filesystem is based.

The Red Hat Linux Directory Structure

4

This section summarizes the generally accepted use for each subdirectory in the root directory.

/ contains the mount point for the major filesystems. In Red Hat, the root directory doesn't contain any files at all, just directories for mounting the other filesystems.

/bin contains the basic commands that are used by all users, such as cat, cp, ping, vi, su, and ls.

> Notice that cd isn't in the /bin directory. cd is a special command that is built right into the kernel.

/boot contains the files used by the boot loader, such as LILO, to boot the system.

/dev contains special files for different hardware devices. If you look in dev, you will see many files for devices that you might not have. For example, there are files in /dev for the amigamouse, atimouse, and atarimouse, different ISDN devices, and different SCSI devices (sda, sdb, sdc, and so on). Since empty device files don't take up much space, it is best to leave the unused device files alone. Otherwise, you will have to re-create the device file when you want to add new hardware.

/etc contains the system configuration files that are used by all users. Sometimes individual users have configuration files in their individual home directories (. files) that override the configuration files in /etc.

/home contains the home directories for all users. You keep your actual working files and other data in your home directory.

/lib contains the shared libraries that are needed to run programs. Different programs share some of the same libraries of functions, so rather than have multiple copies of the libraries in different locations, they are kept together in /lib, then loaded into memory by the programs as they are needed. This also cuts down on memory usage since different programs can share the same libraries in memory.

/mnt contains the mount points for external drives, such as your CD-ROM, floppy, and Zip drives. If you want to mount an external filesystem, such as MS-DOS, you can create the mount point in /mnt. For example, if you have both a Windows system and a Linux system on the same computer, you can easily access your Windows files in Linux by mounting the Windows partition to a mount point in /mnt.

/proc is a pseudo-filesystem, which is used as an interface to the kernel. The kernel creates the /proc filesystem in memory to provide information about the system. Each process that is running on your system has a subdirectory in /proc, which contains pseudo-files with information about the process. Because it is created in memory, nothing in /proc actually takes up disk space.

/root is the home directory for the root user. You should not put ordinary data files in /root.

/sbin contains special commands that are generally used only by root. Some examples are fsck, clock, dump, modprobe, runlevel, and linuxconf.

/tmp is for temporary files. Some people use /var/tmp instead of /tmp.

/usr contains all the commands, applications, documentation, and libraries that are needed to operate the system. The files in /usr are meant to be shared by all users, and are generally read-only. /usr is often the largest partition.

/var contains files that regularly change (hence the name var, for variable or varies). Log files and other temporary files, such as mail and print spools, are usually kept in /var.

A Word About Swap Space

Since we're discussing filesystems and partitions, you may be wondering what the swap space that you created in Hour 2 is used for. Swap space is a special partition on your hard drive that is used as a sort of virtual memory, in addition to your core memory. If you don't have enough physical memory to serve all the programs that the system is running, the kernel writes and rewrites data to the swap space on the hard disk in the same way that data is written and rewritten to your physical memory.

Moving Around the Filesystem

In Hour 3 you learned to use the cd command to change directories. This section explores the cd command further, and you will see what a versatile and powerful command it can be.

When you picture the directory system as a large tree, it makes it easier to visualize how to change directories quickly. Last hour, you used cd to move one directory up and one down. You can jump from place to place in the directory tree by entering **cd**, followed by the full pathname of the directory where you want to go. For example, say you are in the directory /home/judy/mail and you want to go to usr/share/pixmaps. You could enter:

```
$ cd /usr
$ cd share
$ cd pixmaps
```

Or you could enter the entire pathname in one go:

```
$ cd /usr/share/pixmaps
```

Task: Using the .. Directory

Suppose you now wanted to go up one directory, to /usr/share. You could enter:

```
$ cd /usr/share
```

It's kind of annoying to type out the entire pathname again. As a shortcut, instead of typing out the full pathname, you can use the .. directory, which stands for "one directory higher in the directory tree."

1. To go back to /usr/share from /usr/share/pixmaps, type:
   ```
   $ cd ..
   $ pwd
   /usr/share
   ```

2. The .. command comes in handy in many ways. Let's say you now want to move from /usr/share to /usr/src/redhat. You could type:
   ```
   $ cd /usr/src/redhat
   ```

3. Or, you could type:

```
$ cd ../src/redhat
```

This previous command tells Linux to move one directory up from /usr/share to /usr, then to move to src/redhat, which is a subdirectory of /usr.

4. In another example, let's say you downloaded an application, but you can't remember if you put the file in /usr/src/redhat/RPMS/i386 or if you put it in /usr/src/linux/modules. You could type:

```
$ cd /usr/src/linux/modules
$ ls
$
```

5. No new file there. So, using the .. directory, you would go back two directories, then into redhat/RPMS:

```
$ cd ../../redhat/RPMS
$ ls
athlon   i386   i486   i586   i686   noarch
```

6. Now say you can't remember if you put it in i386 or i586.

You could cd to i386, type **ls**, and then try **cd ../i586** and **ls** again.

7. Or, you can use the pathname of the place where you're looking with the ls command:

```
$ pwd
/usr/src/RPMS/386
$ ls ../586
abisuite-0.7.10-1.rpm
```

8. Your file is in /usr/src/redhat/RPMS/586. You can use the full pathname for a file with any command in Linux. So, if you had been in your home directory and wanted to quickly check where that RPM was, you could have typed:

```
$ pwd
/home/judy/mail
$ ls /usr/src/redhat/RPMS/i586
abisuite-0.7.10-1.rpm
```

Task: Using the . Directory

Another useful shortcut is the . directory, which is equivalent to "the present directory." If you recall from the last chapter, we copied a file using the following command:

```
$ pwd
/home/judy
$ cp /usr/X11R6/lib/X11/XF86Config.eg /home/judy
```

1. We could have cut down on our typing by using the . directory instead of
   /usr/X11R6/lib/X11:

   $ cp /usr/X11R6/lib/X11/XF86Config.eg.

2. The . directory is also useful when you want to run a program that is in your home
   directory or another directory that is not in the normal path of executable programs. For example, if you were in a directory called /home/judy/C_programs,
   and you wanted to run the hello_world program, you might have to type:

   $ ./hello_world

   instead of

   $ hello_world

This is because Linux looks for executable programs only in certain directories in the
filesystem. If the executable file is not in one of those special directories, you have to tell
Linux to look for the executable file in the present directory instead. The list of directories where executable programs are kept is called the *path*.

Creating Links

4

In Linux (and Unix) you can use links to give the same file two entirely different names,
or to pretend that a file that is in one location in the filesystem is actually in an entirely
different location.

Linking is useful when you have two different programs that look for the same file in
different places, so you need to make sure the file is in both locations. For example, say
you have a library file in /usr/lib. Most of the programs on your system that use that
file look for it in /usr/lib, but a few programs look for it in /usr/share/lib. You can
create a link from the file in /usr/lib to /usr/share/lib, and then all the programs that
use the file can find it.

In another case, say that you have run out of space in your /usr partition. If you want to
add more files to /usr, you can create a directory in /var, then link the directory to
/usr, and all the files in the linked directory will seem to be in /usr. There are two kinds
of links: the hard link and the symbolic link. Although they do the same job, the way
Linux treats them at a hardware level is completely different, so it is worth exploring the
difference.

Hard Links

A *hard link* is just another name for an existing file. The two files share the same inode,
so in reality they are the same file. This is different from a copy, where there are two
separate files with separate inodes, taking up different blocks on the hard disk. The *inode*

is a special file that tells the kernel which blocks on the hard disk hold the file. Because the hard link to a file is actually the same as the original (target) file, you can't tell which is the original file and which is the hard link.

Every file in the filesystem has two identifying labels: the filename and the inode number. When you want to find a file, you refer to the filename, but when the kernel wants to find a file, it looks in the inode. The inode number is displayed with the ls -i command. Every inode number is unique, but with a hard link you have two filenames mapped to the same inode.

The command to create a hard link is ln. The general structure of an ln command is ln *original_filename link_filename*.

Links are usually used to place the same file in two different places in the directory structure. For example, to create a hard link to a file in the same directory, but with a different filename, enter:

```
$ ln ./plantains ./hardln_plantains
```

A new filename appears in the directory. Figure 4.2 shows that the information in the ls -l output is exactly the same for both plantains and hardln_plantains.

FIGURE 4.2

You can't tell which file is the original and which is the link.

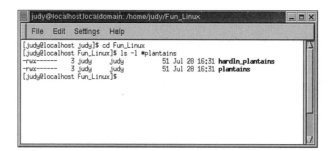

If you eliminate a new link filename and just put a directory, the link filename will have the same name as the original (or target) filename, just in a different directory:

```
$ ln ./bananas /tmp/
$ cd /tmp
$ ls
bananas
$
```

Symbolic Links

A *symbolic link* is different from a hard link in that it is a special file type that contains the name of the original file, somewhat like a shortcut in Windows. When you create a symbolic link, (also called a *symlink* for short), a symbolic link file is created that contains a pointer to the original, target file. If you were to view a symbolic link using the `cat` command (see Hour 3) or open it in an editor, the original file would open. Also, if you make edits to the symbolic link file, the edits also appear in the original file, and vice versa.

To create a symbolic link instead of a hard link, use the `ln` command with an `-s` switch:

`$ ln -s original_filename link_filename`

Symbolic links are labeled in the `ls -l` output with an `l` at the beginning of the permissions string. The target (original) file is listed next to the symbolic link after an arrow, as shown in Figure 4.3.

FIGURE 4.3

Symbolic links are identified by the l at the beginning of the listing and by the arrow, followed by the target file.

In Red Hat Linux, symbolic links appear in light blue by default in the directory listing.

If you delete a target file without deleting the symbolic link, the link is called a dead link. If you try to open the symbolic link with `cat`, you will get an error message. If you delete a hard link, both the link and the target file are deleted.

Understanding Permissions

Linux is by nature a multiuser system. As you learned in the last section, you could potentially have hundreds of different users in the `/home` directory, each owning his own little space in the `/home` filesystem, while sharing the applications, printers, networking, and other services that live on the rest of the filesystem. If you have all these people using the same computer, what's to prevent one user from mucking around in another user's home directory? How can adventurous but clueless users be prevented from accessing and changing vital system files? Even if you are the only user on your system, how can you protect your system from damage while learning? The answer is by using permissions.

Setting permissions enables you to determine exactly who should have access to your files, and exactly what other users on the system should be able to do with your files and directories. Every file and directory on the filesystem has a set of permissions attached to it. Permissions specify who has access to the file or directory and what kind of access the user has.

When you issue the ls -l command, a string of letters appears in the first column of the ls -l output, as shown in Figure 4.4.

FIGURE 4.4

You can tell a lot about a file from its permissions string.

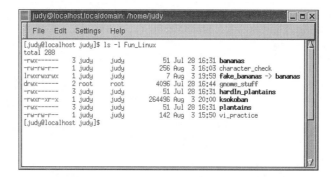

If you look carefully at the string at the beginning of the ls -l output, it looks like one long string. To understand the meaning, however, you should mentally divide the permissions string into four sections. The first section describes the kind of file in one character. You have already learned that a directory contains a d and a symbolic link contains an l. An ordinary file contains a dash (-) in the first section. The next three sections are three characters each, and display the permissions for the three user categories.

Linux classifies three kinds of users for a file: the owner of the file, the group that the owner belongs to, and everybody else on the system.

- The *owner* is the user who created the file.
- Users on the system can float around as individuals, or they can be gathered into groups. A *group* is a collection of users who are working on certain files together. For example, if you have a team of programmers working on an application, the team members should be able share each others' work, without being able to access personal files. The group must have access to each others' files, but you might not want everyone else on the system to have access. By setting group permissions, you can prevent unauthorized users from gaining access to your files, while enabling members of the group you work with to share files.
- The last set of permissions pertains to *everybody* on the system.

As there are three kinds of users, there are three kinds of permissions: read, write, and execute. There are three possible things that that you can do to a file. You can open the file and read it, you can make changes to the file or write to it, and if the file contains a program, you can run the program, or execute it. To correspond with the three kinds of permissions, each of the three user sections contains a string of three characters, which can be a combination of -, r, w, or x characters.

- Read permission, indicated by an r, means that you are allowed to open the file and look at its contents, but that you aren't allowed to make any changes to the file, including making edits or moving the file to another directory. You could, however, make a copy of the file and make changes to the copy.

- Write permission, indicated by a w, means that you are permitted to make changes to the file, including editing, moving, and deleting the file.

- Execute, indicated by an x, means one of two things, depending on whether you are talking about a file or directory. Execute permission on an executable file such as an application means that you are permitted to run the program. Execute permission on a directory means that you have permission to open the directory and look at the contents. If you were to try to open a directory for which you didn't have execute permission, you would get a Permission Denied message.

The dash (-) means that the category of user does not have a particular permission. For example, in the permission string for vi_practice in Figure 4.4, rw-rw-r--, the owner of the file has read and write permission, the group has read and write permission, and everybody else has only read permission. Notice that no one has execute permission. If a file is not a directory or an executable file, it doesn't make sense to give execute permission, because such permission would be meaningless. The files bananas, ksokoban, and plantains/hardln_plantains are all executable files.

Notice in Figure 4.4 that all the permissions for the symbolic link fake_bananas are listed for all users. That is because permissions are meaningless for symbolic links; the target file permissions are what's important. By default, all the permissions are displayed for symbolic links.

Summary

In this hour, you learned how the Linux filesystem is mounted in the root filesystem. You explored the organization of the directory structure, and learned how to use the .. and . directories. You created hard links and symbolic links, and learned the difference between the two. You also learned about permissions and how the permissions system is a necessary basic security tool on a multiuser system.

Workshop

The Workshop contains quiz questions and exercises to help reinforce what you've learned in this hour.

Q&A

Q What is the /opt directory for?

A Some Linux distributions use the /opt directory for operational files, such as applications. The /opt directory isn't really used in Red Hat, but it is included by default.

Q Do I need to bother with permissions if I'm the only user on my system?

A Permissions can still be useful, even if you are the only user on your system. By denying your ordinary user account access to system files, and then making sure that you don't do everyday work while logged in as root, you can prevent yourself from damaging your system through a mistake or carelessness.

Quiz

1. What is a mount point?
2. What is a pathname? In which directory does the pathname start?
3. What is the difference between the commands in /bin and /sbin?
4. With a hard link, how do you tell which file is the original file and which file is the link?
5. What does x permission mean for a directory? What does write permission mean for a directory?

Quiz Answers

1. What is a mount point?

   A mount point is a directory where a filesystem is mounted so it can be accessed.

2. What is a pathname? In which directory does the pathname start?

   A pathname is the path of directories from the root directory to the subdirectory where a file is located.

3. What is the difference between the commands in /bin and /sbin?

   /bin holds the most fundamental commands for all users. /sbin holds system configuration commands that are usually only used by root.

4. How do you tell which file is the original file and which file is a hard link?

You can't—a hard link is just another name for the original file. They are identical in every way, because they are the same file.

5. What does x permission mean for a directory? What does write permission mean for a directory?

Execute permission for a directory means that you have permission to open the directory. Write permission means that you can make changes to the directory: rename it, move it, add or delete files in it.

Exercises

1. Explore the contents of the /bin, /sbin, /usr/bin, /usr/share/doc, /dev, /etc, /lib, and /proc directories.

2. From your home directory, go back to the / directory using only **cd ..**. How many times must you enter the command?

3. Enter **cd ..**. What happens?

4. In your home directory, create the file practice. Create a hard link called hard_practice and a symbolic link called sym_practice.

5. In your home directory, enter ls -l. How can you tell that sym_practice is a symbolic link?

6. While logged into your ordinary user account, look up the permission string for the file /etc/syslog.conf. What is it?

Exercise Answers

1. Explore the contents of the /bin, /sbin, /usr/bin, /usr/share/doc, /dev, /etc, /lib, and /proc directories.

Enter the command cd /bin, then enter ls to display the contents of the directory. For large directories such as /etc or /usr/bin, use ls | more.

2. From your home directory, go back to the / directory using only **cd ..**. How many times must you enter the command?

From /home/user, enter **cd ..**. The number of times entered might vary according to the system setup, but the default number of times is two.

3. Enter **cd ..**. What happens?

You remain in the same directory.

4. In your home directory, create the file `practice`. Create a hard link called `hard_practice` and a symbolic link called `sym_practice`.

   To create the hard link, enter **`ln practice hard_practice`**.

   To create the symbolic link, enter **`ln -s practice sym_practice`**.

5. In your home directory, enter **`ls -l`**. How can you tell that `sym_practice` is a symbolic link?

   There is an `l` at the beginning of the permissions string, and an arrow pointing to `practice` in the filename column.

6. While logged into your ordinary user account, look up the permission string for the file `/etc/syslog.conf`. What is it?

   Enter **`ls -l etc/syslog.conf`** to display the file permissions. By default, everybody should have read access, but only root should have write access (`-rw-r--r--`). On some systems, no one has access except root.

Hour 5

Using the Visual Editor (VIM)

So far you have learned to view, copy, and move files, but you haven't learned how to create and edit files. There are many text editors available for Linux, but the two most widely used are called the Visual Editor Improved (VIM for short) and Emacs. VIM is much like the traditional vi, but with many improvements and extensions. Although people tend to get passionate about their choice of editor, we will only discuss vi (VIM) in this book. You can have a very successful Linux career without ever using Emacs, but you cannot survive without knowing vi. This hour concentrates on using VIM for general editing.

In this hour you will

- Edit and create new files in the Visual Editor Improved (VIM)
- Use the move commands to move around in a file
- Add and delete text to a file
- Undo edits and search for text
- Write (save) changes and quit VIM, and learn where to get more help on VIM

Creating and Editing Files with VIM

Some Linux users are turned off from vi because it is not the most intuitive tool to use. On the other hand, vi is simple, small, and fast, and once you understand the basics it actually isn't hard at all. vi is the Unix equivalent to edit in DOS. The vi used in Red Hat Linux is actually called VIM, for vi Improved.

> If you type :uganda at the VIM welcome screen, you can read about the Uganda Kibaale Children's Fund, which is used to help orphaned children in Uganda. Bram Moolenaar, who was the main creator of VIM, donates any money that is made from VIM to the orphanage, and he asks that if you use and like VIM, you consider donating to the Fund.

To open an existing file in VIM, enter **vi**, followed by the name of the file. If you're not in the directory where the file is located, you must enter a full pathname, such as vi /usr/share/myfile or vi ../../myfile:

$ vi *myfile*

The file is displayed in VIM, ready for editing.

To create a new file in VIM, enter **vi**, followed by the name of the new file:

$ vi *newfile*

An empty VIM screen appears, with tildes running down the left side, as shown in Figure 5.1. The tildes signify that the line is empty, to distinguish an empty line from a line that contains a space. VIM treats a space just like any other character, such as "a" or ";".

FIGURE 5.1

The VIM screen is simple and uncomplicated.

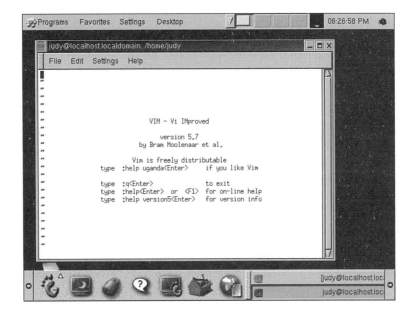

VIM Modes

After you've created a new file in VIM, try typing the word "deluxe." Nothing appears, and you might even hear some annoying beeping sounds as you type each letter. You can't just start typing away in VIM; you must be in the right *mode*. VIM has many modes, but the three most important are the Command mode (also called Normal mode), the Insert mode, and the Command-line mode.

Command mode and Normal mode refer to the same mode. Because they are used interchangeably in the VIM documentation, both terms are used in this chapter.

When you first open VIM, you are in the *Command mode*. In Command mode, VIM interprets everything you type as a command to VIM. There are commands to move the cursor around the text, to delete text, to search, and to copy and paste. There are also commands to save your work and to quit. Not every letter on the keyboard stands for a command; if you type a letter that cannot be interpreted as a command in Normal mode, you might hear a beep, otherwise nothing happens at all.

To enter text into your file, you must be in *Insert mode*. You enter Insert mode by typing an insert command. After you type the insert command, anything you type afterwards is inserted into your document. You must also type an insert command before you type any text in a new file. You will learn some common insert commands in the next section.

When you want to save your file and quit VIM, you must be in *command-line* mode. In command-line mode you give VIM a command to perform some action on the entire file. This is different from command (Normal) mode, where commands are applied to the contents of the file. You enter a command in command-line mode by first making sure you are in Normal mode, then typing a colon, followed by the command.

> People often have trouble with modes when they first use VIM. In some versions of VIM, there is no way to tell which mode you're in until you type something. In VIM, INSERT appears at the bottom of the screen in insert mode, and REPLACE appears when you're in replace mode. In command-line mode, the colon appears at the bottom of the screen. There is no default message for Normal (command) mode.

Moving Around in a File

VIM has dozens of different commands for moving around in a file, but we will discuss just a few of the most useful commands in this hour. To use any of the move commands, you must be in Normal mode. To enter Normal mode from any other mode, press Esc.

> If you're ever unsure of which mode you're in, press the Esc key to bring you back to Normal (command) mode.

The most basic way to move around a file in VIM is to move one character at a time using the arrow keys. In theory, you could use only the arrow keys to move around the file, but it would be a bit like typing with two fingers.

The h, k ,l, and j keys work like the arrow keys, but faster. Type h, k, l, or j to go left, up, right, and down, respectively, as shown in Figure 5.2. You can type a number before a h/k/l/j key to move that number of spaces or lines. For example, to move 5 lines down, then 7 lines up, you would type 5j, then 7k.

Once you get used to them you can move very fast with the h/k/l/j keys, especially since you can use them without ever taking your eyes off the screen.

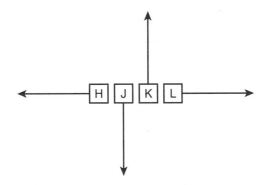

FIGURE 5.2

The h/k/l/j keys can be hard to get used to, but they are much faster than the arrow keys.

To count by words instead of characters, use the w command. w moves you one word at a time along a line. To move two words at a time, type **2w**. To move five words at a time, type **5w**.

A word in VIM is considered to be a string of letters, digits, or underscores, separated by whitespace. Other nonalphanumeric characters, such as apostrophes and quotation marks, are treated as separate words. For example, the word **don't** is considered as 3 words in VIM (by default). The first three letters, don, are a word, the apostrophe is a word, and then the t is a word. The exception to this definition is if the entire word consists of nonalphanumeric characters, such as "*****". In this case, the string is treated like one word.

In a long file, a quick way to move from line to line is to use the G command. To immediately go to the last line in a file, simply type **G** in normal mode. You can also use G to go to a specific line. Type the line number where you want to go, then G. For example, to go to line 22, type **22G**. To go to the first line in the file, type **gg** or **1G**.

The G command is different from the j command. For example, 22G takes you to line 22, from anywhere in the file. 22j takes you 22 lines down from your location in the file.

G is particularly useful when you get an error message that contains a line number. You can just go directly to the line of the program that contains the error.

5

Table 5.1 lists some common commands for moving the cursor.

TABLE 5.1   Commands for Moving Around in a File

Command	Description
h	Move one space to the left
l	Move one space to the right
k	Move one line up
j	Move one line down
7h	Move 7 characters to the left
17j	Move 17 lines down
4k	Move 4 lines up
*n*h/l/j/k	Move n spaces/lines left/right/down/up
0	Go to the first character in the line
$	Go to the last character in the line
G	Go to the last line in the file
*n*G	Go to line n in the file
w	Move to the beginning of the next word
5e	Move to the end of the fifth word from the current position
Ctrl+F	Scroll forwards (down)
Ctrl+B	Scroll backwards (up)

Adding Text to Your File

When you are ready to insert text into your document, there are several commands that place you in Insert mode. After you are in Insert mode, you can enter text anywhere in the document.

Two basic insert commands are a for append and i for insert. a opens Insert mode and enables you to insert text after the cursor. i opens Insert mode and enables you to insert text before the cursor. For example, if you had the word "friend" in a document, and you wanted to change the word to "friendship," you could place the cursor under the d in friend, type `a` to enter Insert mode, and then type **ship**. If you placed the cursor at d and typed **i**, followed by **ship**, it would look like "frienshipd."

After you press an insert command, you can add text to your heart's content. Any character you type is added to your file. When you are ready to save your work, you must go back to Normal mode to save the file. In VIM, saving the file is called "writing" to the file.

Whenever you are in Insert mode or any other mode, to return to Normal mode, press Esc. For example, if you want to move to another place in your file while you are in Insert mode, press Esc to enter Normal mode, move the cursor, then enter an insert command to return to Insert mode. There are key sequences that you can use while in insert mode to move the cursor without leaving insert mode. See the help files or the *VIM Reference Guide*, which is referenced at the end of this chapter.

Table 5.2 lists some of the most common Insert commands.

TABLE 5.2   Insert Commands

Command	Action
a	Append text after the cursor and enter Insert mode
A	Append text at the end of the line and enter Insert mode
i	Insert text before the cursor and enter Insert mode
I	Insert text at the beginning of the line and enter Insert mode
o	Open a line below the cursor and enter Insert mode
O	Open a line above the cursor and enter Insert mode

Deleting Text

There are many commands for deleting text in VIM. Once you become familiar with the more common commands, you will be able to delete much faster than you could with a mouse and graphical interface. Just as for moving text, you must be in Normal mode to delete text.

> To save yourself frustration, you should make a habit of always pressing Esc before typing a delete or move command, unless you are sure that you are already in Normal mode.

To delete one character, go into Normal mode, place the cursor below the character you want to delete and press the x key. You can press x continuously to delete multiple characters.

Using to delete a character is useful for deleting a single typo, but it is as slow as using the arrow keys to move around the file. vi has commands that you can use to delete words, lines, groups of words or lines, and parts of a line.

- dw deletes word by word
- d$ deletes from the cursor to the end of the line
- dd deletes the entire line

If you have four words you want to delete, or three lines in a row, you can enter a number before the delete command to tell VIM to perform the command twice.

For example, in the file below:

```
She sells seashells by the seashore.
Jack Sprat could eat no fat, only lean meats and fish.
His wife could eat no lean.
And so betwixt the two of them
They licked the platter clean.
```

If you wanted to delete only lean meats and fish., you could place the cursor at only, then type:

d$

Alternatively, if you didn't want to retype the period at the end of the line, you could type:

5dw

To delete all lines except the first line, place the cursor at the J in Jack and type:

4dd

This tells VIM to delete four lines of text, starting at the cursor.

Some common delete commands are listed in Table 5.3.

TABLE 5.3   Delete Commands

Command	Description
nx	Delete n characters, beginning with the character at the cursor
n+Delete key	Same as nx
$n$dw	Delete n number of words
d$	Delete to the end of the line
$n$dd	Delete n number of lines

Undoing Mistakes

If you make a mistake in VIM, you can undo it using the u command in Normal (command) mode. u undoes the last edit you made. If you continue to press u, the next to last edit is undone, then the next to next to last, and so on.

vi also comes with the U undo command, which undoes all edits in the current line. U works differently from u, in that it unedits, then re-edits all the changes on the same line. If you press U to undo all the edits on a line, then press U again, all the original edits reappear.

> The trick to using U is that it only remembers edits that you have made on a line if you haven't made edits to another line. Once you make an edit on a new line, you can't go back to a previous line and use U to undo edits on that line.

Task: Replace Text

There are several commands in VIM that enable you to replace, or overwrite, text. Replacing text is often more efficient than deleting and then inserting new text. Replacing text involves another VIM mode, called Replace mode. Replace mode is somewhat different than Insert mode. If you enter text in the middle of a line in Insert mode, the new text is inserted into the old text at the cursor. If you enter text in the middle of a line in Replace mode, the old text is overwritten by the new text.

Use the r command to replace text one character at a time. In Normal mode, place the cursor over the character you want to replace, and type **r**, followed by the character that should replace the original character. For example, in the line:

```
Mari had a little lamb
```

1. To replace the i in Mari with a y, press Esc to go into Normal mode. Place the cursor over the i in Mari. Type **r**, and then type **y**. After you have replaced one character with the r command, you automatically return to Normal mode.

2. You can replace the rest of an object using the c command. To replace the rest of a word, use cw. Place the cursor where you want to begin the change, type **cw**, and then replace the old word with the new word.

3. To change the rest of a line, use the c command with a $ sign (c$).

4. If you have a lot of text to replace, use the R command. After you type **R**, you can continue to overwrite old text with next text until you press Esc to go back to Normal mode.

Table 5.4 lists the Undo and Replace mode commands from this chapter.

5

TABLE 5.4   Undo and Replace Commands

Command	Description
u	Undo the last edit
U	Undo all edits on the current line
*n*r	Replace n number of characters
cw	Replace the word
c$	Replace the rest of the line
R	Enter Replace mode to make unlimited overwrites

Finding Text in VIM

Finding text in VIM is done with the / command. To search for a word, phrase, or other string in a file, in Normal mode type /, followed by the string you are looking for.

To go to the next occurrence of the string, type **n**. To search backwards through a file (from where you are toward the beginning of the file), type **?** followed by the string you want to search for. Type **n** to go to the next occurrence backwards. Table 5.5 lists some of the find text commands.

TABLE 5.5   Find Text

Command	Description
/	Search for a string of characters from the cursor to the end of the file
?	Search for a string of characters from the cursor to the beginning of the file
n	Go to the next matching string of the search in the file

Task: Save Changes and Exit the Visual Editor

1. When you make changes to a file in VIM, the changes aren't made immediately to the file. Rather, a copy of the file is placed in a buffer, and the changes are made to the copy of the file in the buffer.

2. When you are ready to save your changes, you must give a command for VIM to write the file that is in the buffer to the actual file. The :w command instructs VIM to apply the changes that are in the buffer to the actual file, then save the file with the new changes.

3. To save changes you make to a file, press Esc to make sure your are in Normal mode, then type :w.

4. The colon places you in command-line mode. The w tells VIM to write the changes that are in the buffer to the actual file.

5. To exit VIM without saving any changes, enter **:q!**.

6. This command tells VIM to close the buffer without writing the changes to the original file. The buffer file is deleted, and the original file remains as it was when you started (or the last time you wrote changes). The ! command tells VIM to override its default behavior, which is not to exit if the contents of the buffer are different from the actual file.

7. To exit VIM if you haven't made any changes to the file, enter **:q**.

8. To write all your changes and exit VIM, enter **:wq**.

9. You can save the file you are working on in another name by entering :w with a new filename or new directory pathname. The file in the VIM buffer is saved under the new filename.

Table 5.6 summarizes the most basic command-line mode commands.

TABLE 5.6   Writing and Quitting

Command	Description
:w	Write (save) the file
:q!	Quit without saving any changes
:wq	Write all changes to the file and quit
:wq *new_filename*	Save the file with another filename
:help	Open the help window

Getting Help

VIM comes with a detailed help system, although it is somewhat hard to wade through the details when you are a beginner. To open a help window in VIM, type **:help**. The help window appears with a menu of all the help topics, and the file remains open in a window below the help screen. Each topic in the help window is between a set of pipes: |topic|. The pipes signify tags. To jump to a topic, place the cursor between the pipes and enter Ctrl+]. The topic you chose appears in the help buffer.

Alternatively, type **:help** followed by the command you want help on. For example, to get help on the G command, type

:help G

To close the help window, type **:q**. The help window disappears, but your file window remains open. The VIM help window is shown in Figure 5.3.

The help files include a beginner's tutorial that will give you practice in the commands you learned this hour, as well as teach you some new commands. The tutorial, located at /usr/share/vim/vim57/tutor/tutor, is actually just a text file that you can open in VIM. Since you will make changes to the file while doing the tutorial, copy the file to another name first.

You can also get information about VIM, including news, an FAQ, and downloads from http://www.vim.org.

For an excellent reference on VIM commands that is easier to read than the help files, read the *VIM Reference Guide* by Bram Moolenar and Oleg Raisky. You can download the guide at http://www.vim.org

Summary

This hour, you learned how to view and edit files in VIM, which is the GPL version of the vi editor. You learned about VIM modes, how to use keys to move around in a file, how to insert, delete, and replace text, how to write your changes and quit, and how to get help.

Workshop

The Workshop contains quiz questions and exercises to help reinforce what you've learned in this hour.

Q&A

Q Can you copy/cut and paste text in VIM?

A Copying and pasting text in VIM is called *yanking* and *putting*. Yanking and putting requires a bit more knowledge of VIM than what we describe in this hour, so you should read the help files to get a full understanding. To help you get started, use the *n*yy command to yank *n* number of lines, place the cursor where you want them, then type **p** to put them in the new location. To cut and paste, delete the lines using the dd commmand, then put them in the desired location with p.

Quiz

1. Name four VIM modes that were discussed this hour. Which mode are you in when you first open a file in VIM?
2. Can you open VIM without entering a filename? What appears if you do?
3. How do you quit a file without saving changes?
4. What should you do if you don't know which mode you're in? Hint: How do you get back to Normal mode?

Quiz Answers

1. Name four VIM modes that were discussed this hour. Which mode are you in when you first open VIM?

   Command (Normal) mode, insert mode, command-line mode, and replace mode. When you first open VIM, you are in Command mode.

2. Can you open VIM without entering a filename? What appears if you do?

   Yes, the VIM welcome screen appears.

5

3. How do you quit a file without saving changes?

   `:q!`

4. What should you do if you don't know which mode you're in? Hint: How do you get back to Normal mode?

   Press Esc to return to Normal mode.

Exercises

1. Create a new file in VIM called `mary`.

2. Enter the text

   Mary had a little lamb,

   It's fleece was white as snow,

   And everywhere that Mary went

   the lamb was sure to go.

3. Save `mary` without quitting.

4. Put the cursor at the beginning of the first line in the file, then go to "white" using two commands.

5. From the beginning of the file, search for "lamb." Go to the next instance of "lamb."

6. Add this line to the end of the file:

   This is a test_of w's behavior. '"***'

   Go to the beginning of the line and count how many times you have to press w to get to the end of the line.

7. Delete the line from the last exercise.

8. Go to the second line in the file using the `G` command, and then replace "white as snow" with "black as night" using the `c` command. What mode are you in after you type the `c` command?

9. Undo all the changes you just made in Exercise 8. Now use the `R` command to make the same change. What mode are you in now?

10. Save all changes and quit VIM.

Exercise Answers

1. Create a new file in VIM called `mary`.

   At a shell prompt, enter **vi mary**.

2. Enter the text

   Mary had a little lamb,

   It's fleece was white as snow,

   And everywhere that Mary went

   the lamb was sure to go.

   Enter insert mode by typing i or a, then enter the text.

3. Save mary without quitting.

   Press Esc to enter command mode, then type :w.

4. Put the cursor at the beginning of the first line in the file, then go to "white" using two commands.

   In Normal mode, type **1G** or **gg**, then type **j 6w**.

5. From the beginning of the file, search for "lamb." Go to the next instance of "lamb."

   In command mode, type **gg**, then **/lamb**. Type **n** to go to the next occurrence of lamb.

6. Add this line to the end of the file:

   This is a test_of w's behavior. '"***'

   Go to the beginning of the line and count how many times you have to press w to get to the end of the line.

   Type **G** to go to the end of the file, then **A**, then press the Enter key to append new text to the end of the file. Type the line, then press Esc to go to Normal mode. You have to press w 10 times to get to the last word.

7. Delete the line from the last exercise.

   Type **dd**.

8. Go to the second line in the file using the G command, and then replace "white as snow" with "black as night" using the c command. What mode are you in after you type the c command?

   Type **2G** to go to the second line, then type **c$**, then **black as night**. You are in Insert mode. c$ removes the rest of the line and puts you in Insert mode, so you can replace the rest of the line with new text.

9. Undo all the changes you just made in Exercise 8. Now use the R command to make the same change. What mode are you in now?

   Type **U** to undo all changes on the line. Type **R** to go into the Replace mode and overwrite "white as snow" with "black as night."

10. Save all changes and quit VIM.

   Press Esc to go to command mode, then type :wq.

5

Hour 6

XFree86—The Linux Window System

The X Window system is a graphical interface designed to provide the user with a more pleasing and easy–to-use computing environment. When you install the Red Hat Linux system, you are given the option to install the X Window system. When the installation process starts you will have several options. You can perform an install that includes both GNOME and KDE or you can elect to install the one of your choice. Most people wisely choose to install both GNOME and KDE. You get many more games to play and you have much more versatility by using both managers. Without the X Window system and a window manager, you are left with the system (shell) prompt.

In this hour you will learn about the X Window system. It is important that you understand what it is, how it works, and what it can do for you.

In this hour you will

- Discover what the X Window system can do for you
- Choose your monitor
- Configure XFree86

- Understand the XF86Config file
- Use window managers to customize the look of X

Discover What the X Window System Can Do for You

XFree86 is a version of the X Window system produced specifically for Linux. It is a port of X11R6, which can be distributed freely and supports a wide range of video hardware including VGA, Super VGA, and many accelerated video adapters. XFree86 is a complete distribution of the X Window software and contains the actual X server, applications, programming libraries, utilities, and documentation.

> Actually, the X Window system was developed from the beginning as a networking system; the intention was to support networking graphics and provide a base set of communication protocols. With this technology, you can build graphical interfaces for computers that use bitmapped graphics displays. Applications that run under X are called *clients*. These clients do not really draw graphics on your display but communicate with your X server instead. The X server controls your display and manipulates what you see on your screen. If you installed Red Hat Linux in a normal configuration without modifications, your X Window system should reside in the /usr/X11R6 directory.

One of the most useful features of the X Window system is that you can have multiple terminal windows on the screen at once, with each having a different login session. Hundreds of programs are written specifically for Linux and are generally free for you to use. These include games, graphics, utilities, and programming software such as C, Basic, and many others.

What does the window manager do? The X window manager, such as GNOME, exists as a means to control how your graphical user interface (GUI) works. If you have used a graphical user interface such as Microsoft Windows, you are aware of what I am talking about. You will see a better representation of what services are offered by a graphical windows environment such as GNOME, shown in Figure 6.1. When using GNOME or KDE you can use any kind of program, from games to graphics to windows terminals.

FIGURE 6.1

GNOME is a window manager that is installed with Red Hat Linux and allows you to perform many tasks.

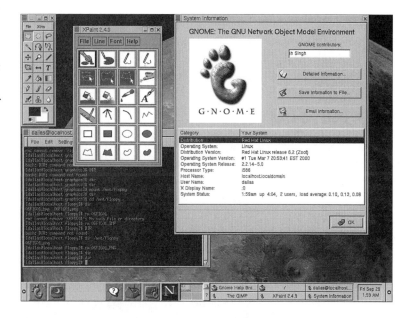

Most UNIX and Linux systems use the X Window system and Red Hat Software, Inc. includes the XFree86 X Window system in its distributions. Red Hat uses the version of XFree86 that is produced by the XFree86 Project. You may see the product referred to as X, X Window, X11, X11R6, or XFree86. If you chose to install the X Window system on your computer during the Red Hat installation, you will have the most current version.

Should you upgrade the X Window system each time it is available? There are times when you may want to upgrade to a newer version of the X Window system. For example, if you purchased a new graphics card that wasn't supported by the old version, you should upgrade.

6

The current version of XFree86 is 4.0.1 (as of July, 2000) and this is the first full upgrade in the XFree86 4 series. This release (4) is a major redesign of the basic architecture of XFree86's original version of the X Consortium's X server. XFree86 4.0.1 has many enhancements that weren't previously available. These include a graphical configuration tool, 3D support by the addition of DRI GLX drivers, security fixes, and additional support for other operating systems such as BSD. You can download the full distribution, patches, and updates from `ftp://ftp.xfree86.org`. However, with Red Hat Linux 7.0, you shouldn't need to upgrade because the current version will be installed when you install Red Hat Linux on your system.

XFree86 is the software that exists between the hardware and the graphical user interface (GUI) that you see when you start the client. When you run a window manager such as GNOME, KDE, or Enlightenment, to name a very few, you are actually running XFree86 because these managers run as XFree86 clients.

Installing X

During the installation of Red Hat Linux, you go through the routine of selecting your window manager, the graphics (video) card, and many other things. When you are doing your installation, you should take your time and make sure that you are careful and very meticulous in your choices. Doing the installation correctly the first time and making the right choices can save you a lot of pain later. Red Hat Linux creates (in a roundabout way) a file called XF86Config. This important file contains all the information about your X Window configuration and determines how your graphics programs will run. If you are lucky in the initial installation, you will have a clean XF86Config file. If you do have problems, you can make changes in this file. Just for the record, this file should be located either in /etc/X11 or the /usr/X11R6/lib/X11 directory. If you launch X as the root operator, the file may be in the /root directory. In my current installation it is located in /usr/X11R6/lib/X11, but yours could be hidden from you. In that case, you get to do a little searching.

When you install Red Hat Linux, you are usually given an option to start the X system automatically, or you can start it from the command line manually. The most common way to start the X Window system from the command prompt is as follows:

```
# startx
```

When you issue the preceding command, it will start the default window manager, which is normally GNOME. You can choose from many window managers, but most people use either GNOME, KDE, or both. In the next section you will discover how to choose and configure the right monitor for your system. If you are using an existing monitor, you will learn how to configure it during the installation process.

Choosing a Monitor

Red Hat Linux 7.0 will support most of the monitors that you are likely to purchase. Numerous hardware compatibility lists are on the Internet, including Red Hat's own site. You can find Red Hat's compatibility list at http://www.redhat.com/. Of course, it isn't always possible to purchase new components for your system because you may already have the equipment on which you are doing the installation. Most monitors are supported by Red Hat Linux, but if yours isn't you may be able to find a driver on one of the numerous Linux Web sites. Another good place to check is the Linux newsgroups. It is likely that if you have the problem, someone else has it, too. And it is even more likely that someone else has the solution, so don't give up. Just keep searching until you get the answer.

Your monitor is configured during the initial installation of Red Hat Linux 7.0. Before you start the installation, you should collect all the information about your equipment that you can, including information about your monitor and video card. Be sure you know the video card's make and model number and the video chipset it uses. You will need to know who the manufacturer is and how much RAM it has. It is also helpful to know if it is a PCI card, an IDE, or if it is on an integrated board. You may have problems with some of the newer computer motherboards (especially the ATX/MMX type integrated systems) because the video is built onto the board, and in some installations, it isn't detected.

> If you have a newer computer system and you are installing Red Hat 7.0, you should have few problems. Red Hat 7.0 actually detects most PCI cards and even most components on integrated boards. It will detect PCI cards and most other Plug-and-Play devices, so you will be up and running in no time. Red Hat Linux 7.0 does a good job of detecting and installing the drivers for AGP cards.

Task: Configuring Your Monitor

If you chose to install Server or Workstation during the Red Hat 7.0 installation, you will be asked to enter the information as outlined in the following task. In most cases, your monitor and video card will be detected during the installation. If you need to perform this operation later because you are having problems with your monitor or video card and you don't want to run install again, here is how to do it:

1. To configure the X Window system you need to run Xconfigurator. You may do this to set up your monitor or video card, or both.

2. From a terminal window or the command prompt, type **# Xconfigurator**.

   Xconfigurator will start, giving you the opportunity to configure the X server for your system.

3. Xconfigurator will present a list of monitors for you to select from. If your monitor is listed, select it and press Enter.

   If your monitor is not listed, press Custom.

6

4. When you select Custom, you will be asked for the horizontal sync range and the vertical sync range of your monitor. You will most likely find this information in your monitor manual. If not, call your monitor manufacturer.

   Do not select a range value for your monitor that is outside these horizontal and vertical requirements for your monitor.

5. After you have selected your monitor, Xconfigurator starts to probe your video card. You can elect to not probe by selecting Do Not Probe and enter the values yourself. If your probe fails, you will have to enter them manually.

   While the probe is in progress, it is normal for your screen to blink on and off several times. Don't panic. Everything is normal with Linux.

6. When the probe is finished, the Probe Finished screen appears. This screen shows you the results of the video card probe. You have three options: Use Default, Let Me Choose, or Back. You can use the settings shown on the screen or choose your own settings. If you choose your own, you will need information about your video card and monitor.

7. Choose Default to accept the color depth and resolution detected during the probe. If you select Let Me Choose, you will be presented with the Select Video Modes dialog.

8. Select the proper video modes that you want to use and press Enter.

9. Once you've made your selection, the Start X dialog box will appear. You have the option of letting Xconfigurator test your configuration or not. Normally, you should select OK to begin the test.

10. If there is an error in the configuration, you will have the opportunity to go back and do it all over again. If not, you will see a small display window asking if you can see the contents of the box clearly. If you do, click Yes within ten seconds (you must be speedy here).

11. You are now given a choice of how you want the X Window system to start. You can start it manually at the prompt by typing **startx** or have it started automatically.

12. You can now reboot your system, log in when asked, and enjoy Red Hat Linux 7.0.

If for some reason your video card wasn't detected, don't worry. This isn't a big problem and you shouldn't be concerned with it. In fact, don't worry about anything where computers are concerned. They may give you problems, but that's just another opportunity for you to learn something new, how to solve the problem, and get the system running again.

Task: Troubleshooting Xconfigurator

If your card wasn't found in the installation process, then you can run Xconfigurator again. Follow these steps:

1. You will need to run Xconfigurator again from the command prompt or a terminal window by typing **Xconfigurator**. You will need to be root or use the su command and enter your password for root.

2. When you ran Xconfigurator before, your system was probed for a video card. If your card was not found or was not listed and you selected Custom, then you will be asked for the amount of memory installed on your video card or the integrated card on your motherboard. Be sure you know the correct memory value to enter here.

3. If you select Custom, the Select Video Memory Dialog will pop up. You will see a list of memory options to select from. Select the correct amount and click OK or Exit to quit without making changes.

4. You may be asked to configure your clockchip in the Clockchip Configuration dialog. In most cases you should select No Clockchip Setting because it should be automatically detected.

5. Click OK or Exit. If you click OK, your settings are saved in the /ect/X11/ XF86Config file. If you need to make modifications in the future, all you have to do is run Xconfigurator again.

The Monitor section of the XF86Config file specifies the characteristics of your monitor. This file is generated by the Red Hat Linux 7.0 Xconfigurator after it probes your system. You will learn more about this in the next section. If you have more than one monitor (with Linux you can have more than one monitor because it is a true multitasking system), you will have multiple sections for Monitor in the XF86Config file. Don't be surprised at this; it is normal to have more than one monitor listed here.

Configuring XFree86

In this section you will learn how to create and edit the XF86Config file, which is the configuration file that tells the XFree86 server what to do. The XF86Config file is the most important file in your X Window program. This file is created when you first install Linux, or you can create it by using Xconfigurator.

Under normal circumstances, everything that your system needs to know will be found out during the Linux installation. The secret to performing a smoother Red Hat Linux installation is to know everything about your hardware that you can. After all, you can't expect Linux to know everything; you have to help it along from time to time.

6

If you took the opportunity to install X when you installed the Linux system, most of your X Window files should reside in the /usr/X11R6 directory. At some point in your Linux career you may need to find out if certain X Window–related files are in this directory. One reason would be if your video card quit working. You can look in this directory to see if some of the files have been deleted, damaged, or if other problems exist.

You can cd to the following directory to look at these files:

```
/usr/X11R6/
```

Your directory should look something like this:

```
bin doc include lib man share
```

You should take a few minutes to look in each of these directories. For instance, Xconfigurator exists in the /share directory on my filesystem. Yours may be different.

If you have an older version of XFree86 on your computer and you want to upgrade it, you do this using Red Hat's rpm (Red Hat Package Manager) command to upgrade it.

Task: Upgrading X Free86 Window System

You can upgrade the XFree86 window system by performing a complete new install or you can do it manually using Red Hat's rpm command. The choice is yours.

Here is how to upgrade your XFree86 window system using Red Hat Linux 7.0 and the rpm program:

1. Insert the Red Hat Linux 7.0 CD into the drive and type this command at the command prompt:

   ```
   # mount /mnt/cdrom
   ```

2. To begin the installation, navigate to the RedHat/RPMS/ directory on the CD. For example: cd/RedHat/RPMS.

3. You should now be in /RedHat/RPMS. Type **dir XFre*** and you should see the XFree86 files. You can also use the ls command if you like.

4. To install the packages from the command line, type the following (assuming you are not logged in as root):

   ```
   #su -c "rpm -1 /mnt/cdrom/RedHat/RPMS/XFree86*rpm"
   ```

   If you are logged in as root, then the following syntax is correct:

   ```
   # rpm -ivh XFree86*rpm
   ```

   The syntax for using rpm is as follows:

   ```
   # rpm -ivh <name of rpm package you are installing>
   ```

5. Your XFree86 files should install and you can reboot your machine in order for them to take effect.

You can also use the Gnome-RPM utility, which is a lot easier to handle and has a graphical interface. See your Red Hat manuals for more information on using Gnome-RPM. Either way, you can get the job done and enjoy the latest enhancements to your X Window system. It is nice to know how to work in both text and graphical modes.

After you have installed XFree86 in the normal manner or as an upgrade, you may want to look in the /usr/X11R6 directory to see what's there. You should find several subdirectories containing files specific to the X Window system.

Note that some or all of the files may be installed in the directories listed in the /usr/X11R6/ directory. You can check out each of these to see what has been installed. The major components of XFree86 consist of many files pertaining to clients, configuration files, header files and libraries, manual pages, and documentation and resource files. Ten X servers are installed.

If your system is working correctly, don't fool with it too much. Of course, you can look at it and even program it, but the safe way is to use the sample XF86Config file that is included in the installation or make a copy of the original file and rename it to something else. You can make several backups of this file and rename them something else. You should never transfer your file to someone else's computer or vice versa. The reason is that rarely are two computers the same. It is easier to reinstall the X Window system or do a complete Linux install or upgrade.

> Okay, now you know how to upgrade the XF86Config file, but what about making some changes to it when you need to? The safest way is to make a copy of the original file and work with the copy. Then when the corrections have been made, you can simply use it.

6

There may be times when you will have to make changes to your XF86Config file. Before doing so, take some time to document information about your system. Following are the items that you should have information about:

- The type, make, model, name, chipset, and manufacturer of the video card that is installed in your computer.
- How much video RAM is installed on your card. This is the RAM that is installed on your card—not in your computer.
- The type of clockchip installed on your video card chipset.
- The type of mouse you are using. This is generally PS/2 or serial mouse.

- All the information that you can get about your monitor. What is usually required is the manufacturer, make, model, and name.
- The vertical and horizontal refresh rates of your monitor. An example is something like 55–100 vertical and 30–60 horizontal.
- Your keyboard type.

You have learned how to install and configure your monitor and video card, what XFree86 is, and how to install or upgrade it using Red Hat 7.0 RPM. Now you will see what is contained in the XF86Config file. Before you begin creating a new XF86Config file, take a look at the section "Understanding the XF86Config File" later in the chapter, which outlines what your file should look like.

What the XF86Config File Contains

The XF86Config file is nothing more than a single text file that contains the following sections:

- **Screen**—Instructs what server is to be used.
- **Device**—Contains information and details about your devices such as video card chip set.
- **Files**—Tells the X server where fonts, colors, and software modules are located.
- **ServerFlags**—On/Off flags that allow or deny special actions such as core dumps and mouse and keyboard configurations.
- **Module**—Tells the server what modules should be loaded.
- **Keyboard**—Contains information about the keyboard and what information the server should use.
- **Pointer**—Tells the server what pointer is used.
- **Input**—For input devices such as scanners and mouse devices.
- **Monitor**—Contains specific details and settings for your monitor.
- **Graphics Device**—Contains a list of devices detected and configured by Xconfigurator. There may be several graphics device sections.

How Xconfigurator Works

Red Hat's Xconfigurator is a unique program that generates an XF86Config file after it probes your system for certain information that it needs. It does most of the work for you, but you may be asked to provide some information. You can now start Xconfigurator and enter your information to set up your monitor and video card. If you aren't logged in as root, you can start Xconfigurator as follows:

```
# su -c Xconfigurator
```

Remember that su means "super user," and you can use it to start programs when you are logged in as something other than root.

When the first dialog screen pops up, you will be informed that the XF86Config generally resides in /usr/X11R6/lib/X11 or /etc/X11. Be sure that you read this and all other information in this program carefully. Figure 6.2 shows the startup screen. This is the first screen that you will see when you first start Xconfigurator.

FIGURE 6.2

The Xconfigurator Start screen gives you some useful information.

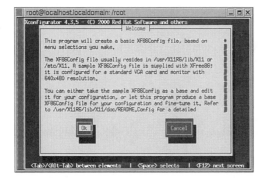

You can use the Tab key to navigate through the menus. You have an OK or Cancel option. Tab down to the OK button and press Enter. Xconfigurator will probe for your video card and report on the results. If it doesn't find your card, you will be presented with a list to choose from. Use the Up or Down arrow keys (or use the mouse for the scrollbar on the right side of the window) to make a choice. If your card isn't listed, you can choose the Unlisted Card option. After making a choice, tab down to OK and press Enter. This dialog is shown in Figure 6.3.

FIGURE 6.3

The second screen asks you to choose a card from the list.

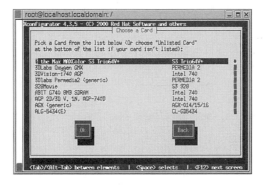

6

You now have to select your monitor. Using the arrow keys, select your monitor type. If you want to enter your own values, select Custom from the list. If possible, select a monitor type without doing anything manually. Click OK. You are now ready to enter the information for your monitor in the Screen Configuration dialog box. You have two options: Don't Probe and Probe. Tab down to Probe and press Enter. The next dialog box will inform you that the system is ready to begin probing (see Figure 6.4). Press Enter to begin the probe. Sometimes you may be asked for information about your video card instead of probing after configuring your monitor.

FIGURE 6.4

Using the Xconfigurator to select your video modes.

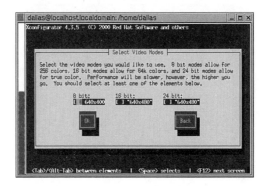

You will see the screen flash from blue to black several times. Don't worry about this; it is a perfectly normal action by a working Linux system. The next screen informs you that the probing is finished and you have three options: Use Default, Let Me Choose, and Back. If the default settings that X has found look reasonable, choose the Use Default button and press Enter.

You will be informed that Xconfigurator is starting X to test the system. Click OK or Skip to proceed.

At this point you will see a gray screen and you will eventually be asked if you can see this box and if you want the X Window system to start when you boot up.

If you chose not to start the X Window system on boot, you will see a blue screen and your system prompt. When the session is over and you are at the system prompt, simply type in **startx** to begin your X Window session with your new configuration. In Figure 6.5, you can see a dialog box telling you that the probe was successful. The new configuration is saved in the XF86Config file.

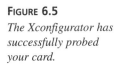

FIGURE 6.5

The Xconfigurator has successfully probed your card.

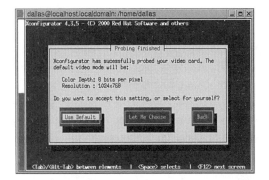

At this point you may be wondering what the XF86Config file looks like. The simplest way to find out is to examine it with a text editor. You can look at it anytime you want, but you'll learn more about it in the next section. So how do you feel now? You have created (successfully, I hope) your first XF86Config file. In the next section you will get away from Xconfigurator and take a look at what it creates in the form of XF86Config.

Understanding the XF86Config File

Now take a look at what you have created or modified, depending on the situation. To examine the file, use any text editor of your choice with the line wrapping turned off. You will need to open the file as root, which you can do very easily like this:

```
# su -c "pico -w /etc/X11/XF86Config"
```

You may have to alter this command line to get it to work, depending on the location of your XF8Config file. This file will be in different locations depending on the version of your Red Hat software. Be careful that you do not edit the sample file; it is just there for you to look at. Read the documentation on your CD for more information about this file.

The Files section tells the designated server where the fonts that it needs are located and where the color name database resides. In most XF86Config files, you will see the name and location of the RGB database under the Files section. If you need to change this at some point, you can do so. Under this you will see the Font Path designation. In older versions of Red Hat Linux you will see this entry, but in later versions Red Hat uses a font server independent of the X server to handle fonts.

The ServerFlags section is used to implement special actions by the X server. The lines are commented with the # sign. You can disable or render useless any command, action, or event by removing this sign. You can use this section to configure special actions allowed by your X server.

6

The Keyboard section allows you to create certain settings that tell your X server what type of keyboard you have and what settings to use. If you scroll through the listing, you will see some of the settings that Xconfigurator has selected for your particular keyboard. If you add a different keyboard, you can edit the keyboard settings to make your new one work without doing a new install. The Pointer section tells the X server what kind of mouse (pointer) you are using. The important thing here is how the buttons are used because some mouse devices can have two or three buttons. In some cases you might be using a trackball or other device. The X server needs to know all about your pointing device.

The Monitor section tells the X server specific information about your monitor. If you are having problems with your monitor, this is the section that you need to pay particular attention to. The Graphics Device section tells your X server about your video card chipset. This information is important because it tells your X server exactly what kind of video card you have and what kind of chipset and options it needs to support.

The Screen section tells the X server important information about what screen resolution to use, such as color depth, screen size, and resolution. The server needs this information before it can start X Window or a window manager.

You can use other methods to configure XF86Config. One of these is the XF86Setup command. This is a graphical interface client that is included in the XFree86 package. If you don't have it on your CD, you can get it from the XFree86 Project site at http://www.xFree86.org/. To try this method, issue the following command as root:

```
# XF86Setup
```

Unless you are the luckiest person in the world, you will have trouble with your computer system. When this happens, think about what the problem is relative to. For example, does the problem relate to the monitor or the mouse? If it relates to the monitor, you have a clue as to where to start your search.

Some of the likely suspects for problems are as follows:

Configuration problems (the most likely culprit)

Display

Fonts

Chipset inconsistencies or problems

Keyboard

Mouse

Monitor

To find out more about handling problems concerning XFree86, you should read the XFree86 FAQ (Frequently Asked Questions); you can get it and a lot of other useful information at http://www.XFree86.org/.

Virtual Consoles and Terminal Windows

Virtual consoles allow you to work in several windows at once or move through many windows one at a time. GNOME features several virtual consoles that you can view simply by pressing a combination of keys. You can access these virtual consoles by pressing Ctrl+Alt+F*n* (where F*n* is any of the first six function keys on your keyboard). When using virtual consoles, you may be asked to log in. After you have logged in, you can use the system normally on any of the virtual consoles. To return to your X session, just press Ctrl+Alt+F7. This may not work if you have programmed your first six function keys for something else, so you may have to change the programming for those keys if you want to use this feature.

You can actually use twelve virtual screens if you have twelve function keys and they aren't programmed for something else. Most distributions of Linux come with five default virtual screens. Virtual screens or consoles have information about your system.

What is in these virtual consoles or screens? During the Linux installation process, Linux makes several kinds of diagnostic messages available to you in five virtual consoles, which include access to the bash prompt. You can switch through these consoles using a single keystroke. Suppose you are working on a document on your desktop and you suddenly need access to the shell prompt. You can access the shell by using the function keys.

Another feature of virtual consoles is useful when you are installing Linux and you have problems. You can switch through the consoles to find information on what and how something was installed. When you are diagnosing installation problems, you should use Alt+F1 because this is a record of the installation process. Following are the five virtual consoles that you have access to:

1. Alt+F1—Installation dialog
2. Alt+F2—Shell prompt

6

3. Alt+F3—Install log (this contains messages from the install log)

4. Alt+F4—System log containing messages from kernel, and so on

5. Alt+F5—Other varied messages

When you want to run a program that you cannot access from the normal window environment, you have to run a terminal program that allows you to run programs and work in a text-based environment. *Terminals* are windows with text-only screens. One of the many terminals available is Xterm. Another you may want to try is the GNOME terminal that is installed when you install GNOME. While in a terminal window such as a GNOME terminal, you can perform all of the functions that you would normally have access to, such as running applications and doing systems maintenance.

> Please don't confuse terminal windows, virtual consoles, and desktop switching. They are all different worlds. Terminal windows allow you to access the shell, such as bash; virtual consoles are windows within windows on your desktop; and desktop switching deals with changing from one window manager to another. An example would be switching from GNOME to KDE.

You should not confuse terminal emulators with terminal programs. *Terminal emulators* are programs that emulate a computer terminal and provide the means for the CPU or computer to talk to the computer monitor. These were and are used mostly by mainframes; they once were called "dumb terminals" because they consisted mostly of a terminal, a keyboard, and maybe a mouse. They do not have the electronics to do anything other than what the software allows them to do.

You may want to run various programs such as word processors, spreadsheets, communication programs, and shells from an Xterm window. If you want to find out more about terminal programs, check out GNOME, KDE, and other window managers. Hundreds of term programs are available free on the Internet, especially where Linux is concerned. Now let's take a better look at the virtual desktop.

The Virtual Desktop

The Red Hat Linux 7.0 distribution allows you to install many types of great window managers. The two most popular desktop managers are GNOME and KDE. The virtual desktop that these two window managers (and other managers) provide you with have specific attributes and features that enable you to control what you see and do while using them.

A *window manager* is the main interface between the X Window system and the user. Without the window manager you would be left with the system prompt, which isn't too productive, especially if you are used to using graphical interfaces. The *screen* is the whole desktop area that you see when you have GNOME or KDE up and running. You can have more than one screen or computer running off one X server, but for the purposes of this chapter, a screen is the viewing area of your desktop. The background area of your screen is called the *root window*; this is the area on which you run your applications, install an icon, or place a picture as a wallpaper image. Your mouse or other pointing device is called the *pointer*.

The window is simply a frame in which your applications reside and from which you can run and use them. The window manager "manages" everything that you see in this window. Within this window environment, you have such things as menus and icons. These menus and icons allow you to view and select your programs and documents.

With most desktop managers, such as GNOME and KDE, you will have a panel at the bottom of the screen. You can add applets to the panel to enhance your productivity and to do other things. You can dock folders, applications, and applets on the panel for easy launching and access. One of the nice features of the GNOME panel is that you can click the left or right arrow at the end of the panel to grow or shrink it. Adding an applet to your panel is as easy as working with any other window environment.

Task: Adding an Applet to Your Panel

To add an applet to the panel, follow these steps:

1. Right-click a clear area of the panel.
2. Select Add Applet and a list of categories pops up.
3. Select an applet to add from the categories.
4. For example, to add the Drive Mount utility to your panel, select Add applet, Utility and select Drive Mount. The Drive Mount applet should appear on your panel. In my case, I can mount/unmount the floppy from the panel, which makes it convenient. Look through the options but don't let your panel get too cluttered or it will be useless.

You can customize the panel by adding one or more panels to your desktop; you can change the orientation from horizontal to vertical or shrink it to move it out of the way.

In this section you have learned a few things about the panel—how to add applets to it, resize it, and make it more personalized. In the next section you will find out what virtual desktops are all about.

6

Using Virtual Desktops

When you are using GNOME, the desktop is bigger than you can imagine. If you doubt me, look at the Pager on the panel. You should see four blocks and one of them should be blue to indicate which screen or desktop you are in. Most of the time you only use about one-fourth of the screen. The Pager allows you to move easily from one part of the desktop to another. For example, drag an open window down to the right side of the desktop until only the top left part of it is visible. Now watch the Pager and you should see a small square overlapping from the left block of the Pager to the right top one.

If your Pager is not on your panel, you can quickly add it like this:

1. Right-click your mouse on a clear area of the panel.
2. Select Add Applet, Utility, and then click Gnome Pager. The Pager should appear on your panel.

The blue corner of the Pager indicates which quadrant of the desktop you are in at the present time. Click on each of the other quadrants or sections of the Pager and look at what is in that section (some quadrants may not have anything in them). If you click the lower-right quadrant, you will see part of the window that is currently scrolled off the screen.

The only time you probably will be interested in the Pager is when you have many windows open and your present desktop is getting cluttered.

 When we are talking about the quadrant, we are referring to the current desktop.

If you take a look at the Tasklist in the panel, you will notice that it shows a button for each window that is currently open. By default, you normally have only four windows available. You can change the appearance or settings for the Pager by clicking the question mark (?) next to the Pager. The Gnome Pager Settings dialog box appears. Please note the Pager and Tasklist tabs at the top of the dialog box. You can set the following options:

- **Show Pager**—Select to show Pager or not.
- **Place Pagers After Tasklist**—Moves pagers to the right of the Tasklist.
- **Use Small Pagers**—Shrinks the size of the Pager when selected.
- **Rows of Pagers**—Determines how many rows of pagers appear in the panel.

There are other options below this that you can look at, but the ones listed above are the main selections that you most likely will be interested in. Once you have made the changes, you have the option buttons OK, Apply, Close, and Help. Now click the Tasklist tab to see the options available there:

- **Show Tasklist Button**—Shows or hides the button. To see how this actually works, click the button and click Apply at the bottom of the window. The Tasklist button will disappear. Click the Show Tasklist Button again and click Apply. It should be back on your panel.

- **Show TaskList**—Shows or hides list of open windows.

- **Show Button Icons**—Shows or hides the little icon at the left of each open window's button.

- **Show All Tasks**—The Tasklist shows all tasks that are currently in normal and minimized windows.

- **Show Normal Tasks Only**—Shows tasks that are in current normal open windows.

- **Show Minimized Tasks Only**—Shows tasks that are currently open in minimized windows.

- **Show All Tasks on All Desktops**—Shows all tasks on all windows on all virtual desktops.

- **Show Minimized Tasks on All Desktops**—Shows minimized tasks on all the virtual desktops.

- **Geometry**—Defines exact size and appearance of Tasklist.

To activate any changes that you have made, click Apply and then OK when you are finished to save the changes. If you have already applied and saved all of your changes, click Close to end the session.

Rather than crowd your work on a single screen, you have the option of using virtual desktops. These options allow you to extend your workspace to multiple desktop areas. You can have your spreadsheet open in one desktop, your word processor open in another one, and access the Internet in still another desktop. By default, you have four desktops available to you, but you can extend this by running your window manager configuration utility. Each window manager has something different, so check your documentation. With Red Hat 7.0, the Enlightenment configuration manager can be run by clicking the middle button on a three-button mouse, or clicking your left and right mouse buttons simultaneously and selecting Enlightenment Configuration. You will need the Enlightenment manager installed to do this. The Enlightenment Configuration Editor dialog pops up. Find the entry called Desktops, and you will be able to increase or decrease the number of windows available to you. The following section describes the simple way to switch desktops.

6

Switching Desktops

The Desktop Switcher is a GNOME utility that enables you to switch desktops. To access the GNOME Desktop Switcher, open the main menu, select System and click Desktop Switching Tool. The Desktop Switcher dialog pops up showing you the current desktop environments available. In Figure 6.6 you can see that I have three window managers available: GNOME, KDE, and FVWM. Click on the window manager you want to change to and click OK. You will need to log out and reboot for the change to take effect. When you type **startx** or your window manager loads automatically for you, the new manager should be in control. You can see what the Desktop Switcher looks like in Figure 6.6.

FIGURE 6.6

The GNOME Desktop Switcher allows you to switch desktops.

Why would you want to switch desktops? The reasons are varied but in general you might have an application that can't be run on your current desktop or maybe you just like the change of scenery sometimes. In this section we have discussed virtual desktops and not only how to switch between windows, but also how to switch between desktops. In the next section you will be introduced to a few ways to customize your X Window environment.

By using the virtual desktop, you can be much more productive—such as playing 10 different games while your boss is not looking. So have fun, but don't get caught.

Customizing the Look of X Using Window Manager

It is pretty straightforward and easy to customize your desktop. This section uses GNOME as an example because most window-based desktop managers are about the same. Some of the things you can do to make your desktop more pleasing and suitable to you is to change the colors, add a bitmap for wallpaper (picture), and change the theme of the desktop.

Both KDE and GNOME offer some extravagant ways to customize your desktop. If you need more specific help, use the Help option in either environment to ensure that you can do what you want to accomplish. One of the enlightening aspects of Linux (all versions) is the help that you get when you press the Help button or look for information on the Internet. If you haven't tried it, click the Help button on a few different applications and I think you will be surprised with the amount of information available. Most of the help that you will ever need is as close as your local bookstore (where you will find many Macmillan books on Linux) and at http://www.mcp.com, where you can find all the help you need in the way of books and other information.

The best way to customize your desktop is by using the GNOME Control Center. You can access it from the Main Menu button (click Settings, GNOME Control Center) or right-click a clear area of the desktop and a dialog box will pop up; then you just select Configure Background Image to make all the changes in the Control Panel.

Summary

In this hour you learned what XFree86 is and how it works to provide you with a full-featured graphical user interface. You learned about some elements of window managers and how to set up and configure your monitor and video card. You learned how to configure XFree86 and what the corresponding XF86Config file is all about. You also received a few instructions on what to do to analyze and solve problems that might result when something goes wrong.

You also learned how to customize the look of your desktop by using the window manager.

Workshop

The Workshop contains quiz questions and exercises to help reinforce what you've learned in this hour.

6

Q&A

Q What is the name of the nonprofit organization that provides XFree86 free for several platforms including UNIX and Linux?

A It is called the XFree86 Project.

Q How many virtual desktops do you have in GNOME by default?

A You have four desktops available to you by default, but you can add as many as you have function keys. If you do not have your function keys assigned to something else, then you can use them for virtual desktops.

Quiz

1. What does a window manager do?

2. What is the current version of XFree86?

3. What command is used to start an X Window session?

4. What is the name of the text file created when you install Linux or when you use Xconfigurator?

5. What types of programs can you use to examine the XF86Config file?

Quiz Answers

1. What does a window manager do?

   It acts like a traffic cop in that it controls the placement of windows; it sizes and moves windows, controls icons, and performs other useful functions.

2. What is the current version of XFree86?

   XFree86 4.0.1.

3. What command is used to start an X Window session?

   `startx`

4. What is the name of the text file created when you install Linux or when you use Xconfigurator?

   `XF86Config`

5. What types of programs can you use to examine the XF86Config file?

   Word processors or text editors.

Exercises

1. Go to the system prompt (#) or run an X terminal such as Xterm from your desktop.

2. Type in **Xconfigurator**.

3. Enter the requested information for your system.

4. Be sure that you enter the correct information for your monitor and your video card.

   Remember that you can use this utility to correct any problems that you may have with the monitor or the video card settings. This information is saved in the XF86Config file.

5. If you entered the correct information, your system should boot normally; if not, try it again and be sure to enter the correct information for your system.

6. Use a text editor to examine the XF86Config file and note any information about your monitor and video card. Does it list the correct information?

7. Exit the program and reboot your machine. If you entered the correct information when you ran Xconfigurator, you should be fine. If not, try running it again and try some of the things that were discussed in this chapter.

6

PART II
Using Red Hat Linux 7.0

Hour

HOUR 7

Using the GNOME Desktop Environment

A desktop environment can make using Linux as easy as using Windows or Macintosh. There are several desktop environments available for Linux, but the two that are included in Red Hat are KDE and GNOME. At the user level, KDE and GNOME are quite similar, although there are differences in overall style and feel. By default, Red Hat supports the GNOME desktop environment.

In this hour you will

- Explore the GNOME desktop environment, including the desktop, main menu, and Panel
- Add applets, launchers, and drawers to the GNOME Panel
- Learn how GNOME works with window managers, and set up multiple workspaces in the Sawfish window manager
- Switch between GNOME and KDE using Switchdesk, and use session management to "save" your GNOME session

Introducing GNOME

As you learned in the last hour, X provides the functions needed for a graphical interface, but it doesn't provide the interface itself. The actual buttons, windows, scrollbars, icons, and other graphical objects are created by the window manager and the desktop environment. The window manager and desktop environment exist as a layer on top of X.

A desktop environment is nothing more than a different way of using Linux. Instead of typing commands into the shell environment, you can point and click in a window with a mouse. All the tools and applications of Red Hat are available within the graphical environment. Some applications, such as AbiWord or Gnumeric, can only be used within an X environment. Other applications, such as Emacs, have both a shell and an X version. You can still access a shell within the desktop environment by opening an X terminal. The X terminal, or xterm, serves as a virtual terminal within X. The GNOME xterm, shown in Figure 7.1, is called GNOME Terminal.

GNOME isn't just a desktop environment, but also a collection of applications that are created using GNOME standards. This means that GNOME applications maintain the same look and feel, and can work together seamlessly. You will be introduced to some useful GNOME applications, as well as other Linux applications in Hours 11, "Linux Applications," and 12, "Linux Productivity Applications."

FIGURE 7.1

The GNOME desktop environment magnifies the things you can do in Linux, while maintaining flexibility.

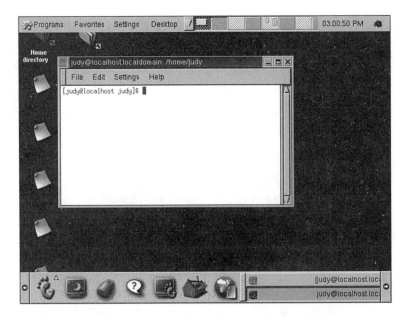

Getting GNOME

If you selected GNOME as one of the package groups to install in Hour 2, "Installing Red Hat Linux 7.0," you're all ready to go. Red Hat uses GNOME as the default desktop environment, so as soon as you start X, GNOME starts by default. If you didn't select GNOME in Hour 2, there are three different ways to install GNOME on your system:

- Run the Red Hat installation program again, select Upgrade as the installation type, and then select GNOME as the package group to upgrade.
- Visit `http://www.helixcode.com` and install Helix Code GNOME directly from the Web.
- Install each GNOME package individually, either from the CD-ROM or from the Helix Code Web site.

Helix Code is a commercial company founded by Miguel de Icaza, founder of the GNOME project. Helix Code GNOME is updated more often than the packages found in the Red Hat distribution, and is much easier to install and upgrade. Even if you would like to use the version of GNOME found in the Red Hat distribution, visit the Helix site to download GNOME Office and other useful GNOME applications.

If you really want to install the packages individually, you can, although it's hard work (there are about fifteen packages). For instructions, see `www.helixcode.com`, or read *Sams Teach Yourself GNOME in 24 Hours*.

Starting GNOME

Starting GNOME in Red Hat is simple. Because GNOME is the default Red Hat desktop environment, all you have to do to start GNOME is start X.

If during installation you chose to make KDE your desktop environment, see the section "Using Switchdesk to Switch to KDE," later in this hour for instructions on starting GNOME.

Getting to Know the GNOME Environment

If you have experience with Windows, Macintosh, or another X desktop environment such as KDE, GNOME should look familiar. There is a desktop area where windows open, with a vertical row of icons, a Panel of buttons at the bottom of the screen, and a

7

Panel of menus at the top of the screen. When you click the Main menu button (it has an icon of the GNOME footprint on it), the GNOME main menu appears.

Figure 7.2 illustrates a simple GNOME desktop, as it appears by default when you first start GNOME in Red Hat.

FIGURE 7.2

The default GNOME desktop in Red Hat is simple, but powerful.

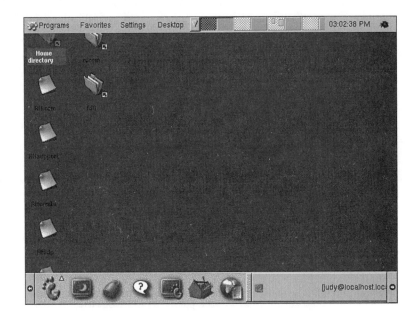

The Desktop

The desktop is the space where you do your work in GNOME. When you start an application, it opens in a window on the desktop. The desktop contains menus, which you can access by right-clicking or middle-clicking an empty space on the desktop. It also contains icons. Icons can be used to open files, list directories, run applications, or open Web pages.

Red Hat automatically includes a row of icons when you first start GNOME, including your home directory, mount points for your CD-ROM and floppy drive, and Web links to various Red Hat, GNOME, and Linux Web sites. When you double-click your home directory icon, the GNOME File Manager opens at your home directory. The File Manager, shown in Figure 7.3, is a graphical directory tree, similar to Windows Explorer.

You can use the GNOME File Manager to manage all your files and directories, as well as drag-and-drop objects onto the desktop.

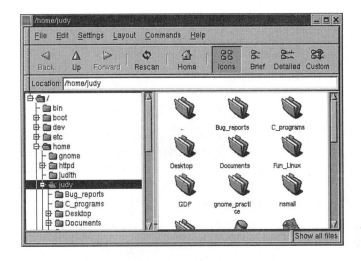

The icons for the floppy disk and CD-ROM can be used to mount and unmount those devices with one click of the mouse. To mount a device, right-click the icon and select Mount Device. When you are ready to unmount, close all device directories, then right-click the device icon and select Unmount Device. After unmounting, you can eject the disk or CD-ROM by right-clicking the icon and selecting Eject Device.

Task: Creating Icons

Red Hat comes with a set of default icons, but you can easily delete some or all of them and create your own. The easiest way to create an icon on the desktop is to drag the file or application launcher from the File Manager to the desktop.

1. Open File Manager by clicking the Home Directory icon or by selecting Programs, File Manager from the Main Menu.

2. Browse for the file, directory, or application for which you want to create an icon.

3. Right-click the entry in File Manager, drag it to the desktop, and select Copy from the drag-and-drop menu.

4. To create an icon for a Web link, right-click an empty space in the desktop and select New URL Link.

5. Enter the URL in the dialog box. An application launcher enables you to start an application by double-clicking the icon.

6. For a new launcher, enter the name of the icon under Name and the command to launch the application in Command. Alternatively, you can open /usr/bin in File Manager, find the executable file for the application, and drag it to the desktop.

7

Although you can create an icon for an application launcher, you might find it more useful to create desktop icons for important files, directories, and URLs, and create application launchers on the Panel.

 Everything in GNOME can be configured and customized until your desktop workspace looks and performs exactly the way that suits *you* best.

The Main Menu

The main menu is divided into different sections, depending on the applications that are installed. The Programs section consists of the shared applications that are installed in /usr/bin. The Panel menu controls the properties of the Panel, as well as the applets and launchers that are on your Panel. Applets lists a menu of all the GNOME applets that you can install on your Panel. Run opens the Run Program dialog box, where you can type the command to run a program. Lock Screen runs the screen lock program. This displays a screensaver that cannot be turned off until you enter your user password. Log Out enables you to log out of X, halt the system or reboot the system, if your user has permission to halt or reboot.

Most sections of the main menu can be altered only by root. The Favorites section, however, is expressly meant for ordinary users to add additional applications to the menu.

Task: Adding a New Program to the Favorites Menu

1. Left-click the main menu foot icon in the Panel.

2. Place the mouse over Favorites and right-click the Favorites title.

3. Right-click the Favorites entry and select Add New Item to This Menu.

4. Enter the name of the program that will appear in the Favorites menu in the Name field.

5. If you want a pop-up to appear with more information about the program, enter it in the Comment field.

6. Enter the command that starts the program in the Command field.

7. Select Application as the Type.

8. If you want an icon to appear next to the menu entry, click the Icon button and select an icon from the menu.

The dialog box to add a new item to the Favorites menu is shown in Figure 7.4.

FIGURE 7.4

The Favorites menu is useful for adding applications that are installed in your home directory, or that don't have an entry in the Programs menu.

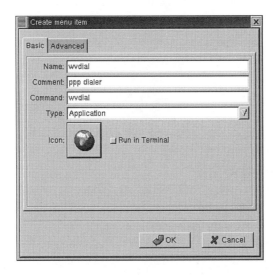

The GNOME Panel

The GNOME Panel is one of the most useful tools in the GNOME environment. You can use the Panel to hold the applications and files that you use every day to keep you focused and organized. The Panel holds the Main Menu, the desktop guide and tasklist, launchers for your favorite applications, and Panel applets. The launchers and applets can be organized into drawers. You can place a Panel along any edge of the desktop, and you can have as many panels as your screen will hold. By default, the Red Hat GNOME desktop starts out with two panels—one along the top of the desktop and one along the bottom. The Panel objects are labeled in Figure 7.5.

- The Main Menu button opens the main menu. To add a main menu button to other panels, right-click the Panel, select Panel, Add to Panel, Menu, Main Menu. You can also add Programs and Favorites to the Panel this way.

- The Log Out button opens the log out dialog box. You can also log out from the Main Menu, Log Out.

- Lock Screen opens an X screensaver to hide the contents of your display. You must type in your user password to unlock the screen.

- The Help System launcher opens the GNOME Help Browser.

- GNOME Terminal opens an xterm, from which you can use the shell from within X.

- GNOME Control Center opens the GNOME Control Center, which contains all the GNOME capplets for configuring and customizing your GNOME desktop environment.

7

- The tasklist contains a button for every task that you currently have open. You can use the tasklist to re-display minimized windows, or to bring to the front what is hidden behind another window.
- Desk Guide contains a miniature image of each of your virtual desktops. To move to another desktop, click the desktop button on the Desk Guide.
- The bug icon opens a menu of the most important GNOME Web pages, such as news, FAQ, and the bug tracking system.
- The mail check applet announces when you have new email. For instructions on configuring the mail check applet, right-click the applet and select Help.

Adding Panel Applets

GNOME comes with a number of applets, which are mini-applications that you can add to the Panel. Some applets are nothing more than quick diversions, others can be extraordinarily useful. To access the menu of Panel applets, right-click an empty space on the Panel and place the mouse over Panel, Add to Panel, Applet. The applet menu is divided by category. To add an applet to the Panel, left-click the menu entry. The applet appears in the Panel.

FIGURE 7.5
The GNOME Panel is powerful and configurable.

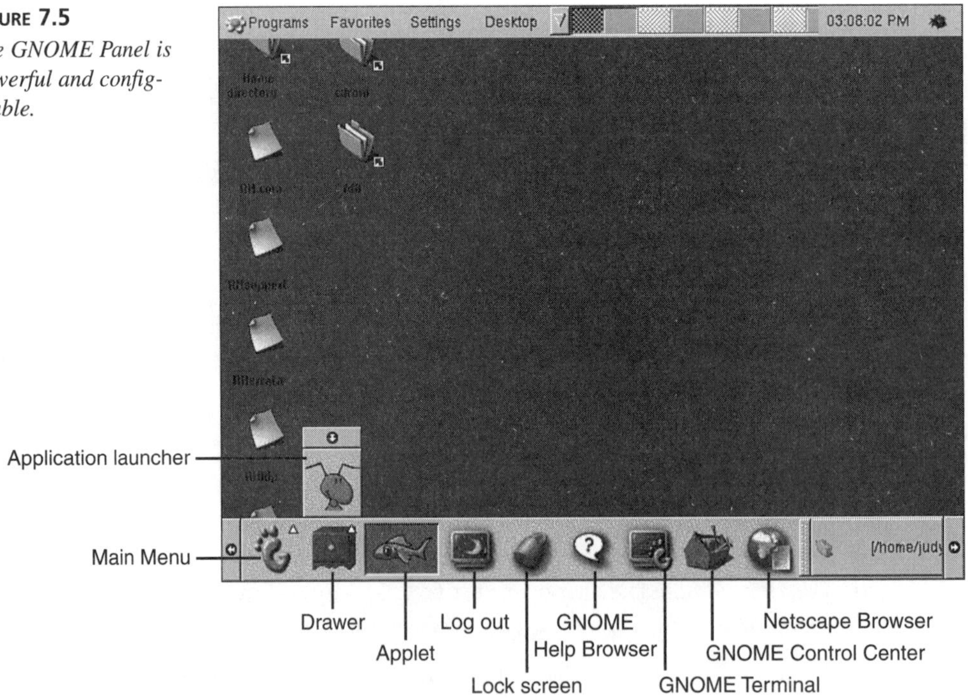
Programs
Favorites
Settings
Desktop
03:08:02 PM
Application launcher
Main Menu
[/home/jud
Drawer
Applet
Log out
Lock screen
GNOME
Help Browser
GNOME Terminal
Netscape Browser
GNOME Control Center

Adding a Launcher to the Panel

Application launchers enable you to quickly open your favorite applications. To create an application launcher, right-click the Panel and select Panel, Add to Panel, Launcher. Enter the name of your application in Name. If you want a ToolTip to pop up when you place the mouse over the launcher, add the ToolTip in Comment. Enter the command that launches the application in the Command field. Select an icon for your launcher by clicking the Icon button and selecting an icon from the icon menu. After creating the launcher, you can modify it at any time by right-clicking it and selecting Properties.

Organizing Launchers and Applets into Drawers

After you have added a few launchers and applets to the Panel, it can get a little crowded. Drawers enable you to organize a group of launchers and applets into one place, to save space on the Panel. When you click the drawer to open it, all the objects in the drawer are displayed. To create a drawer, right-click the Panel and select Panel, Add to Panel, Drawer. An empty drawer appears in the Panel. To add objects to the drawer, open the drawer by clicking it. Right-click the Panel object that you want to move, select Move, then place the mouse over the Panel object, then move the mouse to the open drawer. The Panel object appears in the drawer. Click the object again when it is positioned in the drawer the way you want it.

> There is no need to click the Panel object and drag it to the drawer. If you drag the Panel object to the drawer, the object is copied to the drawer, rather than moved. If you end up with an unwanted extra copy, just right-click it and select Remove from Panel.

If you have more than one drawer, it can get confusing to remember which drawer holds which applets. You can add a ToolTip to the drawer to label its contents and you can also change the icon of the drawer by clicking Properties.

Working with Window Managers

For many people who are new to Linux, the concept of window managers is unfamiliar. In Microsoft Windows, the software that controls the placement and movement of windows is indistinguishable from that which controls the graphical picture that you see on the screen, or the software that makes an application start when you double-click a menu entry or icon. In Linux, the three functions of the desktop, graphical interface, and window operation are controlled by different pieces of software, namely X, the window

7

manager, and GNOME. To further complicate the picture, GNOME is unique among desktop environments because it works with more than one window manager.

GNOME and the window manager work so seamlessly together that you don't need to think of them as separate until you have problems or decide to change window managers. The default window manager for GNOME is Sawfish, although GNOME works with a number of other window managers, including Enlightenment, WindowMaker, FVWM2, and IceWM, among others. Figure 7.6 demonstrates the relationship between the X server, GNOME, and the window manager.

You can switch window managers within the same GNOME session by using the GNOME Control Center window manager capplet. Click Main Menu, Programs, Settings, Desktop, Window Manager. Select the new window manager, then click either Try or OK. If you just want to try the window manager, click Try, Save Session Later. You can then click Revert to go back to your original window manager. To keep the new window manager, click Save Session Now, then click OK on the Control Center.

FIGURE 7.6

X, GNOME, and the window manager work together to create the desktop.

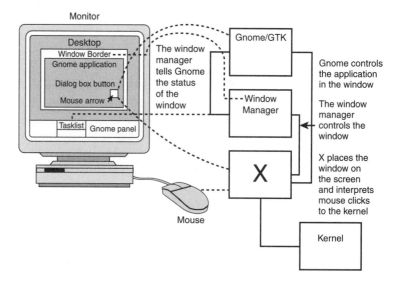

Multiple Workspaces

One of the most useful aspects of window managers such as Sawfish and Enlightenment is the capability to manage multiple workspaces (in Enlightenment, workspaces are called multiple desktops). If you tend to have ten or more windows open simultaneously, or if you are working on several projects at once, you can separate them on different workspaces. Multiple workspaces work somewhat like multiple displays. Each work-space consists of a different desktop, complete with Panel, menu, and desktop space, as if you had multiple displays of the GNOME desktop. With multiple workspaces, you can increase the size of your work area by a factor of two, four, or even twenty.

Task: Adding More Workspaces in Sawfish

By default in Red Hat, Sawfish starts out with only one workspace. To add more workspaces, follow these steps:

1. Click the Settings menu in the upper Panel and select Sawfish Window Manager, Workspaces. The GNOME Control Center opens at the Workspaces capplet.

2. Enter the number of workspaces you want in the Minimum Number of Workspaces.

3. To increase the number of workspaces even further, you can add virtual workspaces. Enter the number of virtual workspaces in Number of Columns and Rows in each virtual workspace.

The Sawfish workspaces capplet is shown in Figure 7.7.

FIGURE 7.7

Use multiple workspaces to keep your desktop uncluttered and to separate projects.

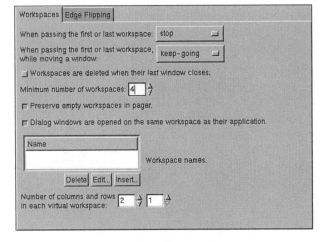

There are differences between a virtual workspace and a workspace, but it's hard to see the difference in Sawfish until you've played around with workspaces for a while. In essence, a virtual workspace appears to increase the size of the same desktop, whereas a new workspace actually adds a new workspace with a new desktop.

7

To move around your workspaces, you can use the Desk Guide, or you can enable edge flipping. To move to a different workspace with the Desk Guide, click the image of the workspace, and that workspace opens on the desktop. To use edge flipping, open the Workspaces capplet in GNOME Control Center and check Select the Next Desktop when the Pointer Hits Screen Edge. To have edge flip move you to the next virtual workspace, select Hitting the Screen Edge Selects the Next Viewport. Selecting Workspace moves you to the next actual workspace when you edge flip.

Using Switchdesk to Switch to KDE

KDE is another major desktop environment that is included in Red Hat. KDE and GNOME share many of the same features; in fact, there is quite a lot of collaboration between the GNOME and KDE projects. Most of the applications developed for one desktop work on the other desktop. For instance, if you like the GNOME desktop, but prefer to use kppp (the KDE modem dialer), you can run kppp in GNOME with no problem. Conversely, you can run just about any GNOME application (including gmc, the File Manager), in KDE.

If you like to switch back and forth between GNOME and KDE, Red Hat has a convenient little utility called Switchdesk that enables you to switch desktops easily, without editing any configuration files. Switchdesk is shown in Figure 7.8.

FIGURE 7.8

Use Switchdesk to switch desktop environments.

To use Switchdesk, install all the Switchdesk RPM packages, if they are not already installed (see Hour 11 for instructions on installing RPM packages). To open the Switchdesk dialog box, Click Main Menu, Run. In the Run dialog box, type `switchdesk`, and then click Run.

> You can use the Run dialog box to run any application. You can also run any application by typing the name of the executable file at a shell prompt in an xterm.

To switch to KDE, click KDE, then OK. You must first log out of X and log back in before the changes take place. Your default desktop will now be KDE, until you use Switchdesk to switch back to GNOME. Follow the same steps to switch back to GNOME, or any of the independent window managers that may be installed (such as FVWM2 or WindowMaker).

Session Management and Logging Out of GNOME

One of the more useful features of GNOME is that of session management. With session management, GNOME remembers all the GNOME-compliant programs you have running before you log out, their position on the desktop, *and* your current place in the file. To use session management, leave your applications running when you are ready to log out of GNOME. Select Log Out on the Main Menu. In the logout confirmation dialog box that appears, check Save Current Setup. The next time you log in to GNOME, GNOME will automatically restart all the applications so that your desktop appears as it was before you logged out of your last session.

Learning More

We have only just touched the surface of the GNOME desktop environment. There are many important topics that are not covered in this book, particularly the GNOME File Manager and the GNOME Control Center. There are many resources that you can use to enable you to get the most out of GNOME:

- The GNOME User's Manual and other application help files, available in the GNOME Help Browser.
- The GNOME Web site at `http://www.gnome.org`.
- The GNOME white papers at `http://developer.gnome.org`.
- The GNOME Documentation Project at `http://www.gnome.org/gdp`. If you would like to contribute to open-source, the GNOME project is a great place to start for user-level documentation.

7

- The Helix Code Web site at `http://www.helixcode.com`.
- *Sams Teach Yourself GNOME in 24 Hours* by Judith Samson.

Summary

In this hour, you learned the basics of how to use the GNOME desktop environment. You learned how to use and create desktop icons, how to add Favorite items to the main menu, and what the default launchers on the Panel mean. You also learned how to add applets, launchers, and drawers to the Panel. You switched between KDE and GNOME using Switchdesk, and saved your GNOME session using session management.

Workshop

The Workshop contains quiz questions and exercises to help reinforce what you've learned in this hour.

Q&A

Q Do I have to use a window manager with GNOME? Can't I just use GNOME?

A GNOME was designed to work with a separate window manager, so it is necessary to have one. Without a window manager, GNOME won't work at all. Sawfish is packaged with GNOME, so you can use GNOME happily without ever thinking about the window manager. Even though you can't use GNOME without a window manager, you can use window managers (with minimum functionality) without GNOME.

Q Can I use sound clips from songs or movies in GNOME?

A You can use any sound clip that is in .wav format as a GNOME sound event, including recordings that you make yourself! From the main menu, click Programs, Settings, Multimedia, Sound to open the sound capplet in the GNOME Control Center.

Quiz

1. How do you access the shell within the GNOME desktop environment?
2. Which GNOME object can you use to mount and unmount a CD-ROM?
3. To which main menu section can ordinary users add items?
4. What is the default window manager for GNOME in Red Hat?

Quiz Answers

1. How do you access the shell within the GNOME desktop environment?

   Open a GNOME terminal using the launcher on the Panel.

2. Which GNOME object can you use to mount and unmount a CROM?

   The CD-ROM icon on the destkop.

3. To which main menu section can ordinary users add items?

   The Favorites menu.

4. What is the default window manager for GNOME in Red Hat?

   Sawfish.

Exercises

1. Use the Home directory icon to open your home directory in File Manager.

2. Open the File Manager to /usr/bin and drag an application onto the desktop.

3. Add a launcher to the Panel by right-clicking the Main Menu and selecting Add to Panel. Now create a drawer and put the launcher in the drawer.

4. Log out and save your GNOME session.

Exercise Answers

1. Use the Home directory icon to open your home directory in File Manager.

   Double-click the home directory icon on the desktop.

2. Open the File Manager to /usr/bin and drag an application onto the desktop.

   Click the /usr/bin directory to open it. Right-click the application you choose, drag it to the desktop, let go of the mouse, and then click Copy in the drag-and-drop menu that appears.

3. Add a launcher to the Panel by right-clicking the Main Menu and selecting Add to Panel. Now create a drawer and put the launcher in the drawer.

   Right-click the Panel and select Panel, Add to Panel, Drawer. Right-click the launcher, select Move, then place the mouse over the launcher and move the mouse to the drawer.

4. Log out and save your GNOME session.

   Log out by selecting Log Out from the main menu. Check Save Current Setup on the logout dialog box, and then click Yes.

7

HOUR 8

Setting Up a Printer and Other Devices

Up to now you have learned many things about the Linux operating system and you will learn much more in the next several hours. In this hour you will learn about devices and filesystems and how to set up your printer and other devices that will make Linux work for you.

In this hour you will

- Examine devices and device drivers
- Learn about filesystems
- Discover how Linux works with printers
- Mount and unmount drives
- Format disks
- Set up a printer
- Configure Zip and CD-ROM drives

Understanding Devices and Device Drivers

The way that Linux is designed makes it unique and different than any other operating system. Everything in Linux is represented as a file, even devices such as hard drives, floppies, or CD drives that a file may reside on. This is a difficult concept for some DOS and Windows users to grasp because of the directory structure of those systems. You'll see, however, that this is really an easy, logical way to handle things, so you won't have any trouble learning and using it.

Linux associates hardware devices with drivers that provide a file interface between the two. That is, any piece of hardware that you have on your system, such as a newly added floppy drive, has to have a driver that tells the kernel what it is and what it can do. Drivers are special files that represent devices (hardware and otherwise) on your system. Without a driver for a particular device, your system will not detect it and the device will be useless. Normally, devices are kept in the /dev directory and are either character or block devices. You can see this represented in Figure 8.1.

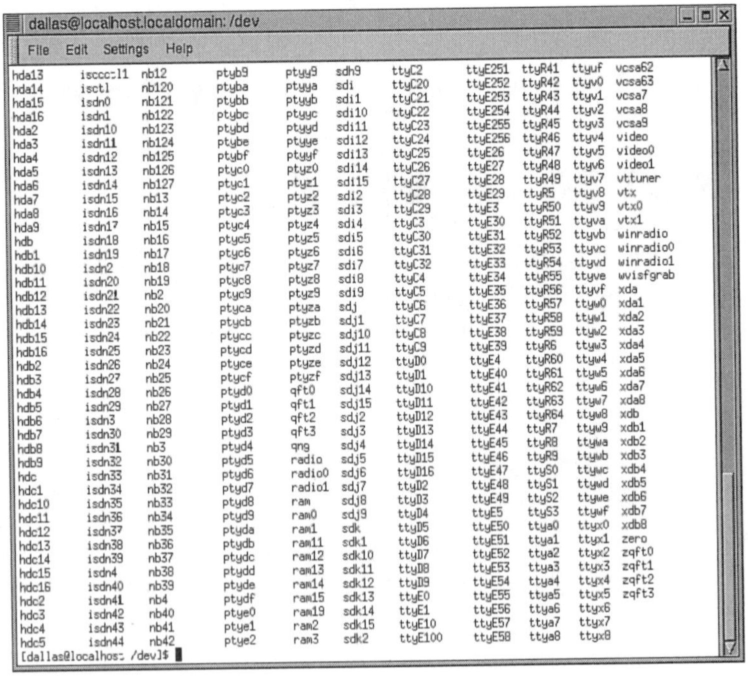

FIGURE 8.1

The device files are all stored in the /dev directory.

> The drivers for the printer are kept in the /var/spool directory. This is the directory where the files are sent to await printing. We will discuss this in detail later in this hour.

8

Characteristics of Devices

There are two kinds of devices: *character* and *block*. Remember that under the Linux hierarchy, each unit or device attached to your computer is abstracted to a device file that has an accompanying device driver in the kernel. Most of the time these drivers are installed when you install Linux, but if you add a piece of hardware later you will have to install a driver for it.

Character devices are also called *sequential access* devices. Everything that is connected to the computer that communicates with Linux is treated as a device. A *block device* is a component of the computer system and has the ability to store data and allows you to access all parts of it equally. They are also called *random access* devices. Some examples of block devices are floppy drives, hard drives, and other storage mediums.

Some of the devices that use blocks of data are tape drives and hard drives. Obviously, the fastest way to send a large chunk of information is to send it in blocks because you can send more data that way. That's why they are called block mode devices.

> You can use many of the utilities found in Linux to configure devices and edit script files, login scripts, and many other things that you really don't have to do. You should get to know how to use the shells and other things mentioned in this book. It will come in handy at making your machine work better.

You may never have to inspect or work with such files unless you write your own device drivers. It is always helpful to know what is going on in your computer and how things work. In today's Linux environment, almost everything is configured for you (such as plug-and-play devices) or you can use a graphical interactive utility such as linuxconf or Xconfigurator to do the hard work for you. You can do most of the device installations on your computer through interactive graphics programs without having to crawl through hundreds of program lines in some script file using a text editor.

Fortunately there are numerous utilities such as the KDE Devices utility that show you the devices on your system. The KDE Devices utility is shown in Figure 8.2.

You can find out more about the devices on your computer. Go to KDE Menus, Settings, Information, Devices and you can view the devices that are on your current system.

FIGURE 8.2

You can view information about the devices connected to your system by using the KDE Devices utility.

If you are having trouble getting a printer, modem, hard drive, or some other device to work, you might want to look in the /dev directory and see whether the device file for that device is there. If not, you may want to try to install it again.

Linux and DOS commands are similar in some instances. You can use the dir command in both DOS and Linux. The Linux ls command gives you about the same results as the dir command. Look at the other commands and note the similarity. If you know a little about DOS, you should feel right at home.

Red Hat Filesystem Structure

Every operating system from DOS to Linux has a method and means of storing files and directories in an organized way. Can you imagine what your hard drive would look like if there wasn't some way to organize things? There are many reasons for this organization, among them keeping track of modifications, additions, and changes to the system.

In Linux, every file is stored with a very unique name in directories that hold other files and subdirectories. This is known as the *tree structure*.

In the tree structure, all of the directories branch off into smaller branches, or subdirectories, and those subdirectories can have subdirectories of their own. Just as a tree has a root, so does Linux. No matter how big your tree is, everything is still connected to the root. In Linux, the root is represented with a forward slash (/).

In Linux, you will notice several references to "root," such as the root password, the root directory, and the root account. Don't let this confuse you. It is just another way of referring to different aspects of the root structure.

8

When you need to operate as root on-the-fly, you can just type **# su** at the command prompt or in a terminal window. You should not forget to log out when you finish doing an operation as root. Staying in root too long can be extremely challenging.

Let's take a look at the root account and how it is set up. If you aren't logged in as root, do so now and enter your password. If you end up at the command prompt (#), then you are where you want to be. You should see something like this:

```
[root@localhost /]#
```

This means you are in the right place.

If you aren't in the root directory, cd to it and type **ls** to see what directories branch off the root directory. You should see several directories with names such as these:

```
# bin dev home lost+found mnt proc sbin tmp var
```

Now let's take a quick look at some of the other useful directories in Linux. You can cd to each directory and do a dir or ls and find out more than I can tell you in one hour. Here is how you can do it:

```
[root@localhost /]# cd sbin
```

By typing in **cd** (changes to directory specified) **sbin**, you will be in the sbin directory. When you are in the directory that you want to be in, just type **ls** or **dir** to see what is in that directory.

The Red Hat filesystem looks something like the following. You can use the cd command to look in each directory in the Red Hat filesystem. Here are the most commonly used directories:

- /boot—The /boot directory contains the Linux Kernel and LILO files needed to boot the system.

- /home—This is your home directory, which contains directories and files that you need.

- /dev—This directory contains filesystem entries pertaining to devices that are attached to the system. You need to have these files installed in order for your devices to be recognized or for the system to function properly.

- /etc—The /etc directory has many configuration files that are used by your local machine.

- /lib—The /lib directory contains files that are needed to execute the binaries in /bin and /sbin.

- /lost+found—When fsck is run, any files that it can't recognize or it doesn't know what to do with end up here.

- /mnt—The /mnt directory contains mount points for removable media such as your CD-ROM or your floppy. The actual directory looks like this: /mnt/cdrom floppy.

- /proc—The /proc directory contains special files that extract or send information to the kernel. You can use the cat command to access information about the operating system in the /proc directory.

- /root—The /root directory is the home directory of the root user. If you are not a superuser (su), you cannot gain access to this directory. It should not be confused with the system root, /.

- /sbin—The /sbin directory contains executable files used only by the root user. It also has files that are needed to boot and mount the /usr directory and for recovery operations. Be careful with this directory.

- /tmp—The /tmp directory stores temporary files. Any user can store temporary files here. These files are removed each time the system is rebooted or shut down.

- /usr—The /usr directory contains shared files or files that can be shared across a whole platform or site. This directory has its own partition (usually) and should only be mounted read-only for obvious reasons.

- /var—The /var directory is used mostly for variable data files such as spool directories, administrative and logging data, and temporary files.

If you are in a terminal window such as GNOME and you have a lot of garbage or characters on your screen, you can remove it by typing clear. The garbage will disappear. Presto!

Both GNOME and KDE have great graphical file managers that you can use rather than working at the command line if you prefer. These are true workhorses that allow you to create, edit, and move your files and directories, among other things.

The GNOME file manager is generally referred to as GMC or GNU Midnight Commander because it is based on the Midnight Commander file manager.

> If you would rather use Midnight Commander, you can start it at the Linux prompt by typing **mc**.

8

Task: Using GMC File Manager

You can use the GMC file manager by clicking on the Main Menu button and selecting File Manager. If you purchased the boxed set from Red Hat, your Red Hat Getting Started Guide has tons of information on the GMC and KDE file managers. Look in Chapter 10 of the guide, "File Managers in GNOME and KDE."

To access the GMC (Midnight Commander) file manager, follow these steps:

1. Click the Main menu button (the GNOME foot).
2. Click File Manager.
3. The GMC File Manager window pops up. In the left pane you will see all of your directories that were discussed previously with either a plus (+) or a minus (-) sign next to them. You click on the plus (+) sign to expand the listing or the minus (-) sign to contract it. Click on the plus sign (+) next to the /mnt directory.

    You should see your subdirectories in the right pane. You should see your cdrom and floppy subdirectories if they were installed. Feel free to explore this window at your leisure.
4. To close your window and end this session, click File, Close Window.

In this part of the hour you learned about the Linux filesystem and two of the file managers that come with Red Hat Linux 7.0. These two file managers are very impressive and useful. You can use either of these managers to move around graphically in your filesystem.

> If you don't have the manuals, don't worry, I'll show you how to get them. Go to http://www.redhat.com/support and look for Red Hat Linux 7.0. You will find all the manuals not only for Red Hat 7.0 but several previous versions as well. You can read them online or simply print them out to your printer. While at the Red Hat Web site you can download the latest version of Red Hat Linux 7.0 or earlier versions. There is a wealth of accurate information here, so take some time to look around.

How Linux Works with Printers

Linux isn't much different than any other operating system when it comes to printing something, depending on the program that you are printing from. It seems that most users want to set up a printer the first thing when they install a new operating system. This is understandable because a printer allows them to produce something. In this part of the hour we will discuss which printers work with Linux as well as how to print with Linux.

Will My Printer Work with Linux?

Under most circumstances, you can get your printer to work with Linux. The quickest way to find out if your printer is compatible is to visit `http://www.redhat.com/support/hardware`. You can find the Linux Printing HOWTO at `http://www.picante.com/~gtaylor/pht`.

Details about Using Printers with Linux

Every printer that is connected to your computer (or any computer, for that matter) has to have a driver. Remember that a printer is a device just like a floppy drive and Linux needs some essential information before it knows it is there and what to do with it. The driver is just a program (which we talked about earlier) that allows the Linux kernel to communicate with the printer. Ghostscript drivers are used mostly these days to drive printers. Ghostscript drivers emulate Adobe's PostScript printing language and supports its Portable Document Format (PDF). You can find out more about Adobe at `http://www.adobe.com/`.

If your printer is supported by the Ghostscript language, it is probably capable of working nicely with your Linux operating system. Macmillan publishes many excellent books that give you tons of information on printers. One book that I get a lot of use out of is *Special Edition: Using Red Hat Linux 6.2*. Another wonderful source is *Red Hat Linux Unleashed 7.0*. These are the best books that you can buy. I still have *Unleashed* books that are more than five years old that are still accurate to some degree. Of course, your best bet in determining printer compatibility is the Red Hat site itself. You will find most of what you want there.

Under Linux, the printers are set up with the following device names, descriptions, and addresses. This information will be important when you are installing your printer(s).

Name	Description	Address
/dev/lp0	First parallel printer	0x3bc
/dev/lp1	Second parallel printer	0x378
/dev/lp2	Third parallel printer	0x278

Have you ever wondered what happens when you tell your computer to print something? Under Linux, a copy of the file is sent to what is called a *print spooler*. If it were sent directly to the printer, you wouldn't get much printed because the printer would be kept pretty busy. The print spooler is a directory that holds the documents that you send to the printer until the printer is available to print them. There are many names and types of print spoolers, among them *print queues*.

On a network such as those under the Microsoft Windows programs, print queues are extremely important because there are always some documents waiting to be printed. Fortunately, there are printer spoolers or queues that hold the documents and release them to be printed when the printer is available. Linux simply stores and prints the files (print jobs) in the order it receives them unless instructed to do otherwise.

You will find the print spool directory under /var/spool. You may notice a file called lpd in the var/spool directory (/var/spool/lpd). This is the line printer spooler daemon, which usually loads when you start the system. Its job is to manage the print jobs.

These are just a few basic facts about how Linux handles your printer. In the next part of the hour you will learn to set up and configure your printer using a utility called print-tool.

Setting Up and Configuring a Printer

When you use any computer you want to be productive with it. You want to write letters, create nice spreadsheets, write recipes, and maybe do a few drawings with a drawing program. In this part of the hour you will learn to set up and configure a printer so you can do just that.

Under the Linux system you can have multiple print jobs running at one time. This is because Linux is a multiuser/multitasking environment. If Linux gets several requests to print something (known as print jobs), it sends the jobs to a print spooler (called spooling or queuing) and then prints them in the order that it receives them. If you are the only user, your print job requests are still sent to the print spool. The jobs are held there until it is their turn to be printed.

In order to understand your printer and how it works you should know these basic facts. Linux loads the lpd (line printer daemon) when it loads the system. The line printer daemon manages the print jobs that lpr receives and sends to it. There are specific input filters that manage printer-specific formatting or handle the way your documents look when they are printed. The printcap file is a configuration file that is stored in /etc (/etc/printcap) and defines your printer configuration among other things.

The print spool is located in /var/spool/lpd/. This is where your files are sent to await printing. You will use the graphical printtool utility to set up your printer, which will modify and configure the printcap file located in /etc/printcap.

> You can learn more about the lpd command by viewing the lpd man pages. To see them, type **man lpd** at a shell prompt.

Task: Using the Printtool Utility

In order to use the printtool utility, you will need to be logged in as root. Let's do that now.

1. From any terminal window, type **su** and press Enter at the system prompt (#). Type your root password when prompted and type **whoami** at the prompt to confirm that you are root. Now, type **printtool** and the utility starts.

2. You should see a screen similar to Figure 8.3. This utility is known as the Red Hat Print System Manager. Since you haven't installed any printers, you won't see any listed. Click Add to add your printer.

3. The Add a Printer Entry dialog pops up. You can select several configurations from the menu. You need to select Local Printer for this installation. Make sure Local Printer is selected and press OK. (You select Local Printer when your printer is connected directly to your computer.)

4. After you have selected your printer type, printtool responds by attempting to detect your printer. You will see these results in the info window that pops up. Click OK to continue.

5. In most cases a printer will be detected at /dev/lp0 unless your printer is on another port.

6. In the Editing Local Printer entry you can specify details about your printer. In the Names box you can specify the print queue where you want your print jobs sent. This will be lp0 or lp1. You can leave this or give it another name. You should leave it as it is for now.

7. In the Spool Directory entry you can specify the default directory where you want the jobs sent. Just leave it as is.

8. Leave the File Limit entry set to 0. You can also leave the Printer Device entry as it is. This will normally have something similar to /dev/lp0 entered in it by the system. Select the Input Filter function by clicking Select.

9. In the Configure Filter dialog, select an exact match for your printer. The make and model of your printer must be selected. If you don't see your printer listed,

scroll down until you find it. If you can't find your particular printer, select one that is close (such as the same manufacturer but a different model).

10. Select the paper size, resolution, and any other options that apply and click OK to continue.

11. Click OK in the Edit Local Printer dialog. You will be in the Print System Manager screen.

12. In the Print System Manager, highlight your new printer entry and click lpd from the menu. Click Restart lpd.

13. To test your new installation, highlight your printer entry in the window (beneath the menu bar) and click Tests. Select Print ASCII Test Page. You should see a message box saying that `Test page printed to lp0` or `Test page printed to lp1` and your test page should print.

If your document fails to print, return to the Configure Filter dialog and try different options.

FIGURE 8.3

The Red Hat Linux Print System Manager dialog box.

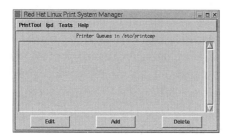

You have learned a few things about how Linux handles the print jobs sent to the spooler and you have learned how to set up and configure your printer. The subject of printers covers much more than I can possibly teach you here and I regret that very much because I love to teach people about Linux. But, if you want or need to know more, read the Linux Printing HOWTO that I told you about previously.

In the next section you will learn how to mount and unmount your filesystems. This will be particularly useful when you are using floppy disks and you are copying files from one type of media to another.

Mounting and Unmounting

The Linux filesystem is so different from the DOS system that it is often hard for people who are familiar with DOS to get used to Linux. In other operating systems, you usually just insert a floppy into your drive and it is accessible by your system. Under Red Hat Linux (and most all Linux versions), you have to mount the drive or device before you can use it and unmount it after you are finished. When you mount a drive or device, you are making the contents of that device available for you to use.

There is a feature in Linux called automounting or automount. One aspect of this concept is that when you click on the CD-ROM on your desktop, your CD-ROM is automatically mounted. Of course, when you are finished, the drive is unmounted.

The program behind this is `autofs`, which uses automount to mount CD-ROM and floppy drives so that when you click on the CD-ROM or floppy icon, it is automatically mounted for you. If you want more information you can find a tutorial at `http://www.linuxhq.com/lg/issue24/nielsen.html`. You can find automount utilities at `http://www.cs.columbia.edu/~ezk/am-utils`. If you need further information you can get it from the Linux Documentation Project (LDP) at `http://www.redhat.com/mirror/LDP/HOWTO/HOWTO`. You can also try the Linux Documentation Project at `http://www.linuxdoc.org`.

When using Red Hat Linux 7.0, there are several ways to mount and unmount your filesystem. The simplest way is to click on the System, Disk Management option from the GNOME main menu. The User Mount Tool dialog box will pop up giving you a choice of mounting or unmounting your devices. If the device you are looking for isn't listed, it probably wasn't installed during install and you will have to reconfigure it or run install again. Please note that you can also format some drives, such as the floppy in your floppy drive. Normally you will see the CD-ROM (cdrom) and the floppy drive (fd0) listed here.

If you recall our earlier discussions, you will remember that all devices under Linux have a device name, driver, and file associated with them. This information is usually of particular interest if you use a graphical mount tool such as the User Mount Tool, but if you have to mount the device from the system prompt, you will need to know what the device is. Here are the device names for some familiar devices:

Device Name	Description
/dev/fd0	First floppy disk
/dev/cdrom	The CD-ROM drive
/dev/hda1	First partition of IDE drive
/dev/sda1	First partition on SCSI hard disk

Each device has a device name and also a mount point. The *mount point* is another directory that is usually in the /mnt directory as a subdirectory. The mount point refers to a place in filesystem where the contents of a disk are made available. When you install Linux, it usually creates two mount points in the /mnt directory called /mnt/cdrom and

/mnt/floppy. When you want to see what is on the floppy in your drive, you simply look in the /mnt/floppy directory. You can see an example of this in Figure 8.4.

FIGURE 8.4

The /mnt *directory should at least have the* cdrom *and* floppy *mount points listed.*

If you find yourself in a situation where you must work from the command prompt, then you can use the following technique. To mount your floppy in /mnt/floppy, enter this at the command prompt:

```
# mount /mnt/floppy
```

To unmount the floppy (which you should do when you are finished with it) just do this:

```
# umount /mnt/floppy
```

The same thing works for the CD-ROM. Just execute the following command:

```
# mount /mnt/cdrom
```

Or to unmount it:

```
# umount /mnt/cdrom
```

If the device that you are trying to mount is already mounted, you will get an error. In such a case you should attempt to access the device before taking other action. If you cannot access it, you may need to have root authority or there may be another problem. You also cannot mount a device from its directory. For example, if I were in the /mnt/floppy directory, I would have to cd out of the directory before I could mount it.

Whenever possible, you should use the graphical utilities provided in GNOME and KDE, but that is not to say that you shouldn't know how to use the commands at the command prompt. Having such knowledge will make you a better Linux person.

In this part of the hour you learned how to mount and unmount devices such as your CD-ROM and floppy drive. Whenever possible you should take advantage of the wonderful graphical utilities such as User Mount Tool and others in your Linux arsenal. Now, let's take a quick look at how to format your disks or prepare them for Linux to use.

You can access a Windows/DOS floppy by issuing the command `mount -t /dev/fd0/mnt/floppy` at the command prompt. Another common way to quickly mount a DOS formatted disk is with `mount -t vfat /dev/fd0 mnt/floppy`.

Task: Formatting Disks

There are several utilities available that will allow you to format disks under Linux. Both GNOME and KDE offer graphical ways to format disks. You can do it under GNOME from the User Mount Tool dialog window. This is probably the quickest and easiest method of performing this chore. You can access the User Mount Tool from the Linux Main menu and then click on System, Disk Management.

In the User Mount Tool dialog box you will see the device and the directory that the device is located in. You have two options here: mount/unmount and format. In most cases you will have to mount the device if it isn't already mounted in order to format it. When you are ready to format the disk, just insert a blank disk, click on the Format button, and follow the instructions. You will be asked to confirm the format because formatting will destroy any information on the disk. Here are the steps necessary to format a disk using Red Hat Linux 7.0:

1. If you aren't already in User Mount Tool, click on System, Disk Management from the Linux Main menu.
2. Insert the disk to be formatted into the a: (fd0) drive.
3. Click the Format button.
4. You'll see a Confirm dialog box. Be sure the Do Low-Level Format option is selected.
5. Click the Yes button to confirm that you really want to do the format.
6. Click the No button if you have changed your mind and don't want to format the disk.
7. The format can take two or more minutes. Upon completion of the format, if the format was successful the Confirm Format dialog box closes and you are returned to the User Mount Tool window. You can now format another disk or exit the program.

If you need to format a disk to the Linux filesystem specifications (ext2) then you can easily use the `fdformat` command to do this. The basic syntax looks like this:

```
fdformat /dev/fdndsize
```

The *n* after fd represents the device number such as fd0 or fd1. The *d* represents the size and density of the floppy disk. The size and density factors that you use here are listed below.

d:	low-density 5.25 inch
D:	low-density 3.5 inch
h:	high-density 5.25 inch
H:	high-density 3.5 inch

In most cases you probably would be using a high-density 3.5-inch disk. For example, if you wanted to format a high-density 3.5-inch disk in drive fd0 at 1440KB, here is the command to do it:

```
fdformat /dev/fd0H1440
```

That's how you format a disk at the Linux command prompt but like I said, if you can you are much better off using one of the graphical utilities provided by either GNOME or KDE.

You can access a Windows/DOS floppy by issuing the mount -t /dev/fd0/ mnt/floppy command at the command prompt.

Configuring a Zip Drive

As we use more and more information, software packages get larger, hard drives get bigger, and it becomes even more important to back up your data on a regular basis. It doesn't make much sense to use floppies today for several reasons. For one thing, it would take you forever to copy all of the contents of even a 1.2 gig drive to floppies. Also, it would be time consuming and expensive. There are several options, such as CD burners, tape backups, and Zip drives.

Zip drives are affordable, but the disks for them tend to be expensive. The Zip drive is ideal for smaller backups. Configuring a Zip drive for Linux is not hard but it is beyond the scope of this book. I will tell you where to find the information that you will need to do the job.

One of the few companies that offer any type of support is Iomega. You will find much useful information on its site at http://www.iomega.com/. Although Iomega clearly states that it does not support Linux for its products, it does offer drivers from third-party developers and is in the process of evaluating these drivers for use on its drives. It is likely that Iomega will offer more support in the near future.

Linux support for most Iomega drives is available from third-party developers at http://www.linux.com/howto/mini/ZIP-Drive.html. For third-party information on Jaz, go to http://www.linux.com/howto/Jaz-Drive-HOWTO.html. You can download the Linux drivers from the Iomega Web site at http://www.iomega.com/software.

The future looks bright for support from major Zip drive manufacturers, it's just a little early. In the meantime, if you want to install a Zip drive on your system, check the Iomega site to see what is supported, and read the mini-HOWTO and other information. You should also read the documentation that comes with your Zip drive and call the manufacturer for other information on Linux support. In the next section, we will look at configuring a CD-ROM drive.

Configuring a CD-ROM Drive

It used to be a nightmare to install and configure a CD-ROM drive. It is much easier now if you follow a few easy-to-do steps. If you are running DOS as another partition on your machine, make sure that it is set up to detect your CD-ROM drive. This is usually done in the config.sys file or even in Windows. If DOS or Windows detects it, then Linux should too. This is probably the easiest situation to contend with. If your CD drive has been detected, you can check this very easily after the installation by looking in the /mnt directory. You should see cdrom, floppy, and other devices listed. You can check th /dev directory for cdrom, which should be listed there. If you have an ATAPI drive Linux should detect it without any problem.

As mentioned many times in this hour, before purchasing any product or device for Linux you should check the Hardware Compatibility section at the Red Hat site to see if it is supported. The subject of setting up and configuring a CD drive is extensive and would fill several chapters this size. The main reason is that there are so many configurations, but in most cases you will not have any problems. In this section I will show you where to find the information that you need if you have problems.

If you do have problems with Linux recognizing your CD drive, read the CD-ROM HOWTO. This is readily available on the Internet and on your CD, and there are many books that cover the subject in its entirety. Your best bet is the CD-ROM HOWTO.

If you are installing a CD-ROM drive for the first time, be sure the computer and other devices are unplugged from the power source. Then read and follow the directions in the manual that usually comes with your CD-ROM drive.

Summary

This hour covered a lot of subjects that are important to knowing and using Linux. You should have a better understanding of what device drivers are and how they relate to the Linux hierarchy. We covered some issues dealing with filesystems and printers, as well as how to mount and unmount various devices. You learned a few things about how to set up a printer and how to get more information on installing Zip drives, CD-ROMs, and other unsupported devices.

Workshop

The Workshop contains quiz questions and exercises to help reinforce what you've learned in this hour.

Q&A

Q When I attempt to access my floppy drive I get a message saying "the major device number is wrong." What do I do?

A Something has happened to change the major device number or the device file in /dev is missing or damaged. Look in the /dev directory to see if the floppy device file is there. You will be looking for device drivers that relate to your floppy drive such as fd0 or fd1. Run linuxconf as root to check the drive's permissions and then (if linuxconf doesn't correct the problem) run install or upgrade again to see if the problem is corrected.

Q I need to format a disk to use on the Linux ext2 filesystem but I don't know what command to use. What command will allow me to do this?

A You can use the fdformat command to format an ext2 filesystem.

Q I'm trying to format a floppy disk using the User Mount Tool but it doesn't do it. What is wrong?

A You probably need to mount it first. Just click on Mount (if it isn't already mounted) and then try formatting it. If this doesn't work try another disk.

Quiz

1. What tool or utility program is best used to configure your printer?

2. What is the definition of a mount point such as /home?

3. What is the command sequence to mount your floppy from the command line?

Quiz Answers

1. What tool or utility program is best used to configure your printer?

   Printtool, which allows you to install and configure your printer, makes certain tests to see if it is operable and provides you with a decent graphical interface. It can be started from the command prompt or from one of the window managers.

2. What is the definition of a mount point such as /home?

   Each device has a device name and a mount point. The mount point refers to a place in the filesystem where the contents of a disk are made available.

3. What is the command sequence to mount your floppy from the command line?

   To mount your floppy in /mnt/floppy, enter this at the command prompt:

   ```
   # mount /mnt/floppy.
   ```

Exercise

1. Use your favorite text editor to look at the /etc/printcap file, which contains all of the configuration information for your printer. This file is created by printtool or when you install a printer. Don't change anything or save the file when you exit. You just want to become very familiar with what it contains. It is important to know what configuration items are written to it when it is created by printtool or by some other method.

HOUR 9

Connecting to the Internet Part 1

Today, no computer system is complete without Internet access, particularly Linux systems, because the Linux community is based on mailing lists, newsgroups, chat rooms, and Web sites. Also, Linux applications tend to be released every few weeks, usually through an FTP site. Of course, you don't need to be networked to use Linux, but you would be selling yourself short if you weren't. In this hour you will learn the basics of networking and how to connect to the Internet. In the next hour, you will learn how to use the Internet in Linux.

In this hour you will

- Get a very basic introduction to TCP/IP networking
- Network over a telephone line by learning how modems work with PPP protocol
- Gather information you will need to connect to your ISP
- Set up /etc/resolv.conf, /etc/hosts.allow, and /etc/hosts.deny
- Connect to your ISP using wvdial and the Red Hat PPP Dialer

Although many options are available for making an Internet connection today, most new users still have dial-up modems, so this chapter will provide instructions for configuring a dial-up modem for Linux. If you have ISDN, ADSL, or a cable modem, you can still make a connection in Linux. See the following documents for help:

LDP Cable Modem HOWTO. All HOWTOs can be found at
http://www.linuxdoc.org.

LDP ADSL Mini-HOWTO

ISDN for Linux FAQ by Matthias Hessler: http://www.isdn4linux.de/faq/

ISDN tutorial: http://public.swbell.net/ISDN/overview.html

For PCMCIA cards, see the LDP PCMCIA HOWTO

Quick and Dirty Networking Concepts

When you connect to another computer via a communication line, you are networking your computer. It doesn't matter whether you are connecting to an ISP server for connection to the Internet, dialing in directly to another computer to access its files, or adding your computer to a private network of servers and workstations—the basic concept is the same. Every network has a few basic similarities. Every computer, or host, needs a method of being uniquely identified in the network—an address. You need some medium by which communication can travel, such as a phone line or fiber-optic cable. You need a set of standards and communication practices that all computers in the network understand—a protocol. You also need a device that can translate the signals inside the computer into signals that can travel on the communications wire, such as a modem or an Ethernet card.

Some modems will not work with Linux. The section "Not Every Modem Works with Linux" discusses which modems will not work with Linux, and how to tell what kind of modem you have.

Because this chapter deals primarily with networking that is done over a telephone line via a modem from a client (your computer) to an ISP server, it assumes that your network is a client connecting to an Internet service provider. The communication medium is an ordinary telephone line connected to a modem. The protocols are the TCP/IP protocols and the PPP and SLIP protocols.

Quick and Dirty TCP/IP Concepts

When you send out data over a phone line via a modem, it appears that a direct line is created between your computer and the computer you are communicating with. You dial up your ISP, enter a Web site URL into your browser, and a page downloads from a remote computer onto your computer. It seems simple, direct, and uncomplicated, whereas in reality the communication path between you and the computer that contains the Web page you requested can involve dozens of intermediate steps. The reason data transmission can seem so simple when in reality it is extraordinarily complicated is the TCP/IP protocol. TCP/IP, as the name suggests, is actually two protocols that work together.

IP stands for Internet Protocol. The Internet Protocol makes it possible for different computers with different hardware to communicate data. A network of computers, or hosts, connected by the Internet Protocol is called an *internet* (an *intranet* is formed with the same idea). Every host on the network is uniquely identified by a number called the IP address. Hosts also usually have alphanumeric names that humans use, called hostnames.

When data is sent over a network, it appears to be a continuous stream, but it is actually broken down into small chunks, called packets. The packets often travel a circuitous route through different servers, gateways, and routers, which direct the packets' data to their final destination, where they are reassembled into the original format the data had when it was sent. The mechanism responsible for all this is the TCP, or Transmission Control Protocol. TCP works on top of IP to make it seem like the complicated route between you and a remote computer is a simple, direct connection.

How Modems Work

At the very lowest level, your computer is nothing more than millions of bits. Each bit has two possible states: on and off. On is represented by a one and off is represented by a zero. Fundamentally, all your documents—email, digital photos, software applications, and even the kernel itself—are seemingly infinite combinations of ones and zeros. This digital way of coding information is called binary code.

Telephones, on the other hand, use a signal called an analog wave to carry voice conversations. The analog wave is an electrical signal that varies in frequency and amplitude in the exact pattern of the frequency and amplitude of the sound waves that your voice makes when you speak into the telephone receiver. For a computer to be able to communicate with another computer over a telephone line, you need a device that converts digital waves to analog waves so that the data from the remote computer (like your ISP's Internet server) can be transported over the phone line and then back to digital again, so that your computer can receive and process the information. Converting signals from digital to analog and back to digital again is the purpose of a modem.

Instructions are sent from the computer to the modem in the form of commands. Commands are sent over the same data line that the modem uses to receive and transmit information. Communications software works by getting input from you via a text or graphical interface and then using the input to send the proper commands to the modem. For example, when you type in the phone number to dial your ISP, the dial-up software uses that phone number as input for the dial-up command, ATDT, to the modem. The actual command that is sent to the modem is ATDT5551234. The initialization string that is sent from the dial-up software to your modem is a command or series of commands used to configure the modem for dialing.

To learn more, check your modem manual for a list of common commands for your modem. If your manual doesn't have a list, your can check the modem manufacturer's Web site.

Not Every Modem Works with Linux

The first step to configuring your system for networking is to ensure that your modem works with Linux. There is a database that provides information on modem types, Linux support, and issues with Linux at `http://www.o2.net/~gromitkc/winmodem.html`.

Basically, your modem must be a hardware modem, not a software modem, or so-called winmodem™, although Lucent Technologies and PC-TEL have released Linux drivers for their software modems, making them "linmodems." See `http://www.linmodems.org` for more information on linmodems.

Issues are also involved with PCI, DSP, Mwave, and Rockwell (RPI) modems. See `http://www.o2.net/~gromitkc/winmodem.html` for more information.

The Serial Port

Modems are connected to the computer via an Input/Output (I/O) device called a serial port. The serial port may not look like much, but it actually has several crucial functions:

- Receive data from the modem and relay it to the computer
- Transmit data to the modem to go out over the phone line
- Hold data in a buffer until it can be relayed to the proper program for reassembly into the original file

- Convert serial data that is being received to parallel data
- Convert parallel data that is to be transmitted to serial data

Data inside the computer is sent in parallel. When you want to send data over long distances over a telephone line, it is necessary to convert the parallel data to serial data so it can fit on one wire—namely, the telephone line. The serial port uses a chip called a UART (Universal Asynchronous Receiver Transmitter) to convert bytes from parallel to serial. The UART is found either on the motherboard or on an internal modem card.

9

The serial port receives 16 bytes of data from the modem at a time. As it is receiving new data, it also has to send the data that it just received to memory. As data is transmitted to memory the buffer is emptied, and new data can come from the modem. This process is called flow control. The speed at which your modem can process the flow of data is one of the factors that limits the speed at which you can receive data from the Internet.

Internal modems don't connect to a serial port via wires, so they emulate the wires and the serial port. The computer can't tell the difference between a real serial port and the internal modem's "virtual" port, so essentially, internal modems work the same way as external modems.

To summarize, when you send an email to a friend, for example, the email message (which is a collection of ones and zeros that can be transmitted digitally) goes from the hard disk on your computer, through the transmit pin of the serial port, to the modem. The modem converts the message into an analog signal, which is like a sine wave. The email, in analog form, travels along the phone line to various places (including your ISP and your friend's ISP.) The modem on your friend's computer receives the analog email through its receive pin, converts and demodulates the signal back to a digital signal, and displays the email on your friend's computer screen.

The Serial Port Number

Each serial port has a name that distinguishes it from all other serial ports. This way, your computer has a distinct "address" for each device (piece of hardware) that is connected to it. Every device has a name, which is included in the /dev/ directory. In Linux, serial ports are named ttyS* in sequence; for example, ttyS0, ttyS1, ttyS2, and so on.

I/O and IRQ Addresses

Along with the serial port number, the serial port has two other addresses, called the I/O address and the IRQ address, that are important to configuring your modem. The I/O address tells the computer the location of the serial port. Each serial port number has an

I/O number that corresponds to it. IRQ stands for Interrupt Request. A device asks for attention from the CPU (Central Processing Unit) by sending requests, or interrupts, on the wire that is assigned to it. When data comes in over the modem, the serial port sends an interrupt to the CPU to let the CPU know that the data is in the serial port buffer and to instruct the CPU to get the data so that the serial port can receive the next set of data (all this happens very quickly; only 1 to 16 bytes of data can be processed at a time). The IRQ number tells the serial port which wire to use to send an interrupt to the CPU so that the CPU knows which device the interrupt comes from.

Every serial device stores its IRQ and I/O number in its memory. The I/O address and IRQ number are determined by jumpers on the device, Plug–and-Play software, or a Plug–and-Play BIOS.

PCI devices work a little differently from ISA devices, but the basic concept is the same.

Configuring Your Modem

With many of the latest BIOSes and Linux distributions, the modem will be automatically configured for you when you start Linux. Either the BIOS will configure the modem at boot or isapnp will configure the modem when you start Linux. However, if things go wrong and you have to configure the serial port manually, this section explains how to do it.

Before configuring your modem manually, test it to make sure that the modem is not already configured. If you get a connection, go directly to the section titled "Using PPP."

Setting the Serial Port Number

If your modem is external, the serial port number is the actual serial port that your modem is connected to on the back of your computer. If you're not sure which serial port is which, connect the modem, power it on, and boot the computer. The BIOS should detect the modem and display the serial port number on the screen during startup. If your modem is internal and it is not Plug-and-Play, set the serial port number and the I/O number by configuring the jumper cables on the modem. Your modem manual will have a list of which jumper settings correspond to which serial ports. Consult your manual for instructions on how to configure the jumper cables.

> If you have external serial ports on your computer, it is a good idea to assign the next higher serial port number to your modem. For example, if you have two serial ports, assign /dev/ttyS2 to your modem. That way, if you need to use the true, physical serial modems later, there will be no confusion about which serial port is which.

9

If you have a Plug-and-Play BIOS and your internal modem is Plug-and-Play, the BIOS will probably set the serial port number, I/O, and IRQ addresses for you. Enter the CMOS setup menu and select the option for non–Plug-and-Play operating system. The BIOS will configure the modem and serial port. If there is no option to specify a non–Plug-and-Play operating system, try disabling Plug-and-Play in the BIOS and making the configurations manually with the jumpers on your modem.

> If you are running Microsoft Windows on another partition, be careful when changing settings on the jumpers or in the BIOS. Make a note of the original settings before you change them, in case you run into trouble with Windows and have to backtrack.

You can also use the wvdial PPP utility to find the correct serial port. wvdial scans all your serial devices automatically until it finds your modem. You will learn more about wvdial in the section "Connecting to the Internet Using wvdial."

Using Setserial

After setting the serial port number and the I/O address in the hardware, use the setserial command to verify that the serial driver has the correct information. If the actual serial port is different from what the serial driver thinks is the port, the device attached there (such as your modem) probably won't work.

It is important to understand that setserial does not set the hardware serial port settings. You must determine the hardware serial port settings and then tell setserial to set them in the serial device driver. Setserial can also help you determine the IRQ of a serial port if you know the I/O address but not the IRQ.

To use setserial to report the current serial configurations, assume root status with su, and then enter the setserial command:

```
$ su
$ [root password]
# setserial -g [devicename]
```

For example, if you were to enter **setserial -g /dev/ttyS1**, setserial would display something like the following:

```
[root@localhost judy]# setserial -ga /dev/ttyS1
/dev/ttyS1, UART: 16550A, Port: 0x02f8, IRQ: 3
        Baud_base: 115200, close_delay: 50, divisor: 0
        closing_wait: 3000, closing_wait2: infinte
        Flags: spd_normal skip_test
```

To change the IRQ, UART, or I/O port number, you would enter

```
# setserial -g /dev/ttySx <parameter> <parameter to be set>
```

For example, the default IRQ number for /dev/ttyS2 is 4. If your modem was in serial port /dev/ttyS2, and you had set the IRQ to 9, you would enter the following command to let the serial device driver know that the actual IRQ number was 9:

```
# setserial  /dev/ttyS2 irq 9
```

Setserial is not difficult to use, but you can render your modem and other serial devices temporarily inoperable if you use it incorrectly. It is beyond the scope of this book to go into great detail on how to use setserial, so if you must use it, be sure to read the serial man pages and the Modem and Serial Port Hosts at http://www.linuxdoc.org.

Create the /dev/modem Symlink

After you have determined and tested your modem configuration, create a symbolic link between the serial port device file; for example, /dev/ttyS, and a file called dev/modem. Enter the following:

```
# ln -s /dev/ttySx /dev/modem
```

In some situations, setting /dev/modem can cause problems, such as when you want others to be able to dial in to your computer. On the other hand, some applications won't work if the symlink isn't there, so you should make the link unless you have specific reason not to. Some Linux distributions create the link automatically. Make sure that /dev/modem points to the correct /dev/ttySx device.

Using PPP

After you have overcome the perils of setting up a modem in Linux, the hard part is over. This section will give you the most basic information you need to set up a dial-up connection, and it will walk you through the process.

The Point-to-Point Protocol, or PPP, is designed to enable computers to communicate with each other over a telephone line via the TCP/IP protocol. PPP converts digital packets of data to analog format so the data can be transmitted over a telephone line.

The PPP daemon, called pppd, controls your PPP connection. When you dial in to your ISP, your PPP connection is called the PPP client. The ISP is the PPP server. pppd negotiates with your ISP's PPP server and attempts to authenticate your computer as a valid client of the PPP server.

> If your company has a PPP server, you can dial in to your company's network using PPP. Contact your network administrator for information on how to set up a PPP client account.

Some ISPs use the older SLIP protocol. SLIP stands for Serial Line Internet Protocol. The procedure for dialing up to a server that uses SLIP is similar to the procedure for PPP. PPP is considered to be an improvement over SLIP, so most ISPs today use PPP. For more information on how to set up a SLIP connection, see the Linux Documentation Project's Linux Network Administrator's Guide (NAG) at `http://www.linuxdoc.org` or on the third CD-ROM of your Red Hat distribution.

Gathering Information About Your ISP

Setting up a PPP connection can be a bit more complicated in Linux than in MS Windows or MacOS. Before you set up PPP connection, you must collect some information about your account from your ISP or system administrator. When you have the following information, you will be ready to create a connection in wvdial, Red Hat PPP Dialer, or another PPP dialing utility:

- **Communication Protocol**—PPP is the most common, but some ISPs still use the older SLIP protocol. If your ISP uses SLIP, contact your ISP for help or see the *Network Administrator's Guide* (see the end of the chapter for reference information) for instructions on how to configure SLIP.
- **Dial-in Phone Number**—The phone number you dial to get a PPP connection.
- **User Name**—The username assigned to you, such as `judith@` or `jsamson`.
- **Password**—Your unique user password that is used to authenticate your computer to your ISP.
- **DNS Server**—You will need the addresses of the ISP's primary and secondary DNS servers. The DNS server translates a computer's hostname into an IP address.

Items you might need are the following:

- **IP Address**—Most ISPs dynamically assign you an IP address each time you log in, but if you have a fixed IP address you will need to include it in the `/etc/hosts` file. (Enter the IP address and your computer's hostname after the localhost entry.)

- **Authentication Protocol**—If you are able to connect but have trouble logging in, you might need to contact your ISP for the authentication protocol it uses, such as CHAP, PAP, or a special login script.
- **Search Domain**—The search domain is used if the DNS server isn't found in the domain. Some ISPs, particularly universities, might have several search domains.

Editing the Configuration Files

To establish a connection, the PPP daemon (pppd) needs information, such as your ISP's domain name server address, your login password, and some security information, such as who, if anybody, should be allowed to log in to your system remotely. The pppd looks for this information in various configuration files in the /etc directory.

> This section assumes that you are the administrator of your machine and that you have root access. If this is not the case, contact your network administrator for help.

You can set up the configuration files manually or by using linuxconf. Each method is described in this section. It is generally easier and faster to enter the information manually into the files, but if you feel more comfortable with a graphical, menu-driven interface, you can use linuxconf. Another advantage to using linuxconf is that you don't have to worry about typos or editing the file incorrectly. You must be able to run X on your computer to use linuxconf.

Task: Entering DNS Servers Using linuxconf

1. To open linuxconf, assume root status with the su command, and then enter the command linuxconf:

```
$ su
$ <root password>
# linuxconf
```

2. Click Networking, Client Tasks, Name Server Specification. The Resolver configuration window is shown in Figure 9.1.

3. Enter your ISP's DNS server address(es) in the IP of Name Server field(s), as well as your ISP domain, as shown in Figure 9.1. If your ISP has alternate search domains, you can enter them in the search domain fields.

4. linuxconf writes the information you enter to the /etc/resolv.conf file.
/etc/resolv.conf lists the IP addresses of a DNS server or servers that will be
able to connect to the Domain Name Service to match hostnames with IP
addresses. Your ISP should provide you with the IP addresses for its DNS servers
when you create your account.

FIGURE 9.1

*You can use linuxconf
to create /etc/resolv.
conf, or simply enter
the information into
the file using a text
editor.*

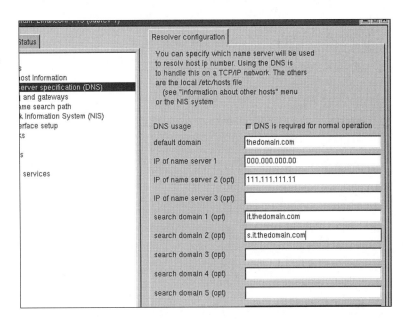

The /etc/resolv.conf file looks like this:

```
domain samsonsource.com
search . judith.samsonsource.com
nameserver 000.000.000.00
nameserver 111.111.111.11
```

Rather than using linuxconf to create /etc/resolv.conf, you can open a text editor and
enter your information as shown. The search line is optional. Enter one nameserver per line.

Adding Basic Security to Your System

After you have completed the /etc/resolv.conf file, you should create two files that
provide basic security to your system: /etc/hosts.deny and /etc/hosts.allow. These
files list the hosts that are allowed to access services on your computer. Also, some PPP
utilities will not work if these files are not in place. Red Hat creates the
/etc/hosts.deny and /etc/hosts.allow files automatically, but it is up to you to enter
the information.

The two files /etc/hosts.deny and /etc/hosts.allow provide your system with basic security. They prevent hostile users from breaking into your system by preventing anyone from remotely logging in. If you do not add them, a cracker could use a password-searching script and log in to your computer via telnet. This is just basic security—you will learn more in Hour 20, "What Every User Should Know About Security." If you want to remotely log in, then add to etc/hosts.allow the specific IP address or hostname that will be allowed to remotely log in.

/etc/hosts.deny should contain nothing but the following line (in all caps):

ALL:ALL

This denies every host access to your computer. Of course, you want to be able to use your own services, so in /etc/hosts.allow, enter this line:

ALL:LOCAL

This means that no host is allowed to use your computer except the local host, which is your local computer. If you want to be able to dial in to your computer remotely, be sure to include in /etc/hosts.allow the hostname or IP address of the computer you are using to dial in!

Connecting to the Internet Using wvdial

wvdial (pronounced weev-dial) is a text-based PPP dialer that searches for your modem, creates your configuration files, and dials your ISP automatically. After you install and configure wvdial, it checks each serial port until it finds your modem. wvdial then automatically initializes the modem, tests the modem speed, and connects to your ISP.

Task: Run wvdialconf

Before you use wvdial to create a PPP connection, you must run the wvdial configuration script to configure your modem and create a login script. You must have root privileges to run the script.

1. Enter the following commands to assume root status and run the wvdial configuration script to create a configuration file called /etc/wvdial.conf:

```
$ su
$ [your root password]
# wvdialconf /etc/wvdial.conf
```

2. wvdial scans for your modem and creates /etc/wvdial.conf, which includes the necessary information about your modem for wvdial to make a PPP connection. As it runs, wvdial sends status reports to the screen. The messages should look something like this:

```
Scanning your serial ports for a modem.

    modemscan<Info>: Ignoring ttyS0 because /dev/mouse is a link to it.
    ttyS1<*1>: AT -- AT -- AT -- nothing.
    ttyS2<*1>: AT -- OK
    ttyS2<*1>: ATZ -- OK
    ttyS2<*1>: ATQ0 -- OK
    ttyS2<*1>: ATQ0 V1 -- OK
    ttyS2<*1>: ATQ0 V1 E1 -- OK
        [more init string testing]
    ttyS2<*1>: Speed 2400: AT -- OK
    ttyS2<*1>: Speed 4800: AT -- OK
        [more baud rate testing]
    ttyS2<*1>: Speed 230400: AT -- AT
    ttyS2<*1>: Max speed is 115200; using 57600 to be safe.
    ttyS2<*1>: ATQ0 V1 E1 S0=0 &C1 &D2 S11=55 -- OK

    Found 1 available modem; using /dev/ttyS2.
    ttyS2<Info>: Speed 57600; init "ATQ0 V1 E1 S0=0 &C1 &D2 S11=55"
```

If you have a serial mouse, do not move it while wvdialconf is running or the scan could cause mouse problems.

Editing /etc/wvdial.conf

wvdialconf creates a file called /etc/wvdial.conf that includes your modem information and blank lines for you to enter your PPP connection information. The autogenerated wvdial file looks something like this:

```
[Dialer Defaults]
    Modem = /dev/ttyS2
    Baud = 57600
    Init = ATZ
    Init2 = ATQ0 V1 E1 S0=0 &C1 &D2 S11=55
    ; Phone = <Target Phone Number>
    ; Username = <Your Login Name>
    ; Password = <Your Password>
```

The Modem, Baud, Init, and Init2 lines are autogenerated during wvdialconf's scan of your modem. For the last three lines, you must fill in the proper information. Delete the semicolon (;) symbol and the blank space before each line and replace the placeholder string with your information. When you are done, /etc/wvdial.conf should look something like this:

```
[Dialer Defaults]
    Modem = /dev/ttyS2
    Baud = 57600
    Init = ATZ
    Init2 = ATQ0 V1 E1 S0=0 &C1 &D2 S11=55
    Phone = 555-1234
    Username = jsamson
    Password = mypassword
```

> You can configure other options for wvdial, such as creating a /etc/ wvdial.conf file that will deal with multiple modems, ISP accounts, users, and so on. For more information, type **man wvdial** at a shell prompt for the wvdial manual page.

Running wvdial

To run wvdial, enter the command **wvdial** at a shell prompt. If wvdial makes a successful PPP connection, you can start your browser or email program and use the Internet. A successful login should look something like this:

```
[root@localhost judy]# wvdial
--> WvDial: Internet dialer version 1.20
--> Initializing modem.
--> Sending: ATZ
ATZ
OK
--> Sending: ATQ0 V1 E1 S0=0 &C1 &D2 S11=55 +FCLASS=0
ATQ0 V1 E1 S0=0 &C1 &D2 S11=55 +FCLASS=0
OK
--> Modem initialized.
--> Sending: ATDT 5551234
--> Waiting for carrier.
ATDT 5551234
CONNECT 24000/ARQ/V34/LAPM/V42BIS
--> Carrier detected.  Waiting for prompt.
max2.RE4-P16-PITTSBURG-MFS.rack7136.MECURY.BBN.COM(BAFTUU.NET)
Login:
--> Looks like a login prompt.
--> Sending: jsamson@emich.edu
jsamson@emich.edu
Password:
--> Looks like a password prompt.
```

```
--> Sending: (password)
    Entering PPP Mode.
    IP address is 4.00.000.200
   MTU is 5678.
--> Looks like a welcome message.
--> Starting pppd at Mon Apr 24 10:42:45 2000
```

To disconnect and end your wvdial session, enter Ctrl+C at a shell prompt.

Solving Problems

If wvdial doesn't work, here are some common problems to help you determine where it failed:

- If /dev/modem already exists, check that /dev/modem is linked to the correct serial port by entering

  # setserial -g /dev/modem

- If wvdial could not detect your modem, something is probably wrong with your modem configuration. Try dialing your ISP (or another number) with minicom or another dialer. If you cannot establish a connection with minicom, go through the steps to configure your modem again.

- If wvdial could not negotiate with your ISP, the login script it uses might not work with your ISP. Read the wvdial README for help and contact your ISP. The wvdial README should be in /usr/share/doc/wvdial. You can also read the ISP Hookup HOWTO, although the directions there are quite terse.

- If wvdial negotiated successfully, but the PPP daemon died soon after login, the wvdial login procedure might not work properly, the ISP could be having problems, or one of your resolver files might be set up incorrectly. Check /etc/resolv.conf, /etc/hosts.allow, and /etc/hosts.deny to make sure that you have them set up properly. Read the wvdial info pages for instructions on adding any special instructions, such as if your ISP has an unusual login procedure. Try to get the login procedure from your ISP or have the ISP give you a login script.

Task: Connecting to the Internet Using the Red Hat PPP Dialer

The Red Hat PPP Dialer is one of the easier PPP dialers to use because it is nothing more than a graphical interface for wvdial. To use Red Hat PPP Dialer, you must first configure an account. The Red Hat PPP Dialer is a graphical version of wvdial. Instead of creating and editing the configuration file manually, the Dialup Configuration tool takes you through a series of dialog boxes and creates an /etc/wvdial.conf file for you.

1. From the GNOME main menu, select Programs, Internet, Dialup Configuration Tool.

2. If you are not already logged in as root, you will be prompted to enter the root password.

3. The first time you use the configuration tool, the program scans your system for modems, as shown in Figure 9.2. If it finds a modem, it displays the modem and serial port.

FIGURE 9.2

The Red Hat Dialup Configuration Tool automatically scans your system for modems if one is not already configured.

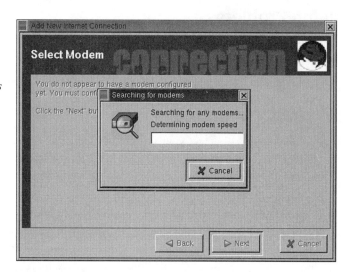

4. If the information is correct, check Keep This Modem and click Next. The Add New Internet Connection dialog box appears, as shown in Figure 9.3.

FIGURE 9.3

The Dialup Configuration Tool creates an /etc/ wvdial.conf file based on the information you enter in the dialog boxes.

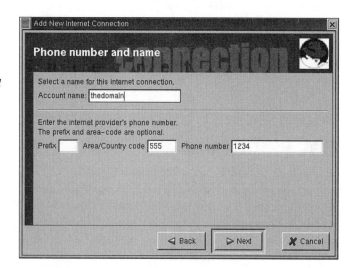

5. Follow the instructions in each dialog box. When you are finished, close the Internet Connections dialog box and click Main Menu, Programs, Internet, RH PPP Dialer. Select the account from the Choose dialog box and click OK. The dialer dials the account.

Summary

In this hour you learned the basics of how the TCP/IP and PPP protocols work to enable you to network with your ISP over a telephone line. You learned how modems work and how to configure your modem to make a connection. You learned how to use wvdial and the Red Hat PPP Dialer to connect to your ISP.

Workshop

The Workshop contains quiz questions and exercises to help reinforce what you've learned in this hour.

Q&A

Q What should I do if my modem is a winmodem?

A Check `http://www.linmodems.org` to see if a Linux software driver is available, although it is unlikely. Chances are that you will have to buy a new modem.

Q How does wvdial know the authentication procedure for my ISP?

A wvdial performs a trial-and-error login procedure that works with most ISPs, based on the information you enter in the configuration file. If your ISP has an uncommon login procedure that wvdial can't figure out on its own, you can enter special instructions in the `/etc/wvdial.conf file`. See the wvdial man pages.

Quiz

1. Which protocol actually forms the Internet network?
2. What does the IP address do?
3. Why do you need a modem to connect to the Internet via a telephone line?
4. Which kind of modem will almost definitely not work with Linux?
5. What is the name of the daemon that controls your PPP connection?
6. Name the configuration file that must be created and edited before you can use wvdial.

Quiz Answers

1. Which protocol actually forms the Internet network?

   IP—the Internet Protocol

2. What does the IP address do?

   It uniquely identifies every host on the network.

3. Why do you need a modem to connect to the Internet via a telephone line?

   Modems convert digital signals to analog and back again, so that data can travel over a phone line.

4. Which kind of modem will almost definitely not work with Linux?

   A winmodem™

5. What is the name of the daemon that controls your PPP connection?

   pppd

6. Name the configuration file that must be created and edited before you can use wvdial.

   `/etc/wvdial.conf`

Exercises

1. Write down the command you would use to find out the IRQ number of `/dev/ttyS1`.

2. See whether `/dev/modem` is on your system. Create it if it is not.

3. Gather the relevant information about your ISP.

4. Enter your ISP's DNS information into the `/etc/resolv.conf` file.

5. Enter the required lines in `/etc/hosts.deny` and `/etc/hosts.allow`.

6. Decide whether you would prefer to make your PPP connection with wvdial or the Red Hat PPP Dialer.

Exercise Answers

1. Write down the command you would use to find out the IRQ number of `/dev/ttyS1`.

   `setserial -g /dev/ttyS1`

2. See if `/dev/modem` is on your system. Create it if it is not.

   Enter **ls -l /dev/modem** to verify that `/dev/modem` is linked to the correct serial port. If it is not there, enter **ln -s /dev/ttySx /dev/modem** (substitute `/dev/ttySx` with the actual device name of your serial port).

3. Gather the relevant information about your ISP:

   Protocol used: SLIP or PPP

   Dial-in phone number

   Your username

   Your user password

   DNS Server IP address(es)

   Your IP address (if fixed)

   ISP Domain

   Search Domain(s)

   (Answer varies with the reader)

4. Enter your ISP's DNS information into the `/etc/resolv.conf` file.

   Open a text editor and enter the information. The file should look something like the following:

   ```
   domain samsonsource.com
   search . judith.samsonsource.com
   nameserver 000.000.000.00
   nameserver 111.111.111.11
   ```

   Alternatively, open linuxconf as root to the Networking, Client Tasks, Name Server Specification page and enter the information there.

5. Enter the required lines in `/etc/hosts.deny` and `/etc/hosts.allow`.

   In `/etc/hosts.deny`, enter **ALL:ALL**

   In `/etc/hosts.allow`, enter **ALL:LOCAL**

6. Decide whether you would prefer to make your PPP connection with wvdial or the Red Hat PPP Dialer.

   Answer varies with the reader.

9

Hour 10

Using the Internet

After you have made a successful connection to your ISP, the difficult part is over and the fun begins. Linux comes with many Internet applications that are often far more powerful than their Windows equivalents. In this hour you will learn the basics of how some Internet tools work in Linux, and you will learn about some useful Internet applications.

In this hour you will

- Discover some of the more popular Web browsers for Linux
- Learn about how email works
- Learn about the Usenet and XRN, the news reader
- Download and upload files with gFTP
- Chat on the Xchat IRC client

Connecting to the World Wide Web

To connect to the Web, you need some sort of Internet browser, which will connect to a Web site and download its contents to your computer. In Linux, you have a lot of choices when it comes to Internet browsers. Some of the most common browsers are introduced in this section.

Netscape Navigator

The Linux version of Netscape Communicator is almost identical to the Windows version. Netscape is included in Red Hat Linux 7.0 and a Netscape launcher is created by default on the GNOME panel. You can use Netscape Communicator for news, email, FTP downloads, and Web browsing, just like in Windows. Java and Javascript are supported, as well as some plug-ins. The Web browser in Communicator, called Netscape Navigator, is shown in Figure 10.1.

FIGURE 10.1

Netscape Navigator for Linux looks just like Navigator for Windows, and you use it the same way.

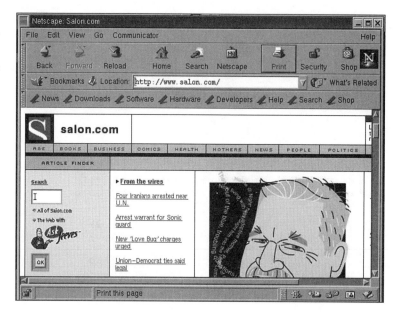

Lynx

If you use a dial-up PPP connection to access the Internet, waiting for graphics to display can seem interminably long, particularly if they are mostly ads. If graphics aren't important to you, consider Lynx as an alternative to graphics-based browsers such as Netscape. When you use the Lynx browser, only the text of a Web site is downloaded and displayed. This makes Web pages load very quickly, and it is also much easier to concentrate on the text. Lynx is particularly useful for reading the news on graphic-heavy sites where the images aren't necessary. Another great time to use Lynx is if you are searching mailing lists or newsgroup archives.

To use Lynx, at a shell prompt enter **lynx**, followed by the URL; for example:

```
lynx http://www.redhat.com
```

Lynx comes with online help and a number of Web pages where you can get information. To use the online help, enter **?** while in Lynx. The Lynx User's Guide is available at `http://lynx.browser.org/` and locally in your documentation directory—by default, `/usr/share/doc/lynx-2.8.4/lynx-help`.

Figure 10.2 shows the Lynx home page, as viewed in Lynx.

FIGURE 10.2

Lynx is small and unbelievably fast, especially if you've grown accustomed to the World Wide Wait.

Mozilla

Mozilla is an open-source browser based on the source code for the Netscape browser. Netscape released the source code for what would have been Netscape 5.0 to mozilla.org for development as a free software browser. Mozilla is still in heavy development, but the project looks promising. The source code is released every day for compilation and testing, but RPM packages are periodically created as well. See `http://www.mozilla.org` to download the latest release.

Sending and Receiving Email

If you are used to using Windows, you probably never really thought about email. You use Netscape Messenger or Microsoft Outlook, and that is that. In Linux, of course, there is much more choice of mail clients, called Mail User Agents (MUA). Although it's beyond the scope of this book, you can even set up your own Mail Transport Agent (MTA), which enables you to send your messages directly over the Internet to the recipient, as well as thoroughly customize your email setup. In this section you learn the basics of email so that you can better understand all the options available to you in Linux. We will also introduce some of the more popular email clients, both graphical and text-based, that come with Red Hat.

When networking was first invented, electronic mail was one of the first uses for networked computers. The features that are available in most mail applications and the kinds of files you can send with email have expanded dramatically, but the basic idea behind email remains the same. You need a way to compose the email, you need a program that will deliver the email from your computer to the recipient's, and you need some kind of transport medium such as TCP/IP to transport the email across the Internet. You also need a mail protocol that every computer and program understands so that the message can be delivered.

The email setup for your system depends on how you send and receive email. When you use an ISP to send email, your ISP accepts email that people send to you over the Internet and stores it on a hard disk. When you want to retrieve your email, you get it from the ISP using POP3 or IMAP protocol. SMTP is used to transport the mail over the Internet. You receive email via POP3 or IMAP and send it via SMTP, both over the Internet. You don't even need to worry about an MTA in this case—the MTA is at your ISP. If you want to use Netscape Messenger, pine, or Kmail, this is a good, simple scenario.

> If you want to use an MUA that does not support POP3 or IMAP, you can use fetchmail to retrieve the mail from your ISP. See the Mail Administrator HOWTO at http://www.linuxdoc.org.

An MUA is what you use to send and receive email. When you think of your email program, you are actually referring to the MUA. MUAs are programs that you use to read, compose, edit, and forward mail. The mail user agent usually has a text editor that you can use to compose an email message.

The Mail Message

The mail message consists of two parts: the message body, which is the message itself, and the mail header, which includes the address of the sender and recipient(s), the subject of the message, and the date. You can also attach a signature to the mail message. A signature is kept in your home directory in the .signature file. Your signature can contain your contact information, such as phone numbers and snail mail address, or a joke, a saying, or a motto.

When you click Send, the MUA attaches some headers to the body of the message and passes it to the MTA. If you send your email via an ISP, the ISP collects your email message; then it uses its own MTA to send the message. The MTA attaches some more headers and then delivers the message to its destination. The transport protocol (usually SMTP, Simple Mail Transport Protocol) is used by the MTA to provide the medium to transfer the mail.

When somebody sends you an email message, your mail is delivered to a mailbox on your ISP's computer. Your computer uses the IMAP or POP3 protocol to pull your email from your ISP mailbox to your local mailbox. Most ISPs use POP3, but IMAP is becoming more popular.

With POP3 or IMAP, your MUA "pulls" mail from your ISP's server. In other words, your email sits on your ISP's mail server until your MUA checks for mail. You can usually configure your MUA to periodically query your ISP's mail server, or to wait for you to manually check for mail. If you don't want to use the POP3 or IMAP, you can use fetchmail to get your email from your ISP.

Fetchmail

The program fetchmail talks to remote mail servers, fetches the mail, and feeds it into the normal mail delivery path using SMTP. Fetchmail is generally better than just using an MUA that uses POP/IMAP. Fetchmail can be run in the background and poll your ISP's mail server, so you can use a mail notifier program such as xbiff or the GNOME mail applet. Also, fetchmail can deal with errors and nonstandard server practices better than MUAs with POP/IMAP capabilities. To learn how to set up fetchmail, see the Mail Administrator HOWTO and the Network Administrator's Guide at `http://www.linuxdoc.org`.

MIME Types

MIME stands for Multipurpose Internet Mail Extensions. It is the officially proposed standard for including different kinds of file types within a standard Internet email message (see RFC 822).

MIME is a collection of standard ways to support different types of messages, such as plain text, binary data files, PostScript files, and so on. MIME also supports messages with different kinds of fonts and messages that include different objects, graphics, and audio fragments. Without MIME types, only standard ASCII text messages could be sent via email.

Mail User Agents

Following are some of the more popular mail user agents:

- **mutt**—A text-based mail user agent that is descended from the original elm. Mutt supports IMAP, POP3, MIME, and PGP (Pretty Good Privacy signed messages). The mutt home page is `http://www.mutt.org`.
- **elm**—One of the original mail user agents for UNIX. Elm stands for electronic mail. Many people still use elm, although mutt is gaining ground.

- **Pine**—A text-based mail user agent that is great for new users because it is easy to use and understand. It also has its own editor for creating email messages and great IMAP support. The home page for pine is `http://www.washington.edu/pine`.

- **Netscape Messenger**—Part of the Netscape Communicator package. Messenger for Linux is identical to that for Windows. Like Windows, Messenger has IMAP and POP3 support, but it doesn't offer aliases and PGP handling.

- **Balsa**—Another mail user agent that is part of the GNOME set of applications. Balsa has been undergoing rapid development in the past six months and is close to a 1.0 release. It supports POP3 and IMAP and has an easy-to-use interface that is similar to Eudora. Because it is GNOME compliant, it works with GTK themes and will also eventually work with bonobo; it will be able to be embedded in other GNOME applications. The home page for Balsa is `http://www.newton.cx/balsa/main.html`.

- **Mahogany**—A graphics-based mail user agent that is quickly gaining popularity among Linux users. Mahogany is available for X11/UNIX platforms (which includes Linux) and Windows. It supports POP3, IMAP, and full MIME support. The home page for Mahogany is `http://mahogany.home.dhs.org`.

Setting Up News

A tool that is somewhat similar to email is Usenet. Usenet contains many discussion groups for every subject under the sun. Although many Linux projects have been gravitating toward mailing lists, Usenet is still an essential tool for keeping up-to-date with the Linux community and getting help.

Usenet is not controlled or governed by anyone; in fact, it is really nothing more than an agreement between many news sites to exchange news. A post to a Usenet newsgroup is called an article. Articles are submitted to a newsgroup, which is set up to accept and post articles that are about a common topic. Newsgroups are organized into hierarchies that indicate the topic for the newsgroup. When you create a news article, you enter your message into a news application called a newsreader—for example, Netscape Message Center. The newsreader formats the message so it can be sent to the news server via TCP/IP.

Nothing controls Usenet. No central body decides which articles are posted (unless a particular Usenet newsgroup is moderated). No central body decides which newsgroups a news server will carry or propagate. Those decisions are made by the owners of the news server. Usenet is like the traditional fence post. Everybody has the right to a place by the fence, but nobody owns the fence or controls what the conversation is about.

Every Usenet site decides which newsgroups to post to the site. Because different sites post different newsgroups, the only limit to which newsgroups are available is made by the administrator of the Usenet site. If you get Usenet from your ISP, your ISP administers your Usenet site and controls which newsgroups you get.

Different Usenet sites carry different groups. Some Usenet sites carry all newsgroups, whereas others carry only selected newsgroups.

A great resource for information on Usenet is the Usenet Help files at `http://metalab.unc.edu/usenet-i/usenet-help.html`.

You can use Netscape News to download and post messages to your favorite newsgroups. Another newsgroup client is XRN.

To run XRN, ensure that you have an Internet connection, then enter the following command at a shell prompt, substituting your news server at *[server_name]*. You can get the hostname for your news server from your ISP.

```
xrn -nntpServer [server_name]
```

XRN is shown in Figure 10.3.

10

FIGURE 10.3

XRN enables you to subscribe to and read messages in a simple, X-based format.

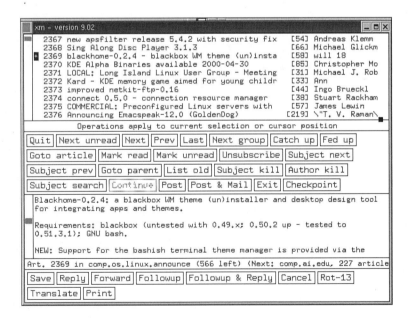

Unfortunately, some users take advantage of the relative anonymity that Usenet provides to post rude, angry, irrelevant, or otherwise obnoxious messages. Please remember that when you post a message to Usenet, you are participating in an ongoing conversation with fellow human beings, and that the normal rules of etiquette still apply. For a really useful but also amusing piece on netiquette, see Brad Templeton's *Dear Emily Postnews* at http://www.templetons.com/brad/emily.html.

Downloading Files with FTP

FTP, which stands for File Transfer Protocol, is used for transferring files and directories between computers via a remote connection such as PPP. You can use the text-based FTP client at a shell prompt, or you can use a graphical FTP client such as gFTP. Because gFTP makes life so much easier than the text FTP, this section describes it in detail while providing the basics of FTP. Following are some of the things you can do with FTP:

- Upload files to another computer.
- Download files from another computer.
- Compare directories on your computer to those on another computer.
- Manipulate files on a remote computer, including changing permissions, copying, deleting, and moving files.
- Edit files on a remote computer.

Upload means to transfer files from your computer to a remote computer via a network connection. *Download* means to transfer files from a remote computer to your computer via a network connection. To *download anonymously* means that you don't need to have a recognized username and password on the remote computer to log in and download files.

Task: Use gFTP to Upload and Download Files

You can think of using anonymous FTP as if you were a guest on another person's computer. You are allowed to look in certain directories, but most are private. You can read and download files, but you can't manipulate files and directories, you can't move files around, and you can't edit files.

When you establish an FTP connection with a remote site that gives you full permissions, that computer's filesystem becomes like an extension of your own. You can copy, move, and delete files and directories. You can create symbolic and hard links. You can open and edit files or upload new files to the remote filesystem.

1. The quickest way to connect to an FTP site via anonymous login is to enter the connection information into the Connect toolbar.

2. Click the Connect button.

3. To make a connection using a username and password, enter them into the fields on the Connect toolbar. If you leave them blank, gFTP will attempt an anonymous login by default.

4. In the left pane, browse to the local directory where you want to download to or upload a file from.

5. In the right pane, browse to the directory where you want to download from or upload to.

6. Click the arrow pointing left to download, or click the arrow pointing right to upload.

gFTP is shown in Figure 10.4.

10

FIGURE 10.4

gFTP is a useful and easy-to-use tool for uploading and downloading files.

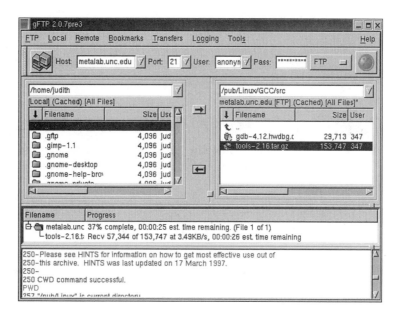

Chatting for Fun and Profit on IRC

IRC, which stands for Internet Relay Chat, enables you to communicate in real time over the Internet to other users all over the world. The media is full of references to chat rooms that are used for pornography, psychobabble, and lonely singles, so many serious people might be reluctant to use IRC. On the other hand, if you are having a problem or question that just can't wait for an email or newsgroup response, if you want to hold a meeting with people in different geographical locations, or if you want to maintain an ongoing sense of community with people who share the same interests as you, you can't beat IRC.

Most of the Linux free software projects maintain a channel for members to hold meetings, make announcements, and discuss problems. If you have a particularly hairy problem, you can often speak in real time to the person who created the software. Just remember that these are usually very busy people, so ask nicely. Also, there are many shortcuts and jargon that people tend to use on IRC, such as "stat" or "a/s/l" for age, sex, where you live, or "brb" for "be right back." If you don't understand something, don't be afraid to ask. People on Linux channels tend to be very nice and friendly, particularly on the help channels.

People use "channels" to form chat groups based on a particular topic. The channels are formed on IRC servers, which you can connect to via a chat client. X-Chat is the most widely used graphical chat client in Linux.

Task: Log in to an IRC Server Using X-Chat

When you first open X-Chat, two windows open: the Server List and the X-Chat window itself; both are shown in Figure 10.5. The servers are grouped by domain.

1. To see the servers that are included in a particular domain, click the domain name to expand the server list.

2. You can open the server list at any time during a session by clicking X-Chat, Server List.

3. Before seeing a list of channels to join, you must log in to a server. You can log in to a server by selecting the server and clicking Connect.

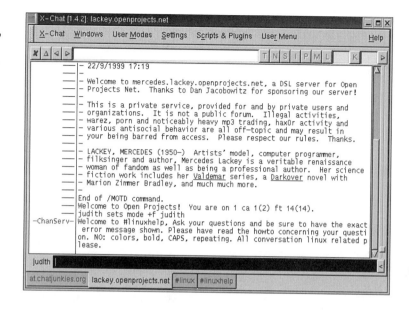

When you type in the X-Chat text box, you can enter two things: commands and messages. A command is prepended by a front slash, which tells X-Chat to interpret what follows as a command, not as a message to the chat group.

Task: Join a Channel

To get a list of possible channels on a server, type /**list** into the message box or click Windows, Channel List Window, Refresh the List. All the channels that are available from that server are listed, including the number of users currently in the channel and the general topic of the channel.

1. To join a list, select the list and click Join Channel. Alternatively, type /**join** *#[channel]* in the text box.

2. You can join multiple channels at once. To join another channel, type /**join** *#[channel]* into the message box, and a new window will open to the new channel.

3. To add a message to the channel (that is, join in the discussion), enter your message into the message box and click Enter. Your message is sent to the channel server and then posted in the channel for everyone in the channel to see.

4. If you want to talk just to a particular person in a channel, you can /msg them. Type /**msg**, the name of the person, and then the message for that person. Your message will be directed to that particular person rather than to the general channel.

When you join a channel, you will see a list of nicknames to the right of the text box. This is the list of people currently logged in to the channel. Channel operators are denoted by a green circle next to the nickname. Channel operators have special status in the channel. The channel operator controls the topic of discussion, much like the moderator of a mailing list. The channel operator can also discipline unruly chatters by kicking them out of the channel.

Some channels are devoted to the Linux community, where people generally go to get help or to help others. Try the #linux and #linuxnewbie.org channels in particular. irc.linux.com hosts dozens of channels for open-source projects.

Getting Help

The IRC Primer is your best reference for useful information on IRC. You can read it online or download it in text, PostScript, or LaTex format from ftp://cs-pub.bu.edu/irc/support/.

If you're really into details, you can read the RFC that outlines the standards and technology for IRC at the same FTP site.

The X-Chat user manual is also useful, particularly as a reference for what all the little buttons and icons on the X-Chat window mean. You can read the X-Chat user manual, FAQs, and some other documents online at http://www.xchat.org.

Summary

In this hour you learned about the various applications and tools you can use on the Internet. You learned about some of the Web browsers that are available in Linux, and you were introduced to how email works and learned about some of the UNIX mail user agents. You learned how to upload and download files with gFTP and how to chat in real time using X-Chat, an Internet Relay Chat client.

Workshop

The Workshop contains quiz questions and exercises to help reinforce what you've learned in this hour.

Q&A

Q Can I use the Internet if I don't run X?

A Every Internet activity that is covered in this hour—browsing the Web, sending email, and using Usenet, FTP, and IRC—can be done in a shell environment. For text-based clients for Usenet, FTP, and IRC, see the Network Administrator's Guide, and the appropriate HOWTOs.

Quiz

1. Which Web browser is text-only?
2. What protocol is generally used to send email across the Internet?
3. What is the difference between a mail user agent (MUA) and a mail transfer agent (MTA)?
4. What is a MIME type?
5. Who controls Usenet?
6. How do you list the channels an IRC server supports?
7. In X-Chat, how do you know who the channel operator is?

Quiz Answers

1. Which Web browser is text-only?

   Lynx

2. What protocol is generally used to send email across the Internet?

   SMTP

3. What is the difference between a mail user agent (MUA) and a mail transfer agent (MTA)?

   You use an MUA to compose and send emails and to read the emails that you receive. Your ISP uses an MTA to actually send the email to the recipient's computer or ISP. You can set up your own MTA on your local Linux system. See the Mail Administrator HOWTO and the *Network Administrator's Guide* at `http://www.linuxdocs.org`.

4. What is a MIME type?

   MIME stands for Multipurpose Internet Mail Extensions. MIME is a collection of standards that enables you to send and receive different types of files via email, in addition to ASCII text.

10

5. Who controls Usenet?

   Nobody. There are groups of people who run Usenet sites who have agreed to do things a certain way; however, no one actually controls or can enforce any standards on Usenet as a whole.

6. How do you list the channels an IRC server supports?

   Open X-Chat. Log on to a server by selecting it from the Server List and clicking Connect. Enter /`list` into the message box, or in the main X-Chat window click Windows, Channel List Window, Refresh List.

7. In X-Chat, how do you know who the channel operator is?

   A green dot is next to the channel operator's name in the list of channel participants.

Exercises

1. Open `http://www.redhat.com` with a graphics browser and with Lynx.

2. Connect to Red Hat's FTP download site or one of the mirror sites listed at `http://www.redhat.com/apps/download`. Download a game that interests you, using gFTP. Suggestion: Xbill at `ftp://ftp.redhat.com/pub/redhat/redhat-6.2/i386/RedHat/SRPMS/SRPMS/xbill-2.0-7.src.rpm`.

3. Join the #linux channel at the `irc.openprojects.net` server or the `irc.linux.com` server.

Exercise Answers

1. Open `http://www.redhat.com` with a graphics browser and with Lynx.

   For the graphics browser, try Netscape or Mozilla (or another graphics-based browser). Open the browser and then type the URL into the location field. In Lynx, type `http://www.redhat.com` at a shell prompt. Make sure that you have an Internet connection first!

2. Connect to Red Hat's FTP download site or one of the mirror sites listed at `http://www.redhat.com/apps/download`. Download a game that interests you, using gFTP. Suggestion: Xbill at `ftp://ftp.redhat.com/pub/redhat/redhat-6.2/i386/RedHat/SRPMS/SRPMS/xbill-2.0-7.src.rpm`.

   Open gFTP from the GNOME Main Menu, Programs, Internet, gFTP. Enter **ftp://www.redhat.com** into the Host field and click the Connect button.

3. Join the #linux channel at the `irc.openprojects.net` server or the `irc.linux.com` server.

   Select the server on the server list under OpenProjectsNet and click Connect. In the message box, enter /**join #linux**.

HOUR 11

Linux Applications

Red Hat Linux 7.0 comes with dozens of applications, but you can download hundreds of additional Linux applications from the Web, and most of them are free software. Linux software usually comes in two forms: the RPM package of binary executable files and the source code. In this hour you will learn how to install RPM packages. In Hour 23, "Compiling and Installing Applications from Source Code," you will learn how to compile and install software from source code.

In this hour you will

- Find Linux applications on the Web and use the wget utility to download RPM packages
- Explore how the RPM package works
- Install new RPM packages
- Query RPM packages for information on the software and files the package installs
- Solve installation dependency errors and uninstall software installed from an RPM package

Where to Find Applications

Red Hat Linux contains numerous applications, but sooner or later you will want to see what else is out there. There are thousands of applications that run on Linux, most of which are free software, created by individuals or volunteer projects. The choices are so dizzying that sometimes it's hard to figure out where to get applications, let alone which applications to get. Luckily, a few central locations are generally recognized by the Linux community as central repositories for Linux software. You will find most available applications in one of the following places.

http://www.freshmeat.net

Freshmeat is the self-proclaimed largest index of Linux software on the Web. Every software package on Freshmeat has an information page, which includes the download link, the description of the application, and the category. Links are provided to the home page for the application, as well as to the project responsible for the application's creation. Users can post comments on the software, which usually include reviews, tips, and workarounds. Freshmeat also frequently publishes articles and editorials about Linux and other areas of technology.

http://rpmfind.net

rpmfind, which was created and maintained by Daniel Veillard, is a marvelous way to find RPMs (more about RPMs later this hour). rpmfind.net is a database of RPMs available for the major Linux distributions that use RPM packages. rpmfind.net works with two clever tools: rpmfind and rpm2html. rpm2html automatically creates a Web page that lists all the dependencies for a particular RPM, along with the RPM packages that fulfill those dependencies. rpmfind enables you to search the rpmfind database for a particular package. Although they make it easier, you don't need rpmfind or rpm2html to use the database—you can look directly at the database listings on the Web.

The only disadvantage to rpmfind is that it is so large that you really must know what you are looking for before you try to use it. Sites like freshmeat.net are better suited for browsing.

You can get rpmfind and rpm2html from the rpmfind.net Web site at
http://www.rpmfind.net/linux/rpm2html/download.html.

http://metalab.unc.edu

Metalab was the original repository for Linux applications and distributions. metalab.unc.edu contains more than 55 gigabytes of Linux software and documentation, free for download. The Linux archive is divided into categories that you can browse, and a search engine can help you find a particular document or software.

http://www.redhat.com

The Red Hat download page contains the entire RH distribution, as well as applications by category, errata, patches, and security advisories. The download page is found at http://www.redhat.com/apps/download/.

The Red Hat Web site also contains all the Red Hat documentation, archives for earlier distributions, developer and user information, and useful Linux links.

Using wget to Download Applications

When you have found an application that you are interested in, you must download it and install it on your local machine. There are several tools you can use to download applications. Later in this hour, you will see how you can download and install an RPM package in one step, without saving the RPM to your hard drive. If you want to save the RPM file to your hard drive, however, a small utility called wget can be your best bet.

wget is a useful utility for downloading large files, particularly if you have an unstable dial-up connection. If your connection is lost during download, wget will read the portion of the file that was already downloaded when the connection was lost. When you reconnect, wget continues where it left off. You can also run wget in the background, and when wget finishes downloading the file, it terminates itself. Best of all, wget prints a dot to the screen for each 10KB of data it downloads, and it shows the percentage of download complete so that you can watch its progress.

To use wget, you must know the complete URL pathname of the file you want to download. You can get the URL via Netscape and then use wget to perform the actual download. From a command prompt, type **wget *[url pathname]***. For example:

```
$ wget http://freshmeat.net/projects/devchanger/download/changer_20000201.tar.gz
```

You can create a file of multiple URLs for wget to download, and you can specify a particular directory to download to (wget saves the file in the current directory by default). See the wget man pages for more options.

The RPM Package

As you will see in Hour 23, installing new applications from source code can be a harrowing experience, even for someone with a lot of knowledge and experience. RPMs make it easy for anyone to add and remove software. An RPM package takes all the files you need to run a piece of software, including the application itself, library files, documentation, and configuration files, and puts them into one file. An RPM package contains information about what is included in the package, what files the package will install on the computer and where they will go, as well as the instructions on how to install and uninstall itself.

In addition to easy installing and uninstalling, RPMs enable you to make sure that your packages are installed correctly—that there are no missing or altered files and that everything is installed where it's supposed to go. RPMs also enable you to verify that a package is actually installed. This is called querying the package.

The RPM Package Filename

The RPM package filename tells you a lot about the package. The RPM filename `apache-1.3.12-20.i386.rpm` is used here as an example. The first part of the filename is the name of the software that the RPM package contains, which in our example is the Apache Web server. Next comes the version of Apache, 1.3.12. After the version number is a dash, followed by a 20. This is the package release number, which signifies the number of times the package was released for the same version of Apache. Thus, this is the twentieth RPM to be released for Apache 1.3.12. New RPM builds for the same software version are usually made to fix bugs that were found in the package itself. Package release numbers start at 1. Next, the i386 signifies that this RPM package was built for an Intel 386 platform or later. Finally, the .rpm tells us that the file is an RPM package.

Task: Installing an RPM Package

To install an RPM, follow these steps:

1. Enter the command

   `rpm -i [package_name]`

2. To upgrade an RPM (recommended even for new installations), enter

   `rpm -U [package_name]`

When installing a package, either by the `-i` or `-U` options, RPM follows these steps:

1. The RPM installer checks for dependencies. Many software packages require files that are not included in the RPM, but that are in another package. The RPM installer first makes sure that all required files are already present in the system. It also checks to make sure that the package to be installed won't replace files that are needed by other packages that are already installed.

2. The RPM installer checks for conflicts. Conflicts occur, for example, if you try to install a package that is already installed or if you attempt to install an older version of a package when the newer version is already installed. Another example of a conflict is if the package installation will overwrite a file that is needed by another, already installed, package.

3. The RPM installer runs any needed scripts or does any other tasks that must be performed before installation.

4. The RPM installer looks on your system for any customized configuration files that are already present for the application. If the RPM installer finds a custom configuration file, it will try not to overwrite it, but it will make another config file with a slightly different name in case you decide to use the RPM's configuration file instead of your own.

5. When everything is in place, the installer unpacks the actual software files and installs them where they belong. The installer also sets permissions for the files according to the instructions in the package.

6. After the installation is complete, the installer performs any required post-installation tasks, such as running a cleanup script or ldconfig, to make new shared libraries accessible.

7. The RPM installer adds information about the newly installed package to the RPM database.

> The actual name of the RPM package isn't important to the installer. For example, if you download an RPM package during a Windows session and the RPM name is truncated or otherwise altered, you can still install the package with no problem.

11

You can install an RPM package via FTP, without downloading and saving the actual package to your computer. Enter the RPM command, followed by the URL where the package is located:

```
# rpm -Uvh http://www.redhat.com/swr/i386/apache-1.3.12-2.i386.html
```

The package will install directly from the download site.

Useful RPM Switches and Options

RPM comes with a lot of switches and options that slightly alter the default behavior of the command, enhance the command, or provide status reports. In fact, you can't use the RPM command without at least one switch to tell the command what you want it to do.

Most people use RPM with the -Uvh options to install, as well as update packages. -U means to update any older packages for the same software and install the package if no earlier version exists. -U fulfills the same function as -i, and you don't have to worry about whether you already have an earlier version installed.

The -v switch tells RPM to go into verbose mode, which causes it to print a status report for each RPM installed. You can get even more information by telling RPM to be very verbose, with the -vv switch, as shown in Figure 11.1. Usually, however, -v is sufficient.

FIGURE 11.1

With -vv, *the RPM installer reports on everything it does to install the package.*

The -h switch tells RPM to print hash marks as it installs the packages. The hash marks assure you that the package is, indeed, successfully installing. After fifty hash marks are printed, the package is installed.

Common options are as follows:

- --test—Performs all the checks that RPM normally performs before installing a package, but stops short of actually running a preinstall script and doing the installation. --test is useful for determining whether the package you want to install has unmet dependencies.

- --replacepkgs—Installs the RPM even if the RPM is already installed. This option is useful if you think files from the original installation have been damaged.

- --replacefiles—Installs the packages even if the package will replace files of the same name that have already been installed from a different package, such as an earlier version of the software. You shouldn't use this option unless you are sure of the results.

- --nodeps—Installs the package without checking for dependencies first. Do not use nodeps unless you are sure or don't care about the results. --nodeps can be useful when you are installing beta software for testing.

Many more switches and options are available for RPM than those described here. See the RPM man and info pages for more information. An excellent resource that very thoroughly explains every aspect of RPM is *Maximum RPM,* by Ed Bailey, Red Hat Press, 1997. The book is geared toward developers; it is a bit out of date but still full of information. Alternatively, you can download a PostScript or LaTex version for no cost at `http://www.rpm.org`.

Querying RPM Packages

If you're not sure about whether to install an RPM, you can get more information by querying it before you install it. To get a list of basic information about the RPM, you can right-click it in GNOME File Manager and select Show Info. The gnoRPM Package Info dialog box appears, which displays basic information about the package, including the following:

- Date and time the package was built
- Description of the package contents
- Total size of all the files installed by the package
- Package group
- Package signature
- Short description of the software
- List of files that the package installs

> The package signature verifies the authenticity of the package—that it was actually built by the listed package builder and contains what the package label says it does. When you check a package, that verifies that the package signature is valid. Always check the package signature before installing a file that you have downloaded from the Web.

An example of a package information box is shown in Figure 11.2.

From the command line, you can enter query options to the RPM command to get the same information. To get basic information about an RPM package, enter **rpm -qpi** **[package_name]**. For example, to get information about the Apache RPM package, enter

```
$ rpm -qpi apache-1.3.12-20.i386.rpm
```

11

FIGURE 11.2

Right-click the RPM package icon in GNOME File Manager and select Show Info to display the Package Info dialog box.

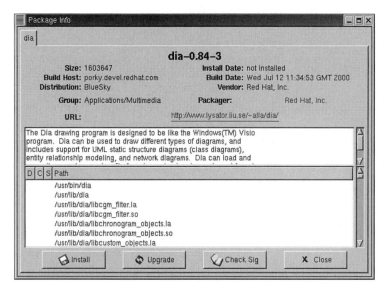

The output is as follows:

```
Name       : apache              Relocations: (not relocateable)
Version    : 1.3.12                  Vendor: Red Hat, Inc.
Release    : 20                   Build Date:
➥Sun 23 Jul 2000 04:19:16 PM EDT
Install date: (not installed)    Build Host: porky.devel.redhat.com
Group      : System Environment/Daemons   Source RPM:
➥apache-1.3.12-20.src.rpm
Size       : 1388176                 License:
➥Freely distributable and usable
Packager   : Red Hat, Inc. <http://bugzilla.redhat.com/bugzilla>
Summary    : The most widely used Web server on the Internet.
Description :
Apache is a powerful, full-featured, efficient and freely-available
Web server. Apache is also the most popular Web server on the
Internet.
```

Install the apache package if you need a Web server.

To list the files that apache-1.3.12-20.i386.rpm installs, enter the following:

```
$ rpm -qpl apache-1.3.12-20.i386.rpm
```

(Use the same command as before, except with a -l switch instead of a -i). The output is

```
/etc/httpd/conf
/etc/httpd/conf/access.conf
/etc/httpd/conf/httpd.conf
/etc/httpd/conf/magic
```

```
/etc/httpd/conf/srm.conf
/etc/httpd/logs
/etc/httpd/modules
/etc/logrotate.d/apache
/etc/rc.d/init.d/httpd
/usr/bin/dbmmanage
/usr/bin/htdigest
/usr/bin/htpasswd
/usr/lib/apache
/usr/lib/apache/httpd.exp
/usr/lib/apache/libproxy.so
/usr/lib/apache/mod_access.so
/usr/lib/apache/mod_actions.so
/usr/lib/apache/mod_alias.so
/usr/lib/apache/mod_asis.so
. . . . .
```

To find out which package a file belongs to, enter the following:

```
$ rpm -qf /etc/httpd/conf
apache-1.3.12-20
```

The package that installed the file, apache-1.3.12-20, is printed to the screen.

Solving Dependency Errors

11

The most common RPM installation error is the dependency error. A dependency error occurs when the package you want to install can't find the files it needs on your system. For example, in the dependency error message shown here, you are trying to install mgetty-sendfax. You get an error message that mgetty version 1.1.21 must be installed, and it cannot be found on the system.

```
# rpm -Uvh mgetty-sendfax-1.1.21.-11.i386.rpm
error: failed dependencies:
        mgetty = 1.1.21 is needed by mgetty-sendfax-1.1.21-11
```

If you install mgetty first, then you can install mgetty-sendfax.

Dependency errors can arise for three reasons. First, errors can occur because an application needs files that are not present at all. Second, errors occur when the RPM installation program can't find the files. Third, errors occur because the application needs files from a more current or an earlier version of a package that is installed.

> If you get a dependency error, pay attention to the files that the RPM installer needs. You might need to install another RPM package first, or you might need a more current or an older version of an RPM package.

It can sometimes be tricky to figure out exactly how to fix a dependency error because the error message doesn't tell you which package the file comes from:

```
# rpm -Uvh gnumeric*
error: failed dependencies:
      libxml.so.0 is needed by gnumeric-0.27-1
[root@localhost RPMS]#
```

In the preceding example, you want to install the gnumeric spreadsheet application, but you are missing the file libxml.so.0. You can enter the command rpm -q libxml to see if there is a libxml package. If so, you can enter rpm -qpl libxml* to see if the libxml.so.0 file is included in the libxml package. If libxml.so.0 is included in the libxml package (and in fact it is), you know that you must install the libxml RPM package before installing the gnumeric RPM.

Most applications contain documentation that lists the package's dependencies. You can also use the rpm2html or gnoRPM utilities to discern which package a needed file comes from.

Removing Software

Applications that were installed as RPM packages are easily removed. To uninstall an RPM package, enter the following command:

```
rpm -e [package_name]
```

When you want to remove a package, do not enter the entire RPM filename, just the name of the software. For example, to remove Apache from your system, enter

```
# rpm -e apache
```

not

```
#rpm -e apache-1.3.12-2.i386.html
```

All files that were installed with the package are removed.

Summary

In this hour you learned where to obtain additional Linux software, most of which is available for free. You learned about the RPM package and how RPM packages install new software. You installed RPM packages using the various options, and you queried RPM packages. You also learned how to solve dependency errors during installation and how to uninstall RPM packages.

Workshop

The Workshop contains quiz questions and exercises to help reinforce what you've learned in this hour.

Q&A

Q Is it possible to install RPM packages that were created for the SuSE distribution? How about Mandrake?

A Before installing an RPM package, make sure that it was created for Red Hat. Other Linux distributions, such as SuSE, have a different directory structure than Red Hat, so their RPM packages will place files in different places than the packages made for Red Hat would. Generally, you shouldn't use RPMs made for another distribution. The exceptions to this rule are RPM packages made for Mandrake, which is based on Red Hat. Mandrake RPMs will usually work fine on a Red Hat system (this may change as Mandrake and Red Hat grow further apart).

Q Many of the applications on Freshmeat have only source code for download. Where can I get the RPMs?

A Many developers release only the source code of an application, and then others make the RPM packages. If no RPMs are available at the home page of an application, check the Red Hat download page at `http://www.redhat.com/apps/download` or `http://rpmfind.net` to see if an RPM is there.

11

Quiz

1. True/False: Any RPM packages that are listed in the rpmfind.net database can be used with Red Hat Linux.

2. What is the difference between `rpm -i` and `rpm -U`?

3. What is a dependency error, and how do you fix it?

4. Must an RPM package have the extension .rpm to work?

5. What does checking the signature of a package do?

Quiz Answers

1. True/False: Any RPM packages that are listed in the rpmfind.net database can be used with Red Hat Linux.

   False. Some RPM packages, such as those made for SuSE Linux or Solaris, cannot be used with Red Hat, or they can be used, but with unpredictable results.

2. What is the difference between rpm -i and rpm -U?

   rpm -i will install only new packages. If you already have an older version of the package installed, rpm -i installs the newer version without removing the older version. This can lead to complications in the future, if you want to install from source code. rpm -U installs a new package and removes any older versions of the software from the system.

3. What is a dependency error, and how do you fix it?

   A dependency error occurs when a package you want to install requires another package to be installed first or requires certain files from another package to be installed first. To fix the error, install the package that contains the dependent files first, and then install the package you originally attempted to install.

4. Must an RPM package have the extension .rpm to work?

   No. The actual filename of the package is unimportant as long as the package's format and contents are valid.

5. What does checking the signature of a package do?

   Verifies that the package actually comes from the source that it claims to come from.

Exercises

1. Find the latest version of gnumeric at http://rpmfind.net. Is the version on your system current?

2. Check the signature of a package from your Red Hat CD-ROM or one that you have downloaded from the Web.

3. Install and then remove the package of your choice.

Exercise Answers

1. Find the latest version of gnumeric at http://rpmfind.net. Is the version on your system current?

   Go to http://rpmfind.net and open the Index by Name at G. Look for gnumeric and note the version number found in the RPM filename. Query gnumeric on your system with the command rpm -q gnumeric*.

2. Check the signature of a package from your Red Hat CD-ROM or that you have downloaded from the Web.

   Locate the package in GNOME File Manager. Right-click the filename or icon and select Check Signature. (Alternatively, enter **rpm --checksig [package_name]** at the command line).

3. Install and then remove the package of your choice.

   Enter **rpm -Uvh *[package_name]*** to install the package, and then enter **rpm -e**
   [package] to remove the package. Remember to use just the name of the software,
   not the entire package filename, when removing the software.

11

HOUR 12

Linux Productivity Applications

Linux has a lingering reputation for being not very useful in an ordinary office environment, despite a proliferation of applications and rapid advances in graphic interfaces and other desktop tools. Many advanced productivity applications are available as part of Red Hat Linux 7.0. In this hour, you will learn about those applications, as well as some commercial office suites that are available for Linux. We will briefly introduce some of the commercial office applications that you can buy for Linux, then we discuss in detail the office applications that come with the Red Hat distribution.

In this hour you will

- Explore the advantages of using Linux office applications
- Discover a few of the commercial Linux applications outside of the Red Hat distribution, including Corel WordPerfect Office 2000, Applixware, and StarOffice
- Learn about GNOME office applications, as well as KOffice and the GIMP

Setting Up the Total Linux Desktop

Ever since the advent of the personal desktop computer, computers have been a fundamental part of every office. Productivity applications have become more complex as software companies scramble to provide as many features as a customer could possibly want.
The end result is huge, disk-space-eating, memory-hogging, bloated software that is
loaded down with features that most users don't need or understand how to use. This
licensed, proprietary software costs hundreds of dollars per user, and often doesn't work
with any other vendor's software, forcing businesses and individual users to buy "office
suites." Few people need all the applications in these suites, but it is easier to just buy a
suite than to try to get the individual proprietary applications of several vendors to work
together.

The problem with modern commercial productivity software can be boiled down to two
issues: complexity and cost. As applications become more complex and feature-heavy, it
gets harder and harder to make updates and improvements and to add new features. The
learning curve for new developers and new users also grows, and the software becomes
more expensive.

Although it's still not as simple as buying MS Office and installing a CD-ROM, the fea-
sibility and advantages of setting up the total Linux desktop are increasing steadily. Not
only are there more Linux office applications appearing weekly, but they are getting better and better. Also, the tools available for integrating Windows and Linux applications,
such as WINE and VMWare, are steadily growing more sophisticated and easy to use.
You will learn more about VMWare and WINE in Hour 19, "Integrating Linux and
Windows."

Free Applications Versus Proprietary Applications

It is important to understand that not all applications that run on Linux are licensed by
the GPL. Some applications that were designed to run on UNIX are just as proprietary as
anything to come out of Microsoft. Other applications, such as Corel WordPerfect, have
licensing restrictions. Still other applications, such as KOffice and GNOME, are free
software, licensed under the GPL. This hour focuses heavily on software that is included
in the Red Hat Linux 7.0 distribution, so most of the productivity applications are part of
the GNOME Office. If you want to go beyond the applications included in Red Hat 7.0,
try one of the three major commercial office suites that have been developed for Linux:
Corel WordPerfect Office, Applixware, and StarOffice.

Corel WordPerfect Office

Corel WordPerfect Office 2000 for Linux is a complete office suite that was developed directly from Corel's WordPerfect Office 2000 for Windows. The suite contains everything you could want in an office suite and more, including the WordPerfect word processor, Quattro Pro spreadsheet, Presentations slide show and drawing creation software, the complete Paradox relational database, and WordPerfect Central scheduler, address book, and contact management applications.

WordPerfect Office is much less expensive than Microsoft Office, and the applications are arguably superior to those in MS Office. The Linux version, while powerful, tends to be a memory hog, and is not yet as stable as could be hoped. Still, if you want to run a Linux office suite with as much power and flexibility as that available for Windows, Corel WordPerfect Office is probably your best choice.

The home page for Corel WordPerfect Office 2000 is `http://linux.corel.com/products/wpo2000_linux/index.htm`. The office suite is not available for free download, but you can download Corel WordPerfect 8 for free at the same site. You can also pick up a copy of *Sams Teach Yourself WordPerfect Office 2000 for Linux* by Alan Golub and Judith Samson, Sams Publishing, or *WordPerfect Office 2000 for Linux: the Official Guide*, by Philip Rackus, Osborne McGraw-Hill.

Applixware

Applixware is a full office suite by VistaSource. It's not available for free download, but you can buy it at `http://www.vistasource.com`.

Applixware includes

- Words: a word processor
- Spreadsheets: a spreadsheet application
- Graphics: an image editor and display tool
- Presents: a slide show presentation creator
- Data: a database program
- Mail: a POP3-compliant email client
- ELF (Extensible Language Facility): a macro programming language that enables you to create custom applications

Applixware is a native Linux application, meaning that it was written from scratch for the Linux operating system. For this reason, it runs faster and is more stable than Corel Office or StarOffice, which run on top of Windows emulators.

12

Applixware office applications use a common object format, so you can embed files made with one tool in the suite into a file in another application.

Applixware is one of the more flexible commercial applications. You can create your own extensions to the office suite and custom applications using the Applixware component library. If you need flexibility and customizability, Applixware is a great choice.

StarOffice

StarOffice is part of Sun Microsystems, and was one of the first Linux office suites to gain popularity. StarOffice 5.2 is available for free download from the StarOffice Web site at http://www.staroffice.com.

Like its counterpart, Corel WordPerfect, StarOffice can import and export all Microsoft Office file formats.

The great advantage of StarOffice over other commercial office suites is that you can download it for free. StarOffice is not released under the GPL or a similar license, however, so there are restrictions to how you can use and redistribute it.

The StarOffice suite comes with the following applications:

- StarOffice Writer word processor
- StarOffice Calc spreadsheet
- StarOffice Impress presentation manager
- StarOffice Draw
- StarOffice Image graphics software
- StarOffice Schedule (Calendar)
- StarOffice Mail and Email
- StarOffice Database
- StarOffice News reader
- StarOffice Math software

GNOME and KOffice

GNOME and KOffice are the free software answers to commercial productivity office suites. Because KOffice is in the early stages of its development, we will only briefly discuss the KOffice suite at the end of this section.

GNOME applications are based on the concept of component software. Instead of large, complex applications that contain every imaginable feature, the GNOME Office consists of a string of small, simple, and lightweight applications that easily integrate together to provide whatever feature you need. If a feature you want is not in an application, it is easily developed and added as a component. You then have this component, or mini-application, available for incorporation into any other application you want. In addition, macros are easily attached to any application using any scripting language that has a CORBA binding, including Python and Perl.

Applications become object containers that you plug components into to get the functionality you want. It then becomes easy to create designer applications that have all the features you want, with none of the fluff. It is also easier to learn a very complex piece of software if you start out with its simpler functions and add complexity as you get more familiar with the components.

With GNOME Office, for example, companies can design individual word-processing applications based on the needs of each person's job function. People who need only the basics can get the core application, and others can add components as they need them. Accountants can get spreadsheet functionality that they can attach to word processing. A secretary might need only the basics of the spreadsheet to create simple documents and not need hundreds of other functions. Graphics designers can get the graphics import component included in their word processing software, whereas managers might not need the graphics import component.

GNOME as a business solution is not quite ready to be unleashed in the office. There are some intriguing aspects to GNOME, however, that deserve notice.

GNOME is free. In the Microsoft era, software is expensive, prohibitively so for the small business owner. Even for large corporations, the price tag for licenses for one new application can run into the hundreds of thousands of U.S. dollars.

12

GNOME is customizable. Imagine having a desktop in which your company's logo—not Microsoft's—appears on every open window, where, in fact, your desktop is "themed" to be uniquely different from anyone else's.

It is easy to understand the GNOME applications inside and out. There are no expensive training courses that teach you the undocumented secrets and tricks of the software, or even the basics. If you want to know everything there is to know about a GNOME application, just look at the source code and the developer documentation.

You also don't have programming language restrictions with GNOME applications. Because the interface for the components is CORBA, any component can be written in any language. So, if you want to design your own add-on to a GNOME application that was written in C, but your developers prefer to work in C++ or even an interpreted language like Perl, they can write the component in whatever language they want.

The biggest disadvantage of deploying GNOME in business is that it is still new. Documentation is still sparse (although it is rapidly being developed), there is no training, and there are few system administrators with experience installing and implementing it.

GNOME Office applications themselves are still in heavy development. Most have not had a 1.0 release yet, although the applications mentioned in this hour are all stable. All the components of GNOME Office are included in Red Hat 7.0, including

- AbiWord
- Dia
- GNOME Personal Information Manager
- Gnumeric

AbiWord

AbiWord is the word processing component of GNOME Office. SourceGear, a for-profit company that produces open-source software, created AbiWord. Based on the GNOME interface, AbiWord is fast and sleek, takes up only 729Kb of disk space, and is intuitive to use for anyone who has experience using a word processor such as WordPerfect or MS Word. It has all the major features you would expect from a word processor, including

- Character formatting
- Dynamic spell check (misspelled words turn red as you type them)
- A rulerbar with interactive tabs
- Type 1 fonts
- Unlimited undo/redo
- Multiple columns
- Widow/orphan control
- Find/Replace
- Easy import of graphics

The big advantages of AbiWord are its speed, small size, and cross-platform capability. AbiWord runs on UNIX (which includes Linux), Win32, BeOS, and MacOS. It can import MS Word 2000 and RTF files and can export documents in RTF, text, HTML, and LaTeX formats.

AbiWord itself is quite simple, but the base AbiWord application is designed to accept as many components as the user wants. AbiWord also easily incorporates objects created in other GNOME applications that the user will eventually be able to modify within AbiWord itself.

AbiWord does have some way to go before it's ready for a 1.0 release, but it is definitely in usable condition for the majority of word-processing needs. Eventually, AbiWord will join Corel WordPerfect and StarOffice as definite Linux rivals to the Microsoft Office universe. The Web site for AbiWord is `http://www.abisource.com`. AbiWord is shown in Figure 12.1.

FIGURE 12.1

AbiWord is small, fast, and easy to use.

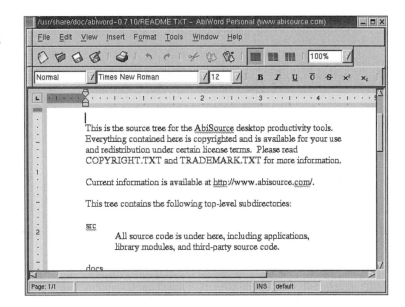

Dia

Dia is a diagram creation application, similar to the commercial Visio. With the current release of Dia (0.84 at the time of writing), you can make entity relationship diagrams, flowcharts, UML diagrams, electrical circuitry schemas, and network diagrams. You can also create your own objects in the XML file format and add them to the collection. Dia files are saved in XML, so it is easy to port and embed diagrams into different applications. Pixmap images can be easily imported and resized quickly, without having to be redrawn by the application.

Although certainly not as powerful as Visio, Dia is much easier to learn (you can learn how to use it in about five minutes), so it is a superior choice for simple flowcharts and diagrams, whereas Visio can be quite unwieldy.

Dia is organized a little differently from Visio. Instead of a screen with a palette on one side and a toolbar at the top, Dia has the palette in a window separate from the diagram grid. To add a shape to the grid, click the object button on the palette, and then click the

12

diagram in the place you want to put the object. To resize the shape, click the Modify Objects button in the Diagram Editor, then click anywhere on the shape and drag it to the size you want.

To import an image, double-click Create Image, browse to find the image file you want, and then click Apply. Click on the grid to drop the image where you want it. Resizing images in Dia is very fast compared to resizing in Visio, and the shapes are not as sensitive as those in Visio, so it is easier for a beginner to use Dia.

The home page for Dia is `http://www.lysator.liu.se/~alla/dia`. Dia is shown in Figure 12.2.

FIGURE 12.2

Dia enables you to create flowcharts and other diagrams.

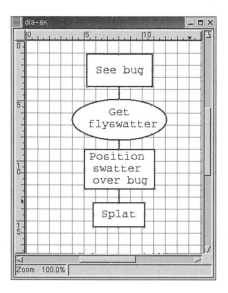

GNOME-PIM: The Personal Information Manager

GNOME Personal Information Manager includes an address book, calendar, appointment scheduler, and task list. GNOME-PIM is fully compatible with Palm Pilot, and files can be downloaded and synchronized with Palm Pilot via the gnome-pilot tool.

For more information on gnome-pilot, see `http://www.gnome.org/gnome-pilot`. The Web page `http://eunuchs.org/linux/palm/index.html` has useful general information on Palm Pilots and Linux.

Another component to GNOME-PIM, GNOME Calendar, is comparable to commercially available calendars, such as Microsoft Schedule or Franklin-Covey Planner. If you are familiar with commercial time management software, GNOME Calendar will look familiar.

The main window of GNOME Calendar contains tabs for daily, weekly, monthly, and annual views of the calendar. The Daily View has an appointment calendar on the left and a To Do list on the right. You can customize the window in Preferences. GNOME Calendar is shown in Figure 12.3.

FIGURE 12.3

Keep yourself orga-nized with GNOME Calendar.

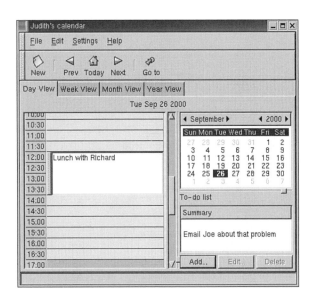

GNOME Address Book works as both a contact management system and electronic business card database, similar to Act or Goldmine. When you open Address Book, all your contacts are listed in the window with columns of information that you can cus-tomize in Preferences. Address Book comes with a sorting feature that enables you to sort your contacts by card name, name of contact, email address, or organization. There is also a Find feature with which you can search for any word or phrase within the entire address book. The Find feature supports shell wildcards such as * or ?.

Gnumeric

Gnumeric is the most advanced of GNOME Office applications. Gnumeric is the brain-child of Miguel de Icaza, the founder of the GNOME Project, so it is usually the first GNOME application to incorporate the latest GNOME concepts, libraries, and features (recall that you learned about GNOME in Hour 7, "Using the GNOME Desktop Environment"). A venerable rival to MS Excel, Gnumeric incorporates most of Excel's

12

features. Gnumeric uses the XML file format, but it can easily import and export Excel files. The design and user interface is similar to that of MS Excel, so if you are familiar with Excel you will feel right at home with Gnumeric.

Gnumeric comes with a full suite of data analysis tools and a "goal-seek" capability. Also, it can be completely automated to work within other applications, if there are CORBA bindings for the programming language the application is written in. Gnumeric comes with an online user's manual and a function reference manual. The Web pages for Gnumeric are `http://www.helixcode.com/apps/gnumeric.php3` and `http://www.gnome.org/projects/gnumeric/`. Gnumeric is shown in Figure 12.4.

FIGURE 12.4
Gnumeric is as advanced as any commercial spreadsheet.

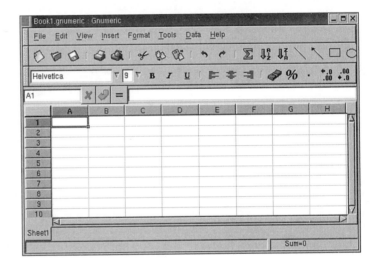

A Quick Word on KOffice

The KDE Project is developing an office suite called KOffice. KOffice includes the following applications:

- Kword—A word-processing application
- Kspread—A spreadsheet
- Kpresenter—For presentations and slide shows
- KIllustrator and KimageShop—For drawing applications
- Kimage—An image viewer
- Kformula—A formula editor

All the KOffice applications are in alpha stage, which means that while they are probably reasonably stable, many of the features are not yet available. Visit the KOffice home page at `http://koffice.kde.org/` for updates and to download the KOffice applications.

GIMP

GIMP, affectionately referred to as "The GIMP," was the application that led to the creation of GTK and GNOME. GIMP is arguably the most advanced application created specifically for Linux. GIMP was designed to be a freeware version of Adobe Photoshop, but many graphics designers find GIMP to be superior to Photoshop.

GIMP is not part of an office suite, but it is one of the oldest and most important productivity applications available for Linux. Gimp is so powerful that it would take an entire book to do it justice, so we will just introduce it here.

> *Grokking the GIMP*, by Carey Bunks, is an excellent guide to using GIMP, up to advanced techniques. The book is available for purchase in hardcover, or online at `http://gimp-savvy.com/BOOK/index.html`. At the GIMP home page, `http://www.gimp.org`, you can find a beginner's tutorial, an overall tutorial, a set of FAQs, and links to another online manual, the GIMP Manual.

GIMP can be used for everyday tasks such as simple image viewing and taking screen shots, or for complex graphics such as creating computer-enhanced film imagery. Some of the features of GIMP include

- Multiple image layers.
- Filters.
- Sub-pixel imaging.
- Anti-aliasing.
- Channel operations and layers.
- Extensibility with scripts.
- A full suite of painting tools.
- Multiple undo/redo.
- Gradient editing and blending.
- Plug-ins for adding new file formats and filters. GIMP comes with 100 pre-defined plug-ins.
- GIMP supports virtually every file format under the sun.

Like most successful free software, GIMP is in a state of constant development. There is usually an unstable, development version that is two or three versions ahead of the stable release, and a new stable release comes out every few months. The best way to keep up

12

to date with the progress of GIMP is to visit the GIMP home page at `http://www.gimp.org`. The latest stable and development versions of GIMP are available for free download there.

GIMP is shown in Figure 12.5.

FIGURE 12.5

GIMP is useful for everything from simple screenshots to the most detailed image manipulation.

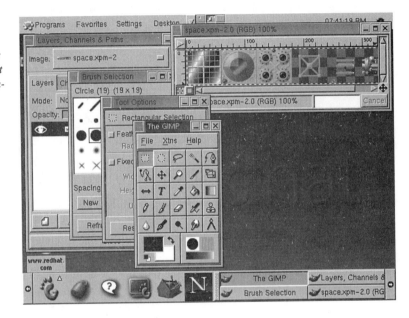

Summary

In this hour, you learned how you can use Linux in your ordinary office computing environment. You learned about some of the advantages of using open-source Linux applications, as well as the disadvantages. You learned about some commercial Linux applications. You also used the GNOME Office applications that are included in Red Hat 7.0.

Workshop

The Workshop contains quiz questions and exercises to help reinforce what you've learned in this hour.

Q&A

Q How could GNOME Office be any good if it doesn't cost anything?

A The purpose of GNOME is to make computing as free and accessible as possible to everybody. The GNOME Office applications have been created by the same people who created the GNOME desktop, and the motivation is a love of computing and a desire to share, rather than financial profit. Commercial companies such as Helix Code are hoping that there will eventually be a demand for customized applications, based on the free basic applications.

Q Can I use Microsoft Office in a Linux environment?

A There are tools such as WINE and VMWare that make it possible to combine the best of Linux and Microsoft products. You will learn more in Hour 19.

Quiz

1. Which office suite discussed in this hour is included in Red Hat 7.0?

2. How much does it cost to download AbiWord?

3. True/False: All office suites available for Linux are licensed under the GPL.

Quiz Answers

1. Which office suite discussed in this hour is included in Red Hat 7.0?

   GNOME Office

2. How much does it cost to download AbiWord?

   Nothing

3. True/False: All office suites available for Linux are licensed under the GPL.

   False. Only GNOME Office and KOffice are licensed under the GPL.

Exercise

1. Download WordPerfect 8 from the Corel Web site at `http://linux.corel.com/download/`.

12

Hour 13

Fun and Games

It is true that Linux offers several applications to make you more productive. Yes, Linux applications can help write reports and manage global networks. But don't forget all the wonderful counterproductivity tools Linux has to offer. I am talking about the huge assortment of games, widgets, and other neat gizmos that are as much a part of Linux as any network tool. There are games for GNOME, KDE, and the X Window system in general. The games vary from single player to huge multiuser environments that span the Internet. Still not enough? With WINE and dosemu, you may even be able to play games intended for other operating systems. And additional commercial games are available for Linux every day.

Clearly, far more games are available than could ever be covered in this chapter. So I will try to hit the highlights and point you to where you can find almost everything else. If you are ever told these games and toys are not important, remember what great stress-relief tools they are. The next time you are stuck on a problem, give them a try. Just be forewarned that most of these games are highly addictive and can really eat your time and processing cycles!

In this hour you will

- Install GNOME and KDE games
- Learn how to network games
- Set up a MUD client

Finding and Installing Games

A long time ago, during the Red Hat install you decided whether to install games. This could have been done on a package-by-package basis or by the main install games option. If you elected not to install some of the games packages, you may find that some of the games and toys covered in this chapter are missing. Don't worry if this happens. It is very easy to install the games later. It is just simpler to do so during the initial install. With this in mind, take a minute to see what is currently installed so there are no surprises later on.

The easiest way to check this is to run gnorpm or kpackage and look at what is installed under Amusements. Although this is not the guaranteed install location of every game in existence, you will find that most of the games and toys are installed here. In the package utility, you can query the packages to find which ones are installed and where they are located, as shown in Figure 13.1. For more information on package maintenance, refer back to Hour 11, "Linux Applications."

FIGURE 13.1

Locate and query game packages with gnorpm.

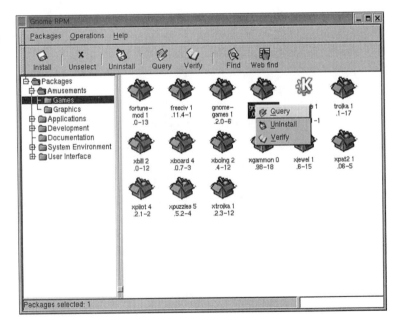

GNOME Games

Red Hat defaults to the GNOME window manager, so you can take a look at its games first. (Most of these games are in gnome-games-1.2.0-6.i386.rpm, so if they are missing, first check to see whether that package has been installed.) You can find them under Games in the Programs menu. As you can see in Figure 13.2, quite a few games are available, as well as multiple versions of many of the popular games. It is a safe bet you will be able to find almost every variant of Mahjongg ever imagined and most of the classic Windows games.

FIGURE **13.2**

So many games, so little time to waste.

One of the things that sets the new GNOME and KDE games apart from most of the older X Window games is their improved graphics. Typically, they are more colorful and have surprisingly smooth animation. A good example of this is gataxx, which is shown in Figure 13.3.

FIGURE **13.3**

gataxx is an excellent example of improved graphics and animation.

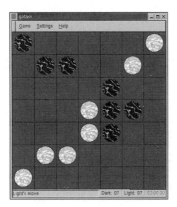

13

KDE Games

KDE offers the same improved graphics as GNOME, with a slightly larger variety of games. Most of the KDE games are in the `kdegames-1.92.20000721-1.i386.rpm`. KDE, like GNOME, offers a wide variety of card games and the seemingly mandatory Mah-jongg variants. Shisen-Sho, a particularly addictive version of Mahjongg, is shown in Figure 13.4. You can find all these games under the Games menu in the KDE main menu. Although you can run KDE games in GNOME, you may want to try KDE as a whole. If you want an easy way to switch between desktops, check out the Switchdesk program.

In addition to strategy and card games, KDE also offers some fun arcade games, such as Asteroids, which is shown in Figure 13.5. Although the graphics are impressive, there is a catch. Some of these games are processor intensive, and if you are on a slower machine, the controls can be really sluggish. If you experience this problem, you can either get frustrated or use it as an excuse to upgrade your hardware. Either way, there are still plenty of other fun games to play.

FIGURE 13.4

Shisen-Sho is a fun way to eat up time.

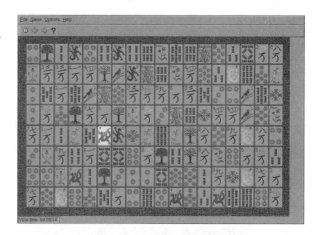

FIGURE 13.5

Asteroids brings back the arcade classics.

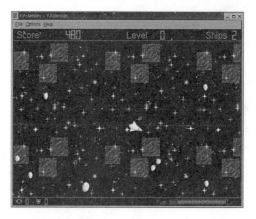

Finding More X Games

Before GNOME or KDE existed, there were X Window games. They are still a lot of fun and they are an absolute must when things get really stressful. At times, a simple game of cards just won't do. Sometimes you really need to pulverize your enemies—death by mouse click. At times like these, you can turn to games such as xboing and xbill. Many other great X games are available, though, so don't stop at just those two.

Unfortunately, Red Hat ships with only a limited number of these games, but a plentiful supply of X Window games can be found on the Web at sites such as `http://www.tucows.com` and `http://www.linuxgames.com`. Running a search for Linux games on any major search engine should turn up plenty of additional links, too.

Networked and Commercial Games

Linux was designed to network, so it makes sense that it has network games. Although many of the original Linux network games such as xpilot are not commonly known, some of the newer commercial games like Quake are establishing Linux as an excellent choice for gaming. For many gamers that demand the maximum performance for network games, Linux is the best choice.

Hard-core game players can configure their Linux machines to run only what is absolutely necessary for their games, and they can devote the maximum amount of resources to the game program. They also have the ability to configure the filesystem and the kernel for maximum performance. To achieve this level of optimization on any other operating system that the games are designed for would be extremely difficult. Keep in mind, however, that even most default Linux configurations will deliver excellent gaming performance.

Currently, most of the available networked games are either commercial shooters and strategy games or the classic MUD. No Linux gaming experience would be complete without a MUD, so you will see how to set one up. You will also learn about some of the commercial games available and where to find more information about them.

13

Setting Up a MUD Client

A MUD (or multiuser dungeon) is a network game that can allow hundreds or thousands of users to interact in a fantasy world. MUD clients can range from the most basic text interface to a highly sophisticated graphical environment. The most important thing to do before getting into MUDDing is to read up beforehand. You should read up on MUDs in general, read about whatever client you choose to use, and most of all, read up on any MUD you want to play. Although most MUD users are tolerant of new users and are willing to help, being a clueless pest in a MUD can be extremely detrimental to your character's health. This may sound like a lot of reading just to play a game, but when you find a MUD you like, that time will be insignificant compared to the time you spend playing.

Task: Playing with Others by Installing kmud

Many popular MUD clients are available these days, but most require some additional configuration. For simplicity purposes, you will be installing kmud.

1. You can find the rpm and the documentation for this MUD at `http://fara.cs.uni-potsdam.de/~uhlmann/kmud/`. At the time of this publication, the current version was 0.4-1. I recommend downloading the latest stable version.

2. To install it, use su to get root access; then in the directory with the file, type the following:

   ```
   $ rpm -ivh kmud-0.4-1*.rpm
   ```

3. Exit su.

4. Type **kmud &** at the command line.

   A window similar to the one shown in Figure 13.6 should appear.

5. Now you are almost ready to MUD. All you need to do is choose a MUD server. A good place to start looking is at `http://www.mudconnect.com`. It has a large, organized database of current MUDs with descriptions.

6. After you have selected a MUD, click Mud Connection Wizard.

7. Select New.

8. Fill in a character name, the title of the MUD, the hostname, and the port.

9. After you complete the entry, click OK.

10. Make sure you are connected to the Internet and then in kmud click Connect. You should see the login screen to the MUD in a few seconds.

Keep in mind that many MUD servers see a lot of traffic, so delays are not uncommon.

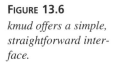

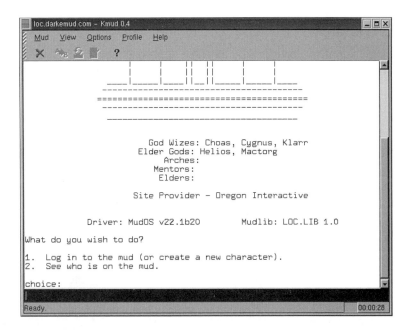

kmud offers a simple, straightforward interface.

Playing Commercial Games

A long time ago, DOOM was ported to Linux. After Quake came along, it was ported to Linux. Since then, many of the popular first-person shooters have been ported to Linux. However, it does not end there. Many new games in other genres, such as Civilization: Call to Power, were developed for Linux and Microsoft Windows at the same time. Many software firms are beginning to see the potential of Linux for gaming; hopefully in a few years, all the major games will be available for Windows and Linux simultaneously. But for now, a great place to start looking for what is currently available is at `http://www.linuxgames.com` and by asking your local retailer.

Obviously not every game has been ported yet, and many may never be ported. So what do you do if your favorite games are not available for Linux? Some people did not want to wait for their favorite games to be ported, so some hard-working developers set out to create WINE in 1993. WINE is an ongoing effort to implement the Windows APIs over an X-based Linux environment, which allows Microsoft Windows applications to run under Linux. Although it might not support all the latest applications, it has had enormous success with many popular programs that may never get ported. In fact, the current database of supported applications contains more than 2,000 entries. To learn more about WINE, go to the main page at `http://www.winehq.com`. There you can find out the latest news on WINE and how to configure it for your system.

13

Linux Amusements

Never underestimate the power of toys to eat time and bring a smile. In this section I will try to show the full gambit. They range from really cool system-monitoring GNOME applets to just plain silly classics such as xeyes. Applets are available for GNOME's Sawfish and Enlightenment window managers. Some of the applets for Enlightenment are shown in Figure 13.7.

FIGURE **13.7**

Enlightenment offers many impressive little applets.

These applets track everything from CPU usage to mouse movements to your email. Many applets are newer versions of older amusements like E-Biff and gEyes. But nothing will ever replace the original xeyes pictured in Figure 13.8. However, xeyes is not the last remaining X Window novelty. You can still find xsnow for those times you need a snow storm on your desktop. There are still many variants of xfish that you can find when you seek an aquarium on your desktop. On the other hand, if a rotating earth is what you seek, check out xearth. If the standard desktop clock just won't cut it, you can find many other clock programs. A good place to start is xdaliclock.

There are many other novelties too, but you will have to look a little harder to find them. Most don't fit well into a category. How would you classify a modified version of DOOM used to kill troublesome processes? You will find these more often by accident than by direct searching. Many Linux news sites occasionally have articles on cool new toys.

FIGURE **13.8**

xeyes is an irresistible laugh.

Summary

In this hour you learned the wide variety of games available for Linux and where to find them. You also learned how to install and configure a MUD client and what your options were on commercial games. Now you know the games included with Red Hat distribution are only the beginning.

You can find many other games and toys at `http://www.X.org` and from other distributions. In addition to all the free games, you can also find a lot of great commercial games ported to Linux. Many retailers are starting to carry games for Linux, so the next time you are at the store, take a look and see what's available—and above all else, remember to have fun with Linux.

Workshop

The Workshop contains quiz questions and exercises to help reinforce what you've learned in this hour.

Q&A

Q Where do I start looking for games on the Internet?

A The search engines return a lot of useful results for Linux games; some of the highlights are

`http://www.linuxgames.com`   Resource for all sorts of Linux games

`http://www.X.org`   Beginning and end of all things X11

`http://www.happypenguin.org`   The Linux Game Tome

`http://metalab.unc.edu/pub/Linux/games`   FTP site of games

`http://www.tuxgames.com`   Great source of commercial Linux games

`http://www.linuxberg.com`   Tucows site for Linux

`http://www.linuxarchives.com`   Source of games and many other programs for Linux

`http://www.winehq.com`   The WINE home page.

`http://linux.davecentral.com`   Another good archive of Linux software.

Q What can I do to get more games ported to Linux?

A Support the games already available for Linux. Many software firms do not offer games for Linux because they do not believe they can make any money from them. For the Linux gaming market to grow, the current games must succeed. Many efforts are also being made to persuade software companies to port their games to Linux. You can always help out with these. Above all, though, you just have to be patient. Porting great games to Linux still takes quite a bit of time.

13

Quiz

1. Where are games installed on a Linux system?
2. How can you get help on a game you don't know how to play?
3. What can I do to get Microsoft Windows-based games to run under Linux?

Quiz Answers

1. Where are games installed on a Linux system?

   Typically, games that install during the initial Linux installation are found in the /usr/games directory. Most games that users install later go in the /usr/local/ games directory. The easiest way to find out where a particular games is installed is to query its package in gnorpm or kpackage. Remember this works only if the games were installed from an RPM.

2. How can you get help on a game you don't know how to play?

   Almost every game has a man page, and many of the GNOME and KDE games have a Help menu option. Many of the more complex games also have a Web site where you can find additional information on how to play.

3. What can I do to get Microsoft Windows-based games to run under Linux?

   Read the Web sites on dosemu and WINE. These packages change often and a lot of online help is available to assist you in getting your favorite programs to work.

Exercises

1. Explore your /usr/games and /usr/local/games directories. Not every game makes it on the GNOME and KDE menus, and often you can find a few fun new things to play with.

2. Search on the Web for MUDs. More than a thousand are available, and you may find one you like.

3. The next time you're shopping for a game, see if it is available for Linux. You may find you prefer playing games in Linux.

PART III
Linux Foundations

Hour

HOUR 14

The Linux 2.4 Kernel

To really understand what's going on in your Linux system, you must develop at least a basic understanding of the kernel. The kernel is the conductor of the orchestra of the Linux system, the director of all the little activities that enable the computer to do useful work and make up the operating system. In fact, many error messages and other problems make a lot more sense if you understand what the kernel is doing.

In this hour you will

- Learn the basics of the kernel, what it does, and how it works
- Learn about processes and memory management
- Use the /proc filesystem and commands that enable you to interact with and learn about the kernel
- Learn about loadable modules and recompiling the kernel

Introduction to the Kernel

The kernel is the heart of the operating system, but it is not the operating system itself. You could say that the operating system is the kernel, plus all the libraries, shells, and system programs that provide an arena for you to run programs that do work. The operating system takes the pile of plastic, metal, and silicon and turns it into a computer that does useful work.

The kernel keeps track of files on the hard disk, starts and runs programs, assigns memory and system resources to the processes, receives packets from and sends packets to the network, and provides the tools that enable services to be built. It also acts as a layer between the hardware and the applications. No applications or other processes can access the hardware directly. They must work with the services that the kernel provides. This method protects individual users and processes from each other. It also makes sure that all processes (hence all users) get fair access to resources. The system programs use the tools that the kernel provides to implement the operating system services. System applications and other user applications run "on top of the kernel."

As you learned in Hour 3, "Linux Basics," a computer consists of a processor, memory, and input/output devices, also called peripherals. The processor contains a clock, which regulates the work that the processor does. The processor performs an action on a process every pulse of the clock. The speed at which the clock pulses is the clock speed of the processor. At each clock pulse, the processor does some work.

 When you buy a system, the feature most usually advertised is the clock speed of the processor, such as Intel 366MHz. That same system might have only 32MB of memory, which kind of makes the fast processor useless. Be careful of this when buying a system, and if you can customize, consider buying more memory and less hard disk space.

Rather than giving user processes direct access to hardware, the kernel runs services that enable the processes to request a service for the hardware. For example, the kernel creates and maintains the filesystem. User processes don't access the blocks on the hard drive directly to access a file—they go through the filesystem, which is controlled by the kernel.

The kernel is one large program linked together from lots of different modules, most of which are written in the C programming language. The kernel is composed of functions that manage memory, processes, the filesystems, and devices. The object modules and libraries are grouped by the function they perform. Linkers link all the objects together when the program is compiling, to make it one big program.

Getting Basic Information about the Kernel

Many beginning Linux users get confused over the difference between the *version of Linux* they are running and the *version of the Linux distribution*. Linux distribution version numbers are arbitrary, and are set by the distribution companies or projects themselves. For example, Red Hat 7.0, Mandrake 7.1, and Debian 2.2 are all the latest versions (at the time of writing) of the respective distributions. They really don't tell you much about the underlying Linux version, unless you are familiar with the distribution. When you talk about the version of Linux you are running, you are generally referring to the version of the kernel.

You can upgrade the kernel just like you can upgrade any other piece of software on your Linux system, although the process is a bit more complicated than simply running and installing an RPM.

To find out what version of the kernel you are running, enter the command

```
# uname -a
Linux localhost.localdomain 2.2.16-22 #1 Tue Aug 22 16:49:06 EDT 2000 i686
unknown
```

The output tells you what version of the kernel you are running, the number of times the kernel has been compiled (#1), and the fact that the machine running it is a Pentium i686. You are also told the name of the machine (localhost.localdomain is the Red Hat default), and that the operating system is Linux.

The kernel version is written using the following convention: *major.minor.patchlevel*. For example, for kernel number 2.2.16, 2 is the major version number, which changes only when something really fundamental changes in the kernel; 2 is the minor version number, which is the strain of the kernel release; and 16 is the patchlevel.

Even-numbered kernel versions are stable releases, patches that contain only bug fixes and no new features. Odd-numbered versions are development versions, patches that contain new code and bug fixes for the code. As soon as the new code is stable enough to be released to general use, the version is named with the next highest even minor number.

For example, take kernel versions 2.2 and 2.3. Any patches to version 2.2 are just bug fixes. Patches to 2.3 include bug fixes and new code, including new device drivers and new features. When kernel 2.3 is stable enough, it will be named to version 2.4. 2.4 will be the new stable kernel, and a copy of 2.4 will be named to 2.5, and development will continue on the kernel version 2.5. This way, if you want to experiment, you can use 2.5, and if you need stable kernel, you can use 2.4.

If you are willing to risk problems with your system, you can use a development kernel, but be forewarned that new features can cause serious problems with previously stable parts of the kernel, so those problems are unpredictable (which can be part of the fun). Use at your own risk.

14

Get information on kernel development and other useful topics about the kernel at http://www.kernelnotes.org.

How Processes Work

A primary function of the kernel is to create, manage, and delete (kill) processes. Linux is a multiprocessing operating system. That means that the Linux kernel can carry out multiple processes at one time. Multiprocessing means that a process is activated until it needs a system resource, then it waits for the resource, and the next process in memory is activated. In a uniprocessing system like DOS, when the process that is running needs a resource, the CPU is idle until the process gets the resource and starts running again.

The kernel schedules the processes, determining which will be run and which must wait in memory. The processes have weights, which determine their importance.

Processes work independently of one another. If one process has a problem, it crashes in its own little address space, and will not cause other processes or the operating system itself to crash. Processes that must interact with each other do so through the kernel, not directly.

The kernel manages each of the processes to make sure that system resources are fairly allocated among all the processes. A system resource is something that a process needs to do its job. A system resource can be hardware, like the CPU, physical memory, or another device. It can also be software, like a file in the filesystem. Because of multiprocessing, your CPU and your memory are used more efficiently than in a uniprocessing system.

A process exists in one of several states, which may include

- Running
- Waiting
- Stopped
- Zombie
- Sleeping

Every process has a process identifier, or pid. The pid is simply a number that identifies the process. You can see the pid number for all the processes assigned to your account by entering **ps -a**, as shown in Figure 14.1.

FIGURE 14.1

The pid is how the kernel recognizes the process.

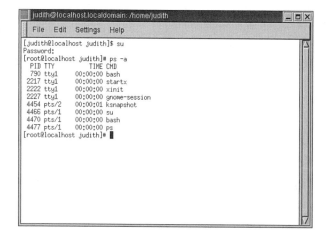

When you talk to the kernel about a process, such as in the command `kill 567`, you refer to the process by its pid.

In Linux, processes don't just appear independently. They must be cloned by a parent process that was already running. The only process that doesn't have a parent is the initial process, or init. Every process has a pointer to its parent, siblings (processes that have the same parent process), and child processes. The child process is a process that the original process creates.

The `pstree` command, shown in Figure 14.2, shows you all the processes on your system, the parents, sibling, and child pointers.

FIGURE 14.2

pstree illustrates the relationships between all the processes on the system.

14

Hardware Device Drivers

The kernel contains a device driver for each kind of hardware that it supports. Hardware drivers are grouped into classes, for the same general types of hardware. Each member of the class has a similar interface to the rest of the kernel, but differs in operations. For example, all disk drivers have operations to "initialize the drive," "read sector X," and "write sector X," but the actual operation procedure may differ from driver to driver.

Memory Management

There are different kinds of memory in your computer. Cache memory is the fastest and also the most expensive. There is usually a small amount of cache memory on the processor chip, and some more cache memory on your system board. Main, physical memory, which comes in cards that are plugged into the system board, is much slower than cache memory. Even physical memory is expensive and there is usually not enough memory for the processor to work at top efficiency, so Linux also makes use of virtual memory, or swap space on the hard disk that is used as memory.

 When shopping for a new computer, pay careful attention to the amount of cache the system has. The more cache, the faster the system will run, assuming there is sufficient physical memory and a processor with a fast clock speed. Cheaper computers tend to skimp on cache and physical memory.

Virtual memory makes the system appear to have more memory than it actually does by sharing the memory between competing processes as they need it. Virtual memory has become more and more important as the need for memory has outstripped the availability of physical memory in most systems. Memory is expensive, so many computer systems don't have enough, if there is such thing as enough.

Each process in the system has its own little chunk of memory, which is the process' virtual address space. The address spaces are completely separate, so that one process cannot affect another process by invading its address space. For example, if these protections were not in place, one process could write over the code and data that is needed by another process.

If you get an error called a segmentation fault (segfault for short), along with a crashed application, that means that the application tried to access a part of memory outside of its address space, so the kernel shut the application down before it could do damage. When this happens, you should report the bug to the maintainer of the application, or to Red Hat's Bugzilla. Instructions for doing this are included in Hour 22, "Troubleshooting and Getting Help."

The kernel swap daemon, called kswapd, is in charge of swapping processes into and out of virtual memory. When you start to run low on physical memory, kswapd tries to free pages of physical memory. kswapd swaps pages to your swap files, and it also makes sure that there are enough free pages in the system to keep the memory management system operating efficiently.

kswapd starts at init. Periodically, kswapd checks to make sure there is enough system memory. If there isn't enough memory, the kernel swap daemon looks for good candidates to swap out or discard. A page fault occurs when a process is scheduled to run, but it has been swapped out. The kernel has to go get the process and reload it into core before it can run. If you get a page fault that the kernel can't recover, you should kill and restart the process.

Getting Information from the Kernel

There are several commands that enable you to get information from the kernel, or to directly influence its work. For example, the nice and renice commands enable you to raise or lower the priority of a process. nice launches a command with a specified priority, and renice lowers or raises the priority of a process that is already running. You must be logged in as root via su to run renice.

The top command enables you to watch scheduler information in real time. top is different from ps, in that ps gives you a snapshot of the processes that were running when you entered the command, but top is continuous. You can renice and kill processes using top. gtop, written by Radek Doulik and Martin Baulig, is a GNOME graphical version of top and is shown in Figure 14.3.

14

FIGURE **14.3**

*gtop enables you to see
everything that is going
on in your system.*

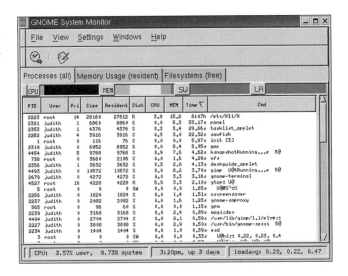

procinfo gathers system information from the files in /proc and prints it to the screen.

The /proc Filesystem

The commands that affect the kernel get their information from the /proc filesystem.
The /proc filesystem is created by the kernel in memory to provide information
about the system. proc stands for "processes." It doesn't exist anywhere on the hard
disk—just in memory.

Every process has a directory in the /proc filesystem, and the /proc filesystem is
dynamically generated and maintained. Every time a new process is added or a process is
deleted, the directories in the /proc filesystem change. The pid is the directory name for
the process directory.

Read the proc manual page for detailed information about the /proc
filesystem.

Process Information in /proc

/proc can tell you a lot about your system. If you look in one of the pid directories,
there are other files that pertain to the process. An example of the subdirectories and
files found in a pid directory is shown in Figure 14.4. If you are an ordinary user, you

can display information only about processes that are yours. If you want to look at all the processes, you must be root. If possible, assume root status with su before you begin your exploration of /proc.

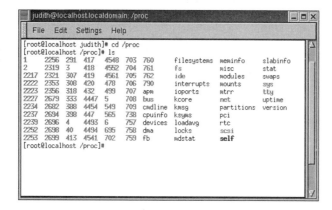

For example, cmdline is a file that contains the command that was entered to start the process. It doesn't matter whether you actually typed the command at the command line, or if you started the process by clicking an application launcher, or if GNOME automatically started the process when GNOME started (session management and so on). It's all the same thing at the kernel level.

environ provides all the environmental variables that are defined for the process in format *VARIABLE=value*. It's kind of hard to look at because the file is not formatted at all, but it's still useful.

exe is a symbolic link pointing to the executable file that starts the process (to get the full pathname of the file, enter **ls -l exe**).

fd is a subdirectory that contains a list of file descriptors currently opened by the process. The syslogd process fd subdirectory is a great example. It lists all the files that syslogd writes to, such as /var/log/messages, /var/log/secure, and so on.

/root is a symbolic link to the root directory used by the process. Usually, the root directory is /, unless a new root directory has been set for the process with chroot. chroot is a command that runs a command or shell with a special root directory, rather than with the / directory.

The status file gives information about the status of the process, such as the state of the process, the name of the executable that starts the process, the PID, and PPID.

cwd is a symbolic link to the directory that the process is currently working with.

14

Hardware Information in `/proc`

The `/proc` filesystem also contains lots of useful information about your hardware.

`/proc/cpuinfo` gives information about your processor, including model, manufacturer, CPU clock speed, and cache size.

Your machine's memory is in `/proc/meminfo`. Included is total memory, swap, amount free and amount cached, and buffers. The `free` command presents the same information as that in `/proc/meminfo`, but in a more readable format, including column headings. The gtop program presents the same information in a color-coded chart.

You can check what devices are using which I/O addresses by looking in `/proc/ioports`.

`/proc/interrupts` lists the IRQ numbers that are in use and which device, or peripheral, is using them. `/proc/dma` does the same for DMA channels.

The command `lsdev` gathers all the information from `/proc/interrupts`, `/proc/io`, and `/proc/dma` and lists the information by peripheral. This is generally a more convenient way to see the information. `lsdev` is part of the procinfo package, which you should install to get useful commands to help you make sense of the information available in the `/proc` filesystem. The `procinfo` command gets system data from the `/proc` directory, formats it, and displays it on the screen. `procinfo` gives you information about your system directly from the kernel as it is running (in real time).

`/proc/devices` lists the device drivers that are configured into the kernel.

`/proc/filesystems` lists the filesystems that are configured into the kernel, which are the filesystems that the kernel supports.

`/proc/kmsg` are the messages that are produced by the kernel. They are also routed to syslog, where they are either printed to the screen, sent to root via email, or written to `/var/log/messages`, depending on their severity (see your `/etc/syslogd.conf` file for more information).

`/proc/modules` tells you which kernel modules are loaded, their usage, and what process used them. The exact same information is shown with the `lsmod` command, but the `lsmod` command adds column headings to tell you what you are looking at.

`/proc/uptime` tells you the amount of time the system has been up since the last reboot.

`/proc/kernel` tells you the version of the kernel.

The `/proc/apm` file tells you about the state of electric power on your system. This is useful if you have a laptop because you can tell whether you are using AC power or battery, the load on your battery, and how much life in minutes you have left in your battery. It's hard to read the contents of /proc/apm, so it's better just to use the apm command, which takes the information in /proc/apm and presents it in a readable format.

Configuring the Kernel

In the past, when you wanted to add support for a piece of hardware to your kernel, you had to recompile the kernel. Now, there are loadable modules for many devices.

A loadable module is a piece of kernel code that is not directly linked into the kernel. Instead of compiling the module as part of the kernel, you compile it separately, then insert it into the kernel as it is running. Many device drivers are now loadable modules, so you can get a device driver without recompiling the kernel.

Why would you want to recompile the kernel? Even if you can load modules without recompiling, you would have to recompile to add new security or other bug fixes, or support for some new devices that don't have loadable modules. If you never recompile the kernel, you will have to wait for a new distribution release to take advantage of changes.

Get rid of device drivers that you don't need. The kernel is loaded into memory when you boot, and there it stays. The memory taken up by the kernel cannot be used by other programs. If you have a bunch of device drivers for devices that you don't have, that wastes space. Also, the kernel is upgraded all the time, and the only other way to get the new kernel if you don't upgrade the kernel directly is to wait for a new distribution release. Newer kernels have more device drivers, which means more device support. They might have better process management or run faster, be more stable, or include fixes for bugs from earlier versions.

The major place to get kernel source code is ftp.kernel.org.

The kernel is compiled with the C compiler, gcc, which we discuss in Hour 23, "Compiling and Installing Applications from Source Code." Before you consider upgrading, check the documentation that comes with the patch or release to make sure that it is worth your while to upgrade.

Also, check *Linux Unleashed*, by Bill Ball, for a detailed discussion on upgrading the kernel. Read the Linux Kernel HOWTO for instructions on configuration and upgrades. Read the Linux Kernel Guide for more information on the inner workings of the kernel. This guide is fascinating reading if you want to learn more about how your operating system really works.

14

Summary

In this hour you learned about the Linux kernel. You learned how the kernel interacts with the processor and your memory to achieve optimal performance. You learned about the /proc filesystem and how you can use it to gather useful information. You also learned about commands that take the information in /proc and present it in readable format.

Workshop

The Workshop contains quiz questions and exercises to help reinforce what you've learned in this hour.

Q&A

Q What happens to the /proc filesystem when I reboot?

A The /proc filesystem is created anew by the kernel during the initialization process every time you reboot. Because it exists only in memory, the /proc filesystem doesn't exist until the kernel creates it.

Q Is it possible to look at the individual parts of the kernel?

A The kernel source code is separated into files called modules. When you compile the kernel, the modules are combined into one big file, which is your kernel. Looking at the modules of the kernel source code is a great way to learn how the kernel works. The source code for the kernel is available as an SRPM (src.rpm) for download from Red Hat at http://www.redhat.com/apps/download. After you install the SRPM, it should appear in /usr/src/redhat/SOURCES. Untar the kernel tar file. The source code for the kernel will be in a directory called linux.

Quiz

1. Name three kinds of memory in your Linux system.

2. What does pid stand for?

3. Where does the /proc filesystem reside?

4. True/False: The kernel is another name for the operating system.

5. How often is the /proc filesystem updated?

Quiz Answers

1. Name three kinds of memory in your Linux system.

   Cache memory, physical memory, and swap space.

2. What does pid stand for?

   Process Identification Number

3. Where does the /proc filesystem reside?

   In physical memory.

4. True/False: The kernel is another name for the operating system.

   False. The kernel is part of the operating system, but the entire operating system also includes libraries, system programs, and shells.

5. How often is the /proc filesystem updated?

   Every time the state of the system changes, the kernel dynamically updates /proc to reflect the change.

Exercise

1. Assume su status, if you have permission. Go through each of the /proc files and directories mentioned in this chapter and view the contents.

14

HOUR 15

Working with Shells

If you have been using Linux or Unix for very long, you probably have heard the term *shell*. If you haven't, I will explain to you what a shell is and how it can help you to use your Linux environment to your advantage. Chances are you have already used the shell when you issued a command at the prompt (#) or worked from a terminal window. In fact, if you have typed **startx** at the command prompt to start the X Window system, you have used the shell to do something. The shell and what you can do with it is one of the most interesting and useful aspects of the Red Hat Linux 7.0 operating system.

In this hour you will

- Understand what shells are
- Learn about bash
- Discover what ksh is
- Explore the tcsh shell
- Discover other types of shells

Understanding Shells

When your Red Hat Linux 7.0 system boots up, the first program to run when you log in is the shell. A *shell* is simply a *macro processor* that executes commands that you enter at the command prompt. A Unix/Linux shell is understood to be both a *command interpreter* and a *programming language*. You can enter commands at the command prompt (#) and the shell will run them. If you have several commands that you need to run, you can put them in a special text file called a *script file* and the shell will run it also. The shell is really good at one thing: running other programs.

There are many choices when it comes to shells—for example, bash, ksh, and others. bash is the default shell that you see when you start Red Hat Linux 7.0. We will discuss other shells later in this hour. You can see the bash shell prompt in Figure 15.1.

FIGURE 15.1

The bash Linux shell prompt.

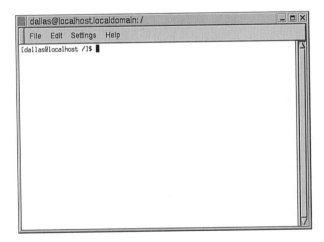

That is basically all you need to know to use the shell except for what commands to type in at the prompt. In Linux, you don't have to worry about learning a lot of commands because most of the help you need is right at your fingertips. Suppose you need help with the ls (list) command. This is the command similar to dir that shows you all of the files in a directory. The following task will show you how to make use of the shell.

Task: Using the Shell

You will need to be in a terminal window or at the bash command prompt to do this.

1. At the shell prompt (#) or in the terminal window type **ls --help | less** and then press Enter.

15

2. To get help for any command, just type the name of the command followed by a space and then two hyphens and the word help. To prevent the text from scrolling off the screen too fast, you pipe it into the less program with the pipe character (|). If the text is too long to see in one screen, you can use the Page Up (PgUp) and Page Down (PgDn) keys to move backward and forward in the document.

3. You should see the word END at the bottom of the document. When you are finished reading you can type a **q** at the END prompt to exit the document.

4. There, wasn't that easy? How about trying another one? Repeat steps 1 through 3, but instead of entering ls as the word you need help on, try **rm**. The rm command removes files from your filesystem, so be sure to type it in like this: **rm --help | less**. I want you to see the shorter document displayed.

As you can see, this document is shorter because there are fewer definitions of the switches and options available to you for this command. When you are finished reading, enter **q** at the END prompt and exit from the terminal. Now you should be able to get all the help that you need for using the shell.

Now you know how to use the shell to execute commands and get help with commands you may not be sure about. Wasn't that a lot easier than you thought it was going to be? What you have learned in the first part of this hour is enough to allow you to run any program that you want, but don't let all that power boggle your mind. I need your attention for the rest of the chapter.

I know using GNOME or KDE is a lot more fun, but here are a few more commands that you can run from the shell prompt:

- If you are ever lost and staring at the command prompt wondering which directory you are in, type **pwd** to find your present working directory.

- If you don't remember whether you are logged in as root, Captain Kidd, or Blackbeard, type **whoami** and Linux will tell you.

- If you want to move from your present directory to another one, use the cd command. For instance, if you are in your home directory and you want to go to your CD-ROM directory, you would type **cd /mnt/cdrom** to get there. If you just want to move to the parent of the current directory, type **cd ..** (one space between cd and ..) and you're there.

- If you want to find out what version of bash you are running, type in the following at the command prompt

   # echo $BASH_VERSION

   and press Enter. You should see a bash version number similar to 2.04.8(1). You can see this in Figure 15.2.

FIGURE 15.2

*Use # echo
$BASH_VERSION to
obtain the current ver-
sion of bash that you
are running.*

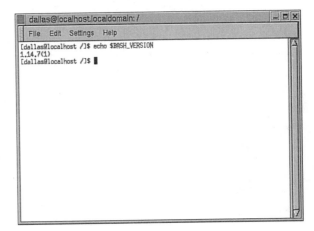

If you're tired of typing in commands, here's something even more interesting: learning about bash script files. In the next part of the hour, you will learn how to run more than one command at the shell prompt and enter only one command to execute them. This is called *script programming* or *scripting*.

Creating Script Files for the Linux Shell

In this section I am going to teach you some basic things about controlling your computer by using shell scripts. Although some people refer to this as programming, it is actually a simple type of programming. The reason I say that is that most shell scripts that are run by the shell tend to be fairly short. Most of these short programs are written to run or execute either commands that are common to Linux or programs that the user has written. For example, you may want to write a small shell script to run your backups at a certain time, print log files to a printer, and notify you that the backup has been performed when you log in the next day. This is a general example of how shell scripts are used.

A shell script or program is a simple text file that contains a series of Linux commands and utilities entered using a text editor. When you have entered these commands and utilities into your favorite text editor and saved it, you can let the shell run it. When the shell runs a script file, the commands are interpreted and executed by Linux and run in sequence, one right after the other. You can write your own shell scripts and execute them like any other command under Red Hat Linux 7.0. If Linux doesn't do what you want it to do, you can more than likely write a shell script to solve the problem.

A shell program has many of the features of other common programming languages, such as Pascal, Cobol, Basic, and C. Shell programming languages have their own syntax. You can assign values to variables and use functions and many other things common to most programming languages. You can even run other scripts from within a shell script.

When you find yourself entering several commands at the shell prompt each morning to accomplish something, that probably is a good time to write a small shell script that you can run by typing in one command.

A script is a program that can be run by a shell or another interpreted language. Since these scripts aren't compiled, they will usually run using bash on any version of Linux created for any platform. This means you can write a script file for bash on Red Hat Linux 7.0 and port it over to bash for Solaris or other operating systems. This makes it a very useful thing to know how to do.

Let's take a look at a simple shell script and then we will discuss shell programming in a little more detail. I don't want to totally confuse you. What you should understand is what a shell is, what scripting is, and how you can use it. One question that may be popping into your mind is, "What can it do for me?" Well, I hope to answer that in this hour.

Task: Creating a Simple Script File

Let's create a simple script to tell us who you are when you run it. This is similar to the famous "Hello World" program used in many computer classes to teach students their first computer program. We'll call your program "talk."

The first line in your script file must be #! /bin/bash. The pound (#) sign is used to tell the shell that this is a comment line, meaning that the shell ignores anything you enter after the pound sign. The exclamation point (!) tells the shell to run anything after the exclamation point and use the rest of the file as input for that command. Next we have a space so make sure that you leave one at this point.

Every script file that you write for bash will begin in this manner so you should get familiar with the procedure. Some other shells begin in a different manner; for instance, most other shells use #!/bin/sh for the beginning line. We won't worry about them now, we just want to know what a simple script file looks like. Now you will write a simple script file to tell the world who you are. Follow these steps:

1. While in Red Hat Linux 7.0 open a text editor such as gEdit or your favorite text editor.

2. Type **#! /bin/bash** and press Enter. This is the first line of your script file.

3. On the second line type **# who am I, created by elaker**.

4. Press Enter to get to the next line in your text editor.

5. Now type **# whoami** on the third line and press Enter. This is the shell command that will tell who is on the system.

6. Save the script file with the filename `talk` and exit the text editor. You can do this in several ways. In most text editors you would click File/Save or File/Save As.

7. Write down where you saved the file and the filename. You will need this later.

This is a very simple script file but it demonstrates how to create script files using a text editor, how to enter the program lines, and how to save it for later use. You can make your own directory to save your files to. I use the home directory but you can create your own personal directory. Type **mkdir elaker**, for instance. This creates a directory called `elaker` where you can save your files.

Every good programmer wants to see the results of their work and you probably aren't any exception. To run your program and see the results of your hard labor, exit the text editor and open a terminal window, and then follow these steps:

1. Click the Red Hat Linux Main menu/Utilities and select Color XTerm.

2. At the command prompt (#) type **cd /home** or the directory where you saved your file.

3. While in your personal directory (mine would be `/home/dallas/graphic`) type the name of the shell you are using and then the name of the shell script that you want to run. For example, type **bash talk** to run your program. You should see the script file run that you programmed or wrote. So there you go, that's how simple it really is.

Your program or shell script file should look like this:

```
#! /bin/bash
# who am I, created by elaker
# whoami
```

Of course this is probably the simplest program that you will ever write but it works. In the next part of the hour we are going to look at how bash works. After you have read the next section you should have a much better understanding of how shells and scripting works.

All About bash

bash is one of many shells that you can run with Red Hat Linux 7.0. This part of the hour will concentrate on learning some of the features of bash. We will not concentrate too much on the history of bash, but instead focus on doing some useful things with it. If you want to know more about bash, check the HOWTOs on your CD and on the Internet.

It would take a full-length book to teach you just the most important topics in bash. It would also take an entire book to teach you about programming, but since you will only be writing short script files you don't need all that knowledge right now. We will focus on learning a few of the commands, functions, and syntax for writing scripts in bash. Once you start writing a few short script files and executing them, everything will start to fall into place and you will be encouraged to learn and do greater things. Trust me.

Later we will take a brief look at some of the other shells. Where is this going to take you and what are you expected to gain from this? When you reach the end of this hour you will have a much better understanding of bash. You also will know the basic syntax and some of the commands you can enter to write a script file.

> bash is an acronym for Bourne-Again Shell, which is the traditional shell that was written by Stephen Bourne. All of the Bourne shell built-in commands are available in all versions of bash.

As a fully featured programming language, bash and most of the other shells support variables. A *variable* is just a place in memory that you tell bash to reserve for some value that you define. This type of variable is called a *user-defined variable* because you (the user) must decide what goes in that memory hole. Variables are used to store information and allow you to manipulate it.

Say you want to have a variable to hold your name. This is called a *string* variable in most languages. You simply give the variable a name and assign it a value, in this case, your name. For example, if your name is Elizabeth Laker, you would define the variable as

`myname=elaker`

The name of the variable is `myname` and the value it holds is `elaker`.

If you want to store a numerical value, you give the variable a name and assign a value to it:

`count=12`

In this example, `count` is the variable name and `12` is the value assigned to it. Starting to make sense?

When using bash you can use any alphanumeric string to make up your variables. That's because in bash and other similar shells you do not have to declare or initialize variables before they are used. In some languages such as C++ you have to declare a variable at the beginning of the program before you can use it. This means that you can't use this variable name more than once in your program to assign a value to. There are two ways you can reference your variable. You can reference a variable by *assignment*, meaning that if you wanted to assign the name `elaker` to a variable called `myname`, this is how you would do it:

```
myname="elaker"
```

In this example, the name or value assigned to the `myname` variable is enclosed in double quotes.

The other way to reference your variable is by *value*. When using bash to output the contents of a variable, you must prefix the name of the variable with a dollar sign ($), which tells the shell that you want the value of the variable to be returned. If you wanted to reference the contents of this variable, you would refer to it as `$myname`. You will see this used in this hour in the "Exploring Conditional and Looping Statements" section.

Shell scripting languages do not use typed variables; that is, they are not defined as just string or just numerical variables. You should be careful that you don't use the same variable name twice in your program. For example, if you defined the variable `count=12` in one part of your program and then defined it in another part of your program as `count=dracula`, at some point when you issued a command to print `count` you would have a problem. This means that you can only use a variable name once in your program. It is true that you could use count1, count2, count3, and so on but this isn't exactly using the same variable name. The best way to prevent this is to use the comment pound sign (#) at the beginning of your program and list the variables in use and what kind they are. For example:

```
# count=dracula, count=12
```

There are three kinds of variables in bash and most of the other shells:

- **User variables**—User variables are defined by the user and can be changed or modified within the script file.
- **Environment variables**—These are part of the system environment. You do not have to define them. They can be used in your shell programs just like any other command and some can be changed, such as PATH, where you would set the path if you need to.
- **Built-in variables**—These are provided to you by the system. These built-in variables cannot be changed or modified at all.

Now that you know how to store information in variables, you might be wondering how to get the information from the user or print it on the screen. The `read` command allows you to take input from the screen and store it in a variable in your script. For example, to read data into the variable `lname` (last name), this will work:

```
read lname
```

Entering this line in your script will prompt the user for his last name. How would you put a line above this prompt to ask the user for his last name? You use the echo command to do this. Here is an example:

```
echo Please enter your last name
```

This line would tell the user to enter his last name and then prompt him for it with the read lname statement.

Now that you know enough about variables to write a script file, let's explore some of the other aspects of bash, such as using conditional and looping statements.

Exploring Conditional and Looping Statements

bash and most of the other shells allow you to use conditional and looping statements that can alter the way your program flows. These used to be referred to as decision-making statements. We will explore a few of these to get you started programming and writing shell script files.

The first condition statement is

```
if ... then ... else ... fi
```

This will test a condition to evaluate it to see if it is true. If it is not true, it will perform some other action.

Most shells allow you to use conditional statements, which further adds to the power of the programming environment. The conditional statements allow you to perform complicated conditional tests in your shell programs. The basic syntax of the if statement is as follows:

```
if [expression]
    then [commands]
elif [expression] (else if abbreviated)
    then [commands]
else [commands]
fi [finished]
```

bash uses a command called test to check variables to see what they contain. You can use test in your scripts to evaluate expressions and return a true or false value depending on the parameters that are supplied to it. Suppose that you want to write a simple script to see if the name laker is stored in the variable $lname. If it doesn't hold the expected value, you will say "you're not laker, sorry I bothered you" and exit.

```
1.#! /bin/bash
2.# if then else loop to test value of $lname variable.
```

```
3.if test "$lname" = "laker"
4.    then
5.  echo "Hi Laker, Please call me at ext. 271."
6.    else
7.  echo "You're not Laker, sorry I bothered you."
8.fi
```

This short program demonstrates the use of the if ... then ... else loop. Please note that you don't need to number the lines in this program. They are just put there for clarity. Most shell script files do not require you to number program code lines.

That is just one kind of conditional statement that you can use to evaluate your data. Let's look at a couple more before moving on to other things.

The while statement can be used to let part of your program execute repeatedly while a certain condition is true. Suppose that you want to restrict a user from entering the word "superuser" at the login prompt. The basic idea is if someone enters superuser, they will be asked to enter something else. The syntax of the while statement looks like this:

```
while ... do ... done
```

Fire up your trusty word processor and, using the example of the script we wrote before, enter this:

```
1.#! /bin/bash
2.# check login name using while ... do ... done
3.echo "Enter Your name ... "
4.logname="superuser"
5.while test "$logname="superuser"
6.do
7.echo -n "Please enter another login name."
8.read logname
9.done
```

Of course this little script file could be run where a user needs root access to get into one of your programs, but it is just an example. There are other conditional loops that you can use but these will get you started. For more information about conditional loops and statements, see the bash reference manual and the Bash-Programming HOWTO on your CD or look for it on the Internet. bash is an extensive but versatile language. You can learn a few commands and start writing scripts immediately. Of course, this will only make you hungry enough to look for more information.

If you want to find out more about bash, look at some of the related HOWTOs at http://www.redhat.com/support. Following are some other interesting sites you can visit:

http://www.gnu.org/manual/bash/index.html (See Figure 15.3.)

15

You can get the most current version of bash at

`ftp://ftp.gnu.org/gnu/bash/`

> The Bash Reference Manual was written by Chet Ramey at Case Western
> University and Brian Fox of the Free Software Foundation. It is definitely one
> of the most complete works that you can read on bash. You can find it on
> several sites on the Internet—just search for "bash reference manual" to
> download it.

FIGURE 15.3

*You can download the
latest version of bash
from the GNU Web site.*

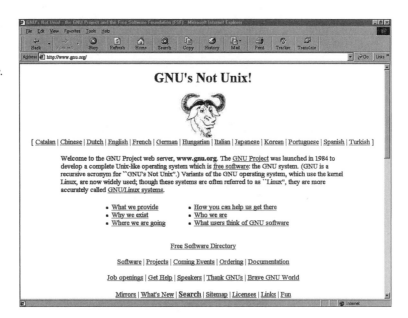

In this part of the hour you have learned enough about what the shell is and how bash
works to allow you to write simple shell scripts. You have enough knowledge about the
topic to allow you to pursue the subject further and write bigger and more effective shell
scripts. In the next section we will look at another kind of shell: ksh.

Another Shell Called ksh

David G. Korn designed and developed the Korn-Shell Language at AT&T Bell
Laboratories. The KornShell was developed for the Unix platform, but today there are
many versions available for other operating systems. There is a public domain distribution for Red Hat called pdksh. You can download the latest version from `http://rufus.`
`w3.org/linux/RPM/pdksh.html`. If you want to find out more about ksh (korn shell) you

can find more than you can probably read at `http://members.xoom.com/dfrench/kshinfo.html`. You can visit the kornshell Web site at `http://www.kornshell.com/`. ksh is a public domain shell that is available for private and public use. You can see the kornshell Web site in Figure 15.4.

FIGURE 15.4

You can find the latest korn shell distribution at its Web site.

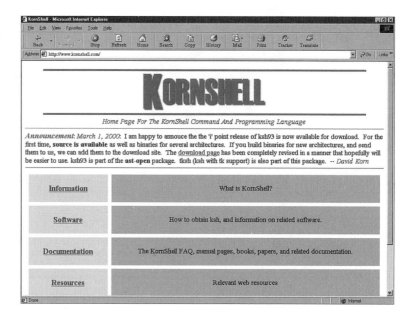

The KornShell (ksh) language is an interactive, complete, high-level programming language that can be used to write shell scripts and programs. It is useful for writing applications, with the development time being less than most other programming languages.

ksh is similar to bash and shares most of the same commands. If you can use bash, you can use ksh. There is a version of ksh called pdksh that you can download. This is the public domain version of the KornShell. If you want to use this program and need to know more, check out the resources mentioned previously in this hour.

Both bash and ksh have what is called *command-line completion*. This means that when you are typing a command at the command line, ksh (and bash) will attempt to guess what you are typing and type it for you. This does not happen automatically. You have to set this up using a method specified for each shell. Consult the documentation for each shell to find out how to do it. It is a little too complex to discuss here. You can read about it in the bash and korn HOWTOs.

In the next section we will look at a shell that is somewhat different than bash and ksh. You will learn some of the more interesting facts about this shell.

Learning About the tcsh Shell

tcsh can be used as an interactive login shell and as a shell script command processor. tcsh is a very well enhanced and completely compatible version of the Berkeley UNIX C shell (csh). This versatile shell includes or supports the following:

- A command-line editor
- Spelling correction
- Programmable word completion
- Job control
- History function and aliases
- Input and output redirection
- Pipelines
- Ability to change prompts
- Key bindings
- Spelling correction

In addition, tcsh features many commands and variables that we will look at in the last part of this hour. We will also look at some features that aren't included in other shells.

Features of tcsh

Most shells support command-line completion and tcsh isn't any exception. Command-line completion can be used in tcsh the same way you use it in bash and ksh—press the Tab key at any point while you are typing a command and tcsh will attempt to complete the command for you.

You can access the command history in tcsh. This means that you can recall the last keys that were pressed or the last commands that were entered by taking some action. The tcsh command history is similar to pdksh and bash. The shell remembers the last commands that you entered into the shell and stores them in a history list. You can invoke the history feature by typing **history [-hr] [n]** at the shell prompt, where the n option is the number of commands to display. If you don't specify how many commands to display, the entire history list will scroll down the screen. Once you have invoked the history feature, you can use the up and down arrow keys to view the commands' history and the left and right arrow keys to edit the commands.

tcsh also contains many history editing and navigation commands. They are too extensive to list here, but you can see the tcsh man page for more about them. Just type in **man tcsh**.

When you use tcsh, you can watch who logs on or off your system. This is very handy if you are on a network. It uses a tcsh variable called `watch`. The syntax of the `watch` command is

```
set watch=(<user> <terminal>)
```

The `watch` variable uses a set of user ID and terminal attributes or pairs to set the conditions for the watch or monitoring. These pairs can contain the word "any," which says to match any user or terminal. The user we are referring to is a Linux user ID and the terminal refers to a Linux terminal device number. If you wanted to see what time your boss got to work each morning, you could use the following example providing your boss is on the network. Enter the following at the command-line prompt:

set watch=(elizabeth laker)

 You could put this type of command in your Linux shell script file to start up when you are running other commands when you log in.

tcsh will check every ten minutes to see if your boss has logged in. You can change this to check, for example, every five minutes using the following:

set watch=(5 elizabeth laker)

Now tcsh will cause `watch` to check every five minutes to see if your boss has logged in.

There are so many features in tcsh that it is impossible to cover everything here, so I would encourage you to read everything that you can find on the subject. This is especially true if you are going to be using it as your shell of choice. Now let's take a look at some of the other shells that are available for Red Hat Linux 7.0.

Other Shells

One of the great things about Linux is its versatility. If you don't like the default bash shell, there are many alternatives. Following is a list of shells that you might like to try out. Please be aware that some shells are written for specific purposes, so check the documentation before installing them. You will find some of these on your Red Hat Linux 7.0 distribution CD, but some you will need to obtain from the Internet.

- **ash**—This is a lightweight Bourne-compatible shell.
- **bash**—The Bourne Again Shell.
- **csh**—The C shell, a symbolic link to tcsh.
- **fsh**—A rsh-compatible replacement for ssh.

- **gsh**—A graphical shell that integrates a terminal window, a normal shell, and various GUI components into a single package.
- **ksh**—A Public Domain Korn Shell that we discussed earlier.
- **pdksh**—A symbolic link to ksh.
- **rsh**—The restricted shell, for network use.
- **sh**—A symbolic link to bash.
- **tcsh**—A csh-compatible shell.
- **zsh**—Designed for interactive use with a powerful scripting language.

If any of these shells are installed on your system, they should be in the /bin directory. If you need to use them and they aren't installed, you will have to install them.

You can use any shell that you want but in most cases, using ksh or bash will provide you with all the resources that you will need. It never hurts to add a few more shells to your collection.

If you want to find out more about Linux and the topics covered in this chapter, two good books that I would like to recommend are *Red Hat Linux 6 Unleashed* (SAMS) and *Special Edition: Using Red Hat Linux* (QUE).

Summary

In this hour you learned what a shell is, how to write some simple script files using shell commands, and how to run them. You also learned about the different kinds of shells and how to get help for the different commands when you need it. In fact, you learned enough to call yourself a programmer—quite an accomplishment for one hour's work. In the next hour you will learn some things about system administration that you will need to know for your Linux career or just to run your own personal computer. Maybe we can get you a promotion from programmer to systems administrator.

Workshop

The Workshop contains quiz questions and exercises to help reinforce what you've learned in this hour.

Q&A

Q What are the two most popular shells?

A People use a lot of different kinds of shells based on their needs, desires, preferences, and requirements. The two most likely candidates are bash, which is based on the Bourne shell, and ksh, which is based on the Korn shell. The csh shell and all its variations is not far behind these two.

Q How do you assign a value to a variable in a shell?

A In most of the shells available for Linux, including bash, you can assign a value to a variable simply by typing the variable name followed by the equal (=) sign and then giving it a value. It looks like this:

```
weekday=3
```

You should be sure that there aren't any spaces on either side of the equal sign.

Q You are hurrying to finish a much-needed script but you can't remember some of the options for a command. How do you get help on the command using bash?

A You type the command like this: `ls --help | less`. The first word is the command itself followed by a space and then `--help | less`.

Q Is the Linux shell a command interpreter, a programming language, a compiler, or all three?

A A Unix/Linux shell is understood to be both a *command interpreter* and a *programming language*. It only interprets the shell script and it is not compiled. You can run a shell script very easily by entering the name of the shell and then the name of the file. For example, `bash dallas`.

Q As a systems administrator, I need a way to see who is logging on the system. I don't know how to program the system yet, is there a simple way to do this?

A In Linux there is always a way. It may not be simple but in this case it is. Put the `watch` command in a simple script file with the following syntax:

```
set watch=(<user> <terminal>)
```

This is an example of using the command:

```
set watch=(elizabeth laker)
```

If you don't remember how to write a simple script file please check how you did it earlier in the chapter.

Quiz

1. Name four Unix or Linux shells that were discussed in this hour.
2. Which Unix or Linux shell is based on the Bourne shell?

15

3. How do you find out the version of your shell?

4. Which man documentation would tell you about tcsh?

5. What does the first line in a shell script look like?

6. What is a good definition for a shell script?

Quiz Answers

1. Name four Unix or Linux shells that were discussed in this hour.

   bash, ksh, tcsh, and ash

2. Which Unix or Linux shell is based on the Bourne shell?

   bash

3. How do you find out the version of your shell?

   At the shell command prompt type

   ```
   # echo $BASH_VERSION
   ```

   and press Enter. This should give you the version number of the shell you are using.

4. How do you find out information about tcsh using man?

   Enter **man tcsh** at the command prompt.

5. What does the first line in a shell script look like?

   You must enter this line in each bash or ksh shell script: #! /bin/bash. Some of the other shells start differently.

6. What is a good definition for a shell script?

   A shell script is a program that can be run by a shell or another interpreted language.

Exercise

1. Just for fun and to help you get some experience with shell programming, create a shell script that you can run when you first login to tell you some things about your system. You might want to know what the time is, who is on the system, what directory you are in, what the other users are doing, what processes are running, and certain things like that. Don't forget to compile your script file as mentioned in the bash section. Also, don't use any destructive commands or commands that can damage your system in your script files, such as any type of delete or format command.

HOUR **16**

Administering the System

In this hour you will learn how to perform the tasks that a systems administrator has to perform to keep the system running. It doesn't matter if you are maintaining a single Linux PC in your office or two thousand PCs in offices scattered around the globe, following some basic techniques will keep your system running with less trouble.

In this hour you will

- Learn how to boot the system
- Learn about filesystem administration
- Manage user accounts
- View the system logs
- Make backups
- Use cron to automate recurring tasks
- Rescue the system

Booting Linux

When you boot Red Hat Linux 7.0, the system processes several files that you need to keep your ever-watchful eye on to see what is happening. It is during this bootup process that you will be able to see error messages and other indications that something is wrong. You can see that things are going right too, which is even better. If you see an error message, write down what the error was and any codes that might be associated with it. This can help you to diagnose and fix the problem later. The one thing that I would like to emphasize in this chapter is the importance of monitoring your system and looking at log files on a regular basis. You can save yourself a lot of trouble by doing that.

> You can monitor your system on a frequent basis if you are running GNOME. Click on the Main menu, and select System, System Monitor. This is a wonderful graphical interface that will let you monitor what system processes are running and other useful information.

Let's take a quick look at the initialization process. When your computer boots up it goes through a process of gathering information just like any computer normally does. Linux uses startup scripts to prepare your system for use. Red Hat Linux goes through a series of installation steps called *runlevels*, which start with runlevel 0 and generally end with runlevel 6, which is reboot.

You can see what runlevels your system uses by looking in the /etc/inittab file, which is an initialization table. This table contains various commands to instruct Linux on how to boot the system. The first startup script is /etc/rc.d/rc.systinit, which is called the system initialization script. This file is run once at boot by the init file. The primary role of the init file is to create processes from the script stored in /etc/inittab. Init starts as the last step of the kernel booting; it is the first command that configures and initializes your system for booting. We won't go into a lot of detail on how this file works, but you can look at its contents by using a text editor.

If you keep a watch on how your system is booting and watch the messages, you will know whether your computer has a clean bill of health. This means that you can spend more time on working on your computer and less time fixing it.

How do you keep your computer booting healthy? One of the things you need to do is make sure that you shut down the system correctly and make sure the filesystems are dismounted correctly. The next part of the hour will take a look at filesystem administration.

Filesystem Administration

Your Red Hat filesystem is normally organized with a place for everything and everything in its place. The trouble occurs when things get disorganized and out of place. As the person responsible for your computer system, you must learn to keep everything organized or you will have problems later on. One thing you can do is create a directory in your /home directory in which to store your personal files. You can do this with the mkdir command. Simply change directory (cd) to your home directory and while there create the directories that you need. For example, if your name is Elizabeth, create a directory called liz in your home directory with the command **mkdir liz**. Now you have your own personal directory in which to save your personal files.

16

You have learned a lot about the Red Hat Linux filesystem in other parts of this book, but we will cover a few more things that you may have missed. If you forget something, please feel free to turn back the pages.

Mounting Filesystems

In Linux, when you want to access a filesystem you have to mount it by using the mount command. When you use the mount command, you need to supply the system with what device contains the filesystem, what type it is, and where in the directory to mount it. The mount command syntax looks like this:

```
mount [-t type] [-o options] device mount-point
```

> Linux filesystems are much different from DOS- and Windows-based systems. When you are finished using a device such as a floppy under Linux, you should unmount (umount) it before removing the floppy. The same is true for the CD-ROM and other devices. This may be hard to remember but after repairing a damaged filesystem or device a few times the message comes through. The main reason for unmounting a device under Linux after you have been using it is that if you are in the process of writing something to it, it may not be saved to the floppy (in particular) until after you have unmounted it. The kernel may be busy and may not have time to schedule the write to the device.

The mount point must be an existing directory or you will get an error. In order to mount a floppy that uses the vfat filesystem you would type the following:

```
# mount /dev/fd1 -t vfat /mnt/floppy
```

The filesystem information is kept in the /etc/fstab file, which is created when you install Linux. If the filesystem information that you want to mount is stored correctly in /etc/fstab, you only need to specify the mount point or the device name. When you use the mount command it reads this information from the /etc/fstab file. When working with filesystems it is very important to know how to correctly mount and unmount them. You can see a simple example of the mount command in Figure 16.1.

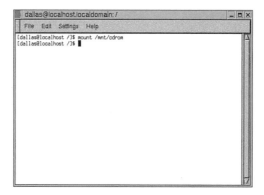

FIGURE 16.1

An example of how to execute the mount *command.*

You probably love working from the command prompt, but using the User Mount Tool can save you some time and energy. You can use it to both mount and unmount Linux filesystems. You access the User Mount Tool by clicking on the Red Hat Linux Main menu and choosing System, Disk Management. You can see this tool in Figure 16.2.

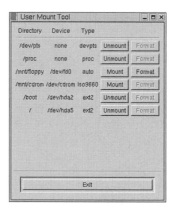

FIGURE 16.2

The User Mount Tool allows you to mount and unmount filesystems under Red Hat Linux 7.0.

The User Mount Tool works just like the mount command because it gets its information from the /etc/fstab file. Don't forget that you can mount and unmount your filesystems from the command prompt if for some reason you don't have access to the X Window system.

In this part of the hour you learned about how to mount and unmount filesystems and devices. In the next section you will learn how to repair filesystems that have become damaged.

Editing Filesystems

There will be times when you will have to create and edit filesystems. There are two basic ways that you can do this and they both involve making changes to the /etc/fstab file. You can edit the file using a text editor or you can use the fsconf utility usually found in the /bin/fsconf directory. You can see what the fsconf utility looks like in Figure 16.3.

16

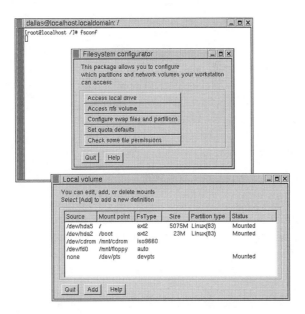

FIGURE 16.3

Use fsconf to make modifications to your filesystem.

The /etc/fstab file is nothing more than a text file, which means that you can make changes to it and save them like you would any other text file. Before you make any changes to this file, you should save previous versions just in case as a backup. You should use a text editor to edit or make changes to it.

Creating and Editing New Filesystems

In some respects, a Linux systems administrator is a filesystems manager and manipulator more than anything else. When the PC crashes it may be due to a corrupted file, a driver that has lost its way, or any number of other circumstances related to the filesystem. Knowing how to create new filesystems and set up the system to use them is very valuable knowledge.

During the install process, Linux creates some new filesystems and sets up the systems so it can use them.

Filesystems are created by a program that opens the block device and adds some structural data to it. This way the kernel will have access to some sort of image of a filesystem when it tries to mount the block device. That is, the device has an image of a filesystem that the kernel and the program can accept. The mkfs command is a generic Linux command that allows you to create a filesystem on a block device. This command has many options that you should become familiar with. Please check your Linux documentation for these options as they are too numerous to mention here.

However, you can type the following to get a list of commands that it executes:

```
# mkfs -v
```

If you want to build an ext2 filesystem (the most likely choice), use the mke2fs command. The two main options you may want to use with this command are the -m and -i options. The -m option tells the program how much space to reserve for the root to use. The -i option is used to set the balance between inodes and disk blocks.

An example of using mkfs is

```
# mkfs -t ext2 /dev/fd0
```

After the command is executed you will see a list of processes that are running.

There is an easier way to create and edit a filesystem using the fsconf utility. By using the fsconf utility, you can add, delete, or edit mounts. You have a list of five tasks that you can perform when you use the file configurator. You see these options when you run fsconf.

Task: Using the fsconf Utility to Make Changes to Your Filesystem

1. Type # **fsconf** at the prompt and press Enter.
2. The Filesystems Configurator dialog appears. Note the different options that you have listed.

   At the bottom of the screen you have the Quit and Help buttons.
3. Click on Configure Swap Files and Partitions to see what you can do to create, edit, and modify your filesystems.
4. Click Add and the Volume Specification dialog pops up. You can choose to add a partition in this dialog. We don't want to do that at this time, so click Cancel. I just wanted you to see how to add a partition.

5. Click on Access Local Drive and the Local Volume dialog box pops up.

6. When you want to make a change all you have to do is click the left mouse button on the partition that you want to edit and the Volume Specification dialog pops up. These partitions are listed in the window. If your list is too long you may have to scroll down to get to the one you are looking for. My first partition is /dev/hda5. Yours may be different. Just carefully left-click your mouse one time on the first partition listed as I said previously.

7. Click on the Options tab and you will be able to set up file permissions for your partition. We won't go through these in great detail because they are self-explanatory.

8. Click on Cancel and Quit for the next three screens. In the terminal window type **exit** to leave that program. Now you should be back where you started. The Volume Specification dialog is shown in Figure 16.4.

FIGURE 16.4

The fsconf Volume Specification screen shown with other related dialog boxes.

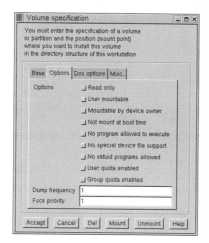

The fsconf graphic utility is a quick and pleasant way to create and edit your filesystems. It is a long way from the old days when everything had to be done from the Linux command prompt.

Repairing Filesystems

There are several reasons why your filesystem can become corrupted. For example, you forgot to shut down properly, lightning knocked out the power (good reason to use UPSs), a storage device such as a floppy was removed before the system was done with it, the reset button was accidentally pressed, the gremlins unplugged it, and a few dozen more too numerous to mention.

In Linux some data is kept in memory before being written to disk. This speeds up the process and is a method used by many systems, including Windows. If the computer is turned off or improperly shut down before the memory content is dumped to disk, the filesystem becomes corrupted because it is missing bits and pieces of data. This is why you must train your users to properly shut down their machines. When you boot your machine it runs fsck, whose main lot in life is to check and repair filesystems. When your machine closes things down during the shutdown process it unmounts all filesystems. During the reboot or startup, fsck knows that these filesystems were unmounted and checked during the shutdown process, so it tells you they are "clean" during the bootup process. It can tell because the kernel writes a special signature on the filesystem to confirm that the data is intact. When the filesystem is mounted again for writing, this signature is removed. The fsck program maintains a watch on the filesystem by doing periodic checks. You can also run this program manually from the command prompt.

You can use the following command to check the root filesystem:

```
# fsck -V -a /
```

For all other filesystems use this:

```
# fsck -R -A -V -a
```

This last command sequence will check everything (-A) except the root (-R) filesystem.

At some point you are likely to see a distressing message from fsck similar to the blue screen of death, which can be frightening if you don't know what it means. This sometimes happens during the bootup process. It looks something like this:

```
***An error occurred during the file system check.
***Dropping you to a shell, the system will reboot
***when you leave the shell.
Give root password for maintenance
(or type Control-D for normal startup).
```

The right thing to do here is to log in with the root password and run the fsck program manually. You can also run the e2fsck program to repair the e2fs filesystems.

After you have entered the root password you will get a prompt that looks like this:

```
(Repair Filesystems) #
```

This might look questionable, but you are being asked to enter a command. You can tell fsck to check everything manually by entering this at the prompt:

```
# fsck -A -V ; echo ==$?==
```

fsck will attempt to manually check all of the filesystems for you. By entering the echo option you are telling fsck to show you what it did. The fsck codes are listed in Table 16.1.

TABLE 16.1   fsck Codes

Code	Explanation
0	No errors
1	Filesystem errors corrected
2	System should be rebooted
4	Filesystem errors left uncorrected
8	Operational error
16	Usage or syntax error
128	Shared library error

16

If fsck fails in its attempt to repair your filesystem, you probably have a corrupted superblock. My best advice here is to try to use a backup superblock that Linux stores in several places. The ext2 filesystem has many backup superblocks placed over the filesystem. If the superblock is corrupted, fsck cannot start its filesystem check.

The e2fsck program is used to check a second extended filesystem under Linux. It is automatically run each time you boot Linux to check the native filesystems before mounting. You should never disable this check in the /etc/fstab file.

Suppose that fsck reports that it could not clean a particular filesystem, such as /dev/foofo. You can start fsck again by using a backup superblock located at (for example) 8193, which is at the start of block group 1. The syntax looks like this:

```
# fsck -t ext2 -b 8193 /dev/foofo
```

You will find this superblock at the start of block group 1 with the first superblock being located at 0. You will find more superblocks located at the start of block group 2, group 3, and group 4. They are spaced at intervals of 8,192 blocks. 8193 is the first superblock backup at the start of block group 1. If one superblock doesn't work, just keep trying another. In every situation that I have personally had (I've had a lot of them recently) the first superblock backup did the trick.

A superblock is just a block of code that Linux can use during the boot and initialization phase to boot the system. Linux scatters several of these around the disk at locations it knows about. Linux uses these superblocks in case the main bootup sequence is corrupted.

After you have manually run fsck, your problem more than likely has been fixed. After the startup scripts have done their job you can type **exit** to end the process and the boot sequence will begin all over again. This is to check the filesystems and make sure that they are all clean.

If you are using the extended filesystem (e2fsck) on your computer, you can use the e2fsck program to diagnose and repair your extended filesystem. You must unmount the partition first before executing the following:

```
# e2fsck -p /dev/hda5
```

Be extremely careful when using e2fsck because the p option can be dangerous and destructive. It means repair without prompting.

If all goes well then you can relax and pat yourself on the shoulder, confident that when the screen pops up again you will know what to do in order to repair the filesystem.

Managing User Accounts

As a systems administrator, one of the most important tasks that you will have is managing user accounts. This can range from a single account such as your own to numerous accounts, perhaps in the hundreds. In the next section you will learn how to use linuxconf to manage your user accounts and perform other functions.

Creating a User Account

When you installed Linux you were prompted to enter a root password. Unless you created other accounts at that time or later, this is the only account available to you. At the time of install you are given the opportunity to add new accounts. I suggest that when you set up new systems that you add an additional account for yourself and all users on the system.

There are a couple of ways you can add users to your system after it has been installed. Perhaps the easiest way is with linuxconf. This graphical feature allows you to create accounts and many other useful things. In any case, you need to be logged in as root to do this administrative task.

You can start linuxconf from GNOME as you will be shown in Hour 17, "Using linuxconf and Graphical Administration Tools," or you can run it from the command line (bash). In this hour you will learn how to run linuxconf from the command line.

Task: Starting linuxconf from the Command Prompt

The first thing you will do is learn how to start linuxconf from the command prompt. I'll admit that it is much easier to use from the X Window system, but there will be times your X Window system may crash and you will have to run programs from the command prompt.

1. Log out of GNOME or KDE. In the Logout dialog box select Logout, and then click OK and Yes. You will then be at the bash system prompt.

2. At the prompt (#), type **linuxconf** and press Enter. Please note that you must type linuxconf in all lowercase and you must be logged in as root.

3. The linuxconf dialog screen pops up. Take a few moments to look at the screen and familiarize yourself with it.

As you may notice there isn't much on this screen that resembles what we are looking for. But with Linux as with everything else, looks can be deceiving. In a few moments you will see what I mean. In the next section you are going to add a user and do some other useful things. Let's get to work making your system work for you.

Using linuxconf to Manage User Accounts

You can use linuxconf to manage your user accounts but looking at the screen you have in front of you now, that would be difficult to see. Before we actually do some useful work let's take a few moments to explore the linuxconf dialog screen. When you are using this screen you can use the mouse as previously mentioned or you can use the Tab and Up/Down arrow keys to move from one selection to another. I find this method works better. When you find a selection that you want to look at, just use the arrow keys to place the highlight over it and press Enter. This will select it for you. You should also notice to the left of each selection that there is a plus (+) sign, meaning that you can click on that selection to expand it. If there is a minus (-) sign beside it, it is already expanded.

If you wanted to access the area where you can work with user accounts and looked at this selection, it might leave you a little confused. But if you look at the first selection, Config, you will see that there is a plus sign beside it. Go ahead and satisfy your curiosity and use the arrow keys to move the highlight over it and press Enter. It expands to show you many more options; the ones that we were looking for.

16

Use your arrow keys to look at the many options available here. Notice the option User Accounts. That is the one you will be working with in the next part of the hour. Also look at the buttons at the bottom of the dialog. You should have the Quit, Act/Changes (Activate Changes), and Help. For more information use the Tab key to highlight the Help button and press Enter. Help is always available to you. Use the arrow keys to scroll through the help screen. When you are finished looking just tab to the Quit button, press Enter, and you are back to the linuxconf screen again.

In the next part of this hour you are going to learn how to set up a new user account using linuxconf, which you ran from the bash command prompt. You can use any other shell but since bash is the default, I will refer to the shell as bash.

Using linuxconf to Set Up a New User Account

When you need to set up a new user account or make changes to an existing one, you can do it as shown in the following Task. You should already have linuxconf running. If you don't have it running, refer to the previous instructions on how to do it.

> You should not confuse running linuxconf from the command prompt and using linuxconf to make changes and executing commands such as adduser from the command prompt. They are two separate and different things. You can issue commands such as adduser elizabeth to add a user named Elizabeth from the command prompt.

Task: Setting Up a User Account Using linuxconf

This example assumes that you have a computer network in a small office. You have just hired a lady named Elizabeth Mary Laker. You need to create a new account for her and give her a password so she can begin work.

1. Use the arrow keys to move the highlight bar over the Config option.

2. Move the highlight bar over User Accounts and press Enter.

3. Look at the User Accounts screen (see Figure 16.5). At the top of the screen it tells you the things that you can do in this screen. Below that you have the categories Account (name), Name (of the person or account), Uid (user identification), and Group. You can assign each account to a group. For instance, you may have several groups in a network setting and in a business these are usually based on the departments. In most businesses you at least have a personnel (HR) department, and

receiving, payroll, shipping, and accounting departments. In your office you probably do most of these jobs yourself so you could have two groups, maybe personnel and accounting. So, since Elizabeth is a secretary, let's add her to the HR group.

Next notice the accounts that you already have in the box below the names at the top of the box. You can scroll down and look at these but don't make any changes. Now look at the options at the bottom of the screen. You have the options Quit, Add, and Help.

16

4. You are going to add the `elaker` account, so Tab to the Add button and press Enter.

    The User Account Creation screen pops up with a list of items that you can add on the left side of the screen and a screen to the right of that where you can enter the information. At the bottom of the screen you have Accept, Cancel, Del (delete), Tasks, and Help buttons to direct you through the process.

5. Your cursor should be somewhere under the Base Info section in the window at the right side of the dialog. Use the arrow keys to move it down to the line below (X) The Account is Enabled. You will notice that this is in line with the Login name to the left. So let's enter her login name.

6. Enter **elaker** and use the arrow keys to move down to the next line and enter her full name. Enter **elizabeth mary laker** in that line and move down to the next line. Here you can enter a group, but it is optional. However, for the sake of experience enter **hrd** for Human Resources Department. Let's make it look official.

7. If the Command Interpreter line is blank enter **/bin/bash** and arrow down to the next line and enter **em1556** for the User Identification. This could be any number to identify the user.

8. In the Password Management section you can add other restrictions, but you can skip this for now. You can change it later as you develop policies and procedures for your system and users.

9. Use the arrow keys to move down to the Privileges section. In the first section, General System Control, you can grant or not grant certain rights to the user. All of the privileges should be denied (indicated by a zero (0) in the option on the left). The only privilege I would personally give this user is May Shutdown because it is a small office and she may be the only one working sometimes. Use the arrow keys to move down to that option and use the right arrow key to move to the Granted option. The zero (0) should move to the Granted slot.

10. Use the arrow key to move down to the Miscellaneous section and give her access to the Message of the Day.

11. Let's leave everything else Denied. Now Tab to the Accept button and press Enter. If this is a new Group, the Create Group dialog pops up. Tab to the Yes button and press Enter. You have created a new group.

12. Now you will be asked for a password for the new user elaker. For this example, let's just use emlaker for the password. You will need to enter the password twice to verify or confirm it. After you have entered the password, press Accept to finish the process.

You now have created a new account and assigned the user a password. Wasn't that easy?

If you want to set up a new user from the command prompt (bash), type this at the command prompt:

```
# adduser elaker
```

You will be able to add the information to create a new account.

In the next part of the hour you will spend some time learning how to modify, change, or edit an existing account.

FIGURE 16.5

Setting up a new user account using linuxconf.

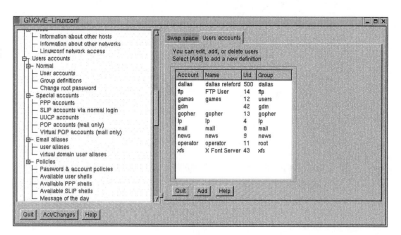

Task: Modifying a User Account

When you need to modify a user account, here is how to do it running linuxconf from the command prompt. Please note that if you are using linuxconf from GNOME the sequence will be slightly different.

1. Start linuxconf from the command prompt and open Config and User Accounts under Normal.

2. Press Enter when you have User Accounts highlighted. The User Accounts dialog box appears.

3. Highlight the account that you want to modify and press Enter.

4. Make the changes using the procedures you learned in the last section. Tab to Accept and press Enter when you have made the modifications.

Task: Changing the User's Password

There will be times when you will need to change the user's password and using linux-conf will save you some valuable time.

Here is the way to make modifications to the password while running linuxconf from the command prompt:

1. From the User Accounts dialog screen move the highlight bar to the account you want to change and press Enter.
2. The User Information screen appears. Tab down to the Passwd button and press Enter.
3. Enter a new password for the selected account. You will need to enter it a second time to confirm it.
4. Tab down to Accept and the User Accounts dialog screen will pop up confirming that the password was correctly changed. Be sure to remember your passwords.

You have now changed a password for your user.

In the next section you will learn how to change the root password should you ever need to. You should change your root password frequently to protect your system.

How to Change the Root Password

Changing the root password is fairly straightforward in linuxconf. To do this simply go to Open Config, Users Accounts, Normal, Change Root Password and enter the request-ed information. Use the information in the previous task to change the root password.

In Hour 17 you will learn how to use linuxconf from GNOME and the X Window system. If for some reason you can't get the X Window system to run, you can run linuxconf from the bash prompt. You can use linuxconf to maintain your system when you can't do it from the X Window system.

Viewing the System Logs

In order to correctly and efficiently diagnose a problem that has occurred with your PC or system, you need to know what happened to cause the problem. One way to do this is to look at and analyze the system logs, the configuration file, and other files. The system logs provide you with a wealth of information about what the system was doing when it crashed.

Following is a list of some of the more important log files that you can review using a text editor. For more information, consult your HOWTOs and other books on the subject.

- `/etc/syslog.conf`--This file defines where logs and most messages are routed. Use this to find other important logs. You can use the `cat` command to view this file by entering $ `cat /etc/syslog.conf`.
- `/var/log/messages`--These are mostly administrative-type files.
- `/var/log/maillog`--This contains mostly mail files.
- `/var/logboot.log`--This shows boot-up information.
- `/var/log/secure`--This is a security related log.

All of these files can give you important information about security, bootup information, and various other system information that can give you clues to how your system is functioning.

Making Backups

No one can deny that making effective backups is essential to the safe operation of any system, whether it is a single PC or many PCs on a network. You have to be sure that the system files, programs, and data are backed up on a timely basis in order to restore the system should it crash.

Most standardized Linux distributions do not have regular backup programs with them. There are still utilities such as the GNU `tar` that you can use to backup your system.

Probably the first chore that you need to do is to make a decision as to what kind of media you will use to do the backups, whether it be disks, tape, or CD. If you have Linux on a single PC, you probably can back up your data files to floppy disks, but your system files will more than likely require a tape backup drive. CD writers are falling in price even as I write so that may be an option that you will want to look into. The actual CD can be bought at a very low price for the content you can store on them. Zip disks can be used for some backups and DVDs may be another option in the future, but for now they may be too expensive and are virtually unsupported. Zip disk drives are becoming more supported for the Linux system as some companies are realizing there is a market there.

Your best bet in any case is using tape backups. They are fairly cost effective and reliable. The other and probably most important advantage is that you can store a lot of information on them. The type or brand of media you use is up to you, but it is imperative that the tape drive be able to handle large capacity tapes in excess of 1GB because even most small systems today have more than that amount of programs and data stored on them.

Before purchasing a tape drive, as with any hardware, check with the manufacturer to make sure it supports Linux systems.

I would suggest that you read the HOWTOs relative to the `tar` command, which will teach you how to use it to do backups. The `tar` command actually means *tape archive* so it is well suited for this purpose.

For more specific instructions on how to use `tar`, please consult the man pages, the Red Hat Linux Web site, the GNU Projects home page, and your Linux manuals.

The next issue concerning backups is when to back up and how often. How many times a week you backup depends on how much information you generate that needs to be backed up. If you generate a considerable amount of data, you should back up at the end of each working day so that you don't lose any data. If you generate less data, you may not need to backup so often. You will also need to purchase new tapes when the old ones start to wear out. You should check your tapes periodically to determine whether the data is being saved. Older tapes may become worn out and need to be replaced. You should test your backups at least once a month to make sure that everything is working as planned.

When you have your system and data files backed up you will feel much better knowing that your data is safe.

Using Cron to Automate Recurring Tasks

At some point you will need to run programs or processes automatically at a pre-scheduled time. Fortunately, Linux provides a way to do this very efficiently and effectively with a daemon called cron.

Cron is a process of the Linux system that can execute a program at a predetermined time. In order to use cron you must write a text file that describes the program that you want to execute and the times that you want it to activate. In order to use the text file that describes the jobs that you want to run, you must use the crontab program to load the text file into cron.

Here is what your cron job responsibility text file should look like:

```
[min] [hour] [day of month] [month] [day of week] [program to be run]
```

Using cron is too involved to discuss in detail here, but you can learn more about using cron by reviewing the cron man page. There is a lot more information on the Internet and in the form of HOWTOs as well.

You can make your administrative life much easier by taking advantage of the cron daemon to help you automate processes on your system. One very efficient use for cron is to automate your backups. Once you have determined what backup method you will use, such as using `tar` to manage the backup sequence, just put that command in your text job file and sit back and relax.

Rescuing the System

Sooner or later the time will come (usually when you aren't there or are busy) when the system will come crashing down and you will go looking for your latest backup tapes. Did you remember to back up the whole system periodically? Have you made a recent backup of the system? Have you checked the log files to make sure the daily data backups are working correctly? These are all essential questions that will race through your mind. If the answer to any one of them is no, you'll have a very long day ahead of you and maybe an uncertain future.

A restore is the exact opposite of a backup. When you do a backup you copy files from a disk to a backup media such as tape. When you do a restore you copy files from the tape to the disk. Simple logic, but sometimes things go wrong and that is why you should back up every day for larger systems. If your previous day's backup didn't work, you can resort to the one before that and hope that it worked. You may lose some data but that is better than losing all of it.

You should also make a set of boot-up and restore disks to use in an emergency. This is not a complicated thing to do and it can save you a lot of headaches later. Please check your Red Hat Linux 7.0 manuals for instructions on how to do this.

For more information on how to restore your system or data files using `tar`, please refer to the `tar` HOWTO on your CD or read such books as *Red Hat Linux 7.0 Unleashed*.

Summary

This hour covered many subjects dealing with Linux including filesystems, backing up the system, and automating tasks. You also learned a few things about data storage using tape and Zip drive backups. You learned that you can easily use cron to automate such tasks as backing up your data and running script files. Now get comfortable (but not too comfortable) and we will see how much you have learned.

Workshop

The Workshop contains quiz questions and exercises to help reinforce what you've learned in this hour.

Q&A

Q What is the name of the program that checks the filesystems upon startup under Linux?

A Either fsck or e2fsck, with the latter checking extended filesystems.

Q What runlevel are you in during the shutdown process?

A You are in the runlevel 0 stage. You can learn about runlevels by watching what is happening during bootup and shutdown operations.

Quiz

1. Why must you unmount (umount) a floppy before removing it from the drive?
2. What kind of script files does Linux use during the bootup phase?
3. If fsck should fail in its attempt to repair your filesystem, what is the most likely problem?
4. Where is the filesystems information kept?

Quiz Answers

1. Why must you unmount (umount) a floppy before removing it from the drive?

   Because the kernel may not have had a chance to write the information to it yet.

2. What kind of script files does Linux use during the bootup phase?

   Linux uses startup script files during the boot and initialization phase to prepare your system for use.

3. If fsck should fail in its attempt to repair your filesystem what is the most likely problem?

   You probably have a corrupted superblock. Please see the instructions in this chapter to learn how to fix it.

4. Where is the filesystems information kept?

   In the /etc/fstab directory.

16

Exercises

1. Just for the fun of learning, create a script file using bash to backup some files from your hard drive, create a text job file, and use cron and crontab to initiate it automatically. Remember to use `tar` as the backup tool.

2. Using linuxconf create a new account for yourself to use in addition to the root and your personal account. You will use this account to do minor maintenance such as adding users, changing passwords, and so on.

   Don't give yourself full superuser privileges but just enough rights to do the jobs that you consider routine.

   You can use this account instead of running root.

HOUR 17

Using linuxconf and Graphical Administration Tools

Performing system maintenance and general system administration duties may seem to be one of the scariest and most complex tasks a new system administrator would ever have to perform. Thankfully, system administration in most cases is neither complex nor scary. This is largely because of the graphical system administration tools that have arisen in recent years. Sure, you can still control the entire system from the command line, but now you have excellent alternatives for most tasks. Granted, the graphical tools are not perfect, but if you are like me, Lord of the Typos, it is often preferable to let the tools edit your configuration files rather than doing it manually. Especially because damaging some configuration files can leave your system unbootable and can be rather frustrating to fix.

In this hour you will

- Perform administration tasks with linuxconf
- Learn about KDE administration tools
- Learn about GNOME administration tools
- Learn where to find other X-based tools

This hour explores various graphical tools such as linuxconf. Most of the hour will concentrate on linuxconf, but keep in mind that linuxconf is not the beginning or end of administration tools. It is a good tool with a lot of features and provides an example of what you can expect from graphical administration tools. Many other choices are available, so try some of the other tools, too. New tools are also being developed all the time, so if the tools covered in this chapter do not suit your purposes, search the Internet for others. Odds are the search will be worth your while.

Starting linuxconf

In most previous versions of Linux, linuxconf was started by typing `linuxconf` into a terminal window. In Red Hat 7.0, you start linuxconf by typing `linuxconf-auth` into a terminal window. `linuxconf-auth` is just a script that causes linuxconf to prompt for the superuser password if it was not run from the superuser account. It eliminates the need to use `su` before starting linuxconf. So right now, type in **linuxconf-auth** and look through the interface. As long as GNOME is installed, linuxconf should look like Figure 17.1.

FIGURE 17.1

The linuxconf main menu provides almost all necessary administration features.

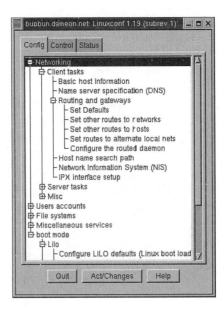

When you first open linuxconf, you will see that the menu is organized into three major categories: Config, Control, and Status, which reside on the tabs at the top of the window. Below each you will find a listing of items presented in a collapsible directory structure. You can expand or collapse nodes by double-clicking them. When you select one of the items, the appropriate module will appear as part of the current window or cause information to be displayed in a separate window. After you are through editing configuration information, you can select Quit to exit. At this point you will be asked if you want to activate the changes. If you have changed anything, activate the changes before exiting. One of the nice features about Linux that becomes apparent at this point is that most configuration changes do not require a reboot. This is a huge timesaver, especially when you want to try a few different configurations.

Administration with linuxconf

17

Just from a brief look at linuxconf, it is obvious that covering all its capabilities would take several chapters. Some day linuxconf will probably have its own book. But for now, I would like to show you how to perform some common tasks with linuxconf. You will find using many of the other features very similar to these examples and linuxconf has a Help system, so if you are stuck, try checking it. Before we get into setting anything up, however, we need to know what is happening on the system. Click the Status tab and expand logs to see what logs are available for viewing. If you have to perform system administration duties, always take time to read the logs. It will prevent a lot of suffering and help you to better configure the system. In Figure 17.2, the kernel boot message is displayed, which is a good place to check to see whether hardware was properly detected at boot.

FIGURE 17.2

The kernel boot message reveals a lot of useful information.

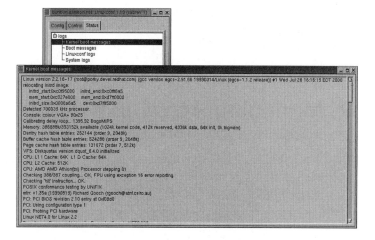

Now that you know the current state of the system, you can set up a network card and edit user accounts with linuxconf. If you click Config and then expand Networking and Client tasks, you will have access to everything necessary to configure a basic network client. First, select Basic Host Information and fill in the hostname if it has not already been entered. Then move on to Adaptor 1. You should now see something similar to what is shown in Figure 17.3. Here you can assign the device a name and an alias. You also have the choice to manually configure the IP address information or to choose DHCP or Bootp for automatic configuration. Net Device specifies the type and number of the device being configured. Typically, this is eth0 for a regular Ethernet connection. Kernel Module specifies which module to use to control the card. Remember to enable the device after you configure it! Yes, I have made that silly mistake before.

FIGURE 17.3

The Basic Host Information screen can configure most network adaptors.

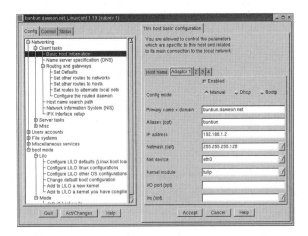

You can specify the DNS servers under the Name Server specification item and set the default route under Routing and Gateways, Set Defaults. This is another common oversight when setting up the network. If this seems too brief, don't worry, all of this will be covered in greater detail in Hour 18, "Setting Up a Simple Network."

Task: Managing Accounts with linuxconf

Another useful feature of linuxconf is its capability to manage accounts. To manage accounts, do the following:

1. Expand the Users Accounts menu item and its submenu item. The choices available here allow the superuser to manage every type of account and control the policies.

2. Select User Accounts.

3. Click an account to edit it or click Add to create a new account. Be careful not to edit any of the accounts made for the daemons, such as gdm and mail. They are configured the way they are to allow certain programs to run, and changing them could cause serious problems later on. Figure 17.4 shows how all the necessary information can be edited in a convenient manner.

FIGURE 17.4

The linuxconf makes managing accounts a breeze.

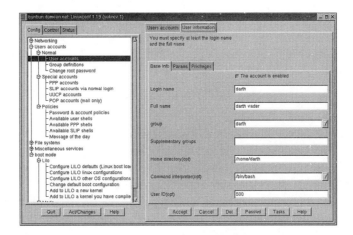

17

4. From here, you can specify login, group, shell, UID, and home directory.

5. You can also assign account parameters and privileges, toggle account status, and change the password. Granted, all this can be done from the command line, but it is nice to be able to double-check everything at once before accepting the changes. Configuring groups and other types of accounts is very similar and should be very intuitive.

Another important feature linuxconf offers is the capability to configure LILO. LILO is the program used to boot your system and load the kernel. LILO can be configured to boot additional operating systems or other Linux kernels. The default boot behavior can be changed as well. Take a few minutes to look through all the things you can configure. You will find these features under boot mode. If you want LILO to wait for you to choose an OS, or if you just want a different delay, you can configure that now. Choose to expand Mode and select Default Boot Mode. You should see something similar to Figure 17.5. Set the prompt timeout to however long you want it to wait in seconds before booting to the default configuration. As you can see in the figure, it is set to 0, which means wait until a decision is made.

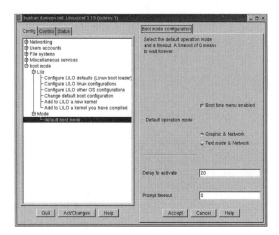

The biggest convenience of linuxconf, however, is its capability to control system activities. The options under the Control tab allow practical management of multiple profiles
and system services. Shutting down unwanted services is a great way to improve system
performance. Just make sure that you really don't need a service before you shut it down.
To view the available services and their status, expand Control Panel and select Control
Service Activity. You should see something similar to Figure 17.6. The window lists all
the services currently available on the system and their status. By clicking any of them,
you can view their configuration options and change their status. This is also a good
place to learn what the various services do; each configuration screen typically has a
short explanation of what the service does.

FIGURE **17.6**

*linuxconf provides a
convenient method to
track and control
services.*

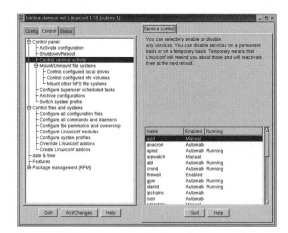

kInetEd for inetd. kfirewall, shown in Figure 17.8, is another young application, but it offers an easier way to test rule sets than hacking and slashing on the command line. You many not appreciate this now, but if you ever manually set up a firewall, the advantages will quickly become clear.

FIGURE 17.8

kfirewall is another example of how a simple GUI can take a lot of frustration out of configuration.

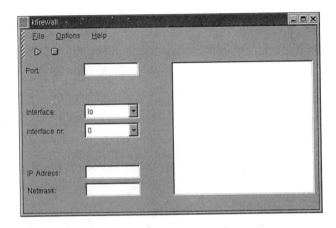

A crontab editor, known as kcrontab, is also under development and many other useful GUI front ends should also become available. Linux is designed for tools to be improved and expanded, and in this area things look very bright.

GNOME Administration Tools

GNOME offers its own assortment of configuration tools. Most of these are part of the standard Red Hat install and can be found in the Utilities or System menu under Programs. Many of the GNOME tools very closely match KDE counterparts. For instance, gdiskfree displays the usage of space on all partitions in a dial format. gw displays who the active users are and is generally a good thing to check while performing maintenance. Earlier in this chapter, you learned the importance of reading system logs. GNOME offers logview for this purpose. It is very simple and has an easy–to–read format; it is shown in Figure 17.9.

KDE Administration Tools

A wide variety of alternatives to linuxconf are available in KDE; however, KDE uses an assortment of smaller utilities rather than one massive one. You can also run linuxconf from KDE as long as you have all the required libraries installed. KDE's utilities are scattered across several menus, but you can find most of them under the Preferences menu. Many of the tools are geared more to monitoring system status than actual configuration. Good examples of this are kdf (Disk Free), which shows the free space on all mounted partitions, and ksysguard, which does an excellent job of tracking system load and current process. ksysguard, shown in Figure 17.7, can even show the load on individual devices and kill out–of-control processes. It is also friendlier on resources than many other process-tracking utilities.

FIGURE 17.7

ksysguard provides a very attractive interface for system monitoring.

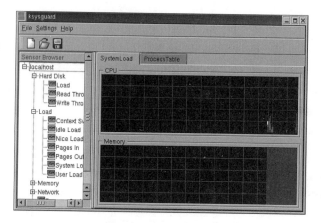

A good selection of KDE administration utilities are available, but only a few are included in this distribution of Red Hat. However, you can obtain these utilities from sites such as http://www.kde.org. KLILO is a convenient GUI configuration tool for LILO. It provides an excellent alternative to manually editing /etc/lilo.conf. kpackage is an excellent package maintenance tool that handles both RPM and DEB packages. kuser (KDE User Manager) allows you to add, edit, or delete any user or group at the click of a button. Although it does not offer quite as many features as linuxconf, it is still a good tool to do the job. It is still fairly early in its development, so more features will be added soon.

The other exciting development in the KDE world appears to be an effort to create a GUI front end for all the major command-line based network configuration tools. Currently, work is underway on kbindconfig to handle bind, kfirewall to manage ipchains, and

FIGURE 17.9

logview is one of many ways to read the daily logs.

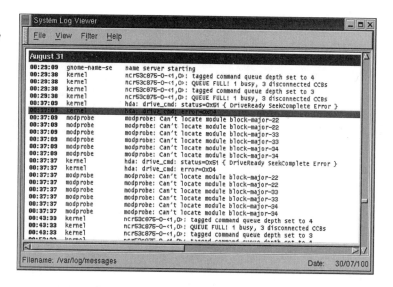

In addition to status monitors, GNOME offers search tools such as gsearchtool. Most power users may be experts with `find`, `whereis`, `locate`, and so on and have no need for this tool. But for new users, this will allow you to search like the pros. GNOME also offer utilities to determine drive and hardware information, such as idetool and guname. guname provides reasonably detailed system stats. Between the logs and the various hardware tools, no hardware information should be difficult to obtain.

GNOME also provides excellent package maintenance capabilities with gnorpm. This utility can be used to install, remove, query existing packages, and even search the Web for new packages. It provides a quick-and-easy method of tracking what you have installed, instead of querying one package at a time on the command line. It can also verify whether a package is still installed correctly on the system, which is always handy when an install goes wrong.

Probably the biggest time-saver for the administrator that GNOME has to offer is the update tool known as up2date from Red Hat. It can minimize the tedious process of searching for newer packages and security updates. After configuring it with server and login information, it can go and find the latest update packages and install them on its own in most cases. up2date is shown in Figure 17.10.

17

FIGURE 17.10

FIGURE 17.10

up2date takes all the hassle out of search for the latest packages.

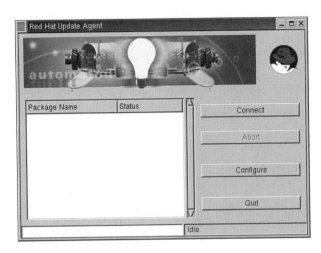

In addition to the GNOME tools included with Red Hat 7, you can find information and links to many more at http://www.gnome.org. There you will find utilities for kernel configuration, printer setup, and many network tools, such as a graphical front end to samba. Each entry has a link to its home page and may have screen shots to look at. You will also find many applets on this site.

Applets are the other handy system administration lifesavers GNOME has to offer. Although they may not configure the system for you, they are a handy way to monitor little details while you're working. They have the advantage of being small and easy on resources. Depending on the window manager being used, they may be part of the menu or be a window on their own, but they are always small and do not clutter the desktop.

Other X Tools You Can't Do Without

Before there was linuxconf or GNOME or KDE, there were the original X-based configuration tools. Although many of these are turning into KDE or GNOME tools, some are still around. Two classic examples are the Red Hat printer tool, printtool, and netcfg. Although some newer printer tools are coming out, for a long time printtool truly offered the easiest way to set up and test a printer. It is still a preferred backup when the autodetection utilities fail; it is shown in Figure 17.11.

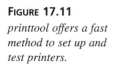

Figure 17.11

printtool offers a fast method to set up and test printers.

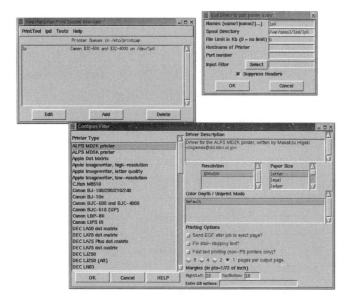

17

netcfg provides an alternative to linuxconf for setting up a network. It can set most network options and it can activate and deactivate the interfaces much faster than linuxconf can, which makes it an ideal choice when you're testing network configurations. There are also the traditional system load viewers, such as xosview. You can find more by searching the Web and checking the site http://www.rpmfind.com.

Summary

In this chapter you learned that performing system administration duties on Linux machines does not have to be a tedious, painful experience. You learned how to perform common tasks with linuxconf. You learned about the many other choices of graphical tools. The only thing that should be overwhelming now is the sheer volume of graphical tools available. By all means, try linuxconf and explore your menus and the Web to find others. Take the time to learn the tools available and find tools that you are comfortable with. Also, keep in mind that you should still make an effort to learn about the relevant configuration files and how to perform administration tasks on the command line. Remember, the graphical tools are supposed to make tedious tasks easier; they are not there to replace the knowledge of how the system works. If you ever get into a situation where you have to fix the system from the command line, you will be glad you learned how to work from the command line. Putting in a little extra effort here can really make your experience with Linux a lot more pleasant.

Workshop

The Workshop contains quiz questions and exercises to help reinforce what you've learned in this hour.

Q&A

Q Why should I use graphical tools over the command line?

A You don't have to use graphical tools if you don't want to, and many experienced system administrators prefer the command line. However, the graphical tools will not make typos in critical files, and they make it a lot easier to double-check your work. When it is just your machine, you can do what you want, but when you have numerous users dependent on you, they will not appreciate experiments gone wrong.

Q Why do I have to learn how the configuration files work and how to work from the command line?

A Some day the system may go down and you will have to boot from a floppy, or you can't get the X Window system running. If that happens, you can't use graphical tools to fix the problem. Then you have to know how to configure the system by editing the configuration files, or you will have to reinstall the system. Understanding the configuration at this level will help you to build a more reliable and more secure system.

Q I tried a graphical tool, but it complains about the files it is configuring. What's wrong?

A If you have manually edited a configuration file, you may have changed the format of the file so that the tool can't read it. Some graphical tools are very strict about how the files they edit are formatted. So always back up your configuration files before editing them. Otherwise, you may create problems for yourself later on.

Q I don't like linuxconf. Where do I find alternatives?

A `http://www.kde.org` A good place for KDE-based tools.

`http://www.gnome.org` Has links to many GNOME-based utilities.

`http://www.rpmfind.com` A large RPM repository; if it exists as an RPM, a link should be there.

`http://www.redhat.com` Red Hat often bundles commercial tools with its distribution. Searching around the site could lead to some very nice commercial tools.

Quiz

1. Why didn't typing `linuxconf` work?

2. What is the advantage of netconf?

3. Where do I learn more of the details about how the configuration files work?

Quiz Answers

1. Why didn't typing `linuxconf` work?

   To save the trouble of having to `su` before running linuxconf, it is now launched by `linuxconf-auth`, which will prompt for a password if you are not logged in as root.

2. What is the advantage of netconf?

   It allows you to quickly test network settings.

3. Where do I learn more of the details about how the configuration files work?

   To start with, read the man pages. Most important configuration files have man pages, or go to `http://www.linuxdoc.org`. The documents there should cover the configuration files in documents related to what they configure. The documents also are searchable. You can find more detailed information in advanced Linux books like Sams Unleashed series.

Exercises

1. Before you add or edit users or groups, take a look at the `/etc/passwd` and `/etc/group` files. Then after you are through, look at how they have changed.

2. Read everything in `/var/log` regularly! If you don't like listing it in a terminal, plenty of graphical tools will display the logs. The more users that depend on your system, the more you need to depend on the logs to tell you what is going on.

3. If you have Ethernet configured, study the `/etc/hosts`, `/etc/networks`, and `/etc/resolv.conf` files to see where the configuration information goes.

17

HOUR 18

Setting Up a Simple Network

Computer networks have connected the world. They are everywhere, in businesses, offices, libraries, and even in the home. Networks can be complex and sometimes even mind-boggling. Would you like to have your own network? Of course you would. If you happen to have a couple of PCs sitting around, I'll show you how to do it.

Learning to set up a computer network for the first time can be an exciting and rewarding experience, so let's have some fun.

In this hour you will

- Set up and install your own home network
- Install your Ethernet card
- Set up a virtual private network (VPN)
- Learn about IP masquerading
- Build your own firewall to protect your system

Setting Up Your Own Simple Network

Before you begin to set up your network, there are a few things that you need to know. You may already have used the largest network in the world without really realizing it—the Internet. That's right, the Internet has grown to be the largest network of all. But what is a network?

A network is nothing more than two or more computers connected with a cable or other type of conductor. Each of these computers must have a unique address (just like a house has an address and is connected to other houses by telephone lines) so that other computers can communicate with it.

In reality, computers on a network send data to each other by sending electrical signals over the cable. The technology involved here is very complex and we will not get into exactly how all this works. Libraries are filled with books on the subject and the Internet abounds with such information. It is sufficient for us to understand what we need to know to build a simple network. You will know enough to build your network and understand how it works.

There are some questions here that you may have already been asking yourself. For instance, how does one computer know whether another computer has received a message it sent? Or, by what path did it travel to reach its destination? How do the computers on a network know the addresses of the other computers? All of these questions and many more are answered by one single word: protocol. A *protocol* is just a set of rules that defines how computers and everything on the network behave or conduct themselves. A protocol is a common language that each unit or device on the network must use.

If one computer spoke one protocol and another computer spoke a different one, they would not be able to communicate. All units on the network will be able to communicate effectively if they use the same protocol or set of rules. Table 18.1 defines some of the more common protocols you will most likely come into contact with.

TABLE 18.1 Common Protocols

Protocol	Definition or Meaning
FTP	File Transfer Protocol
HTTP	Hypertext Transfer Protocol
LAN	Local Area Network
MAN	Metropolitan Area Network
OSI	Open Systems Network
SMTP	Simple Mail Transfer Protocol
WAN	Wide Area Network

You can further define protocols as a set of standards that defines how each computer or node identifies itself to everything else on the network. It also defines the data format and how the data is processed when it reaches its destination within this framework. Data is normally transferred in what are called "packets," which are sent and received by nodes of the network.

Types of Networks

You will need to know some of the details about what makes a network before you can proceed with building your own. Knowing what constitutes a network will help you to better understand how to build one. Figure 18.1 shows a simple network composed of two computers connected to a hub. There are many kinds of networking topologies, of which Ethernet is only one. Ethernet is probably the most popular, cheapest, and easiest to build, which is why we're covering it here. It is beyond the scope of this book to cover all the different types.

FIGURE 18.1

A simple network composed of a hub and two computers.

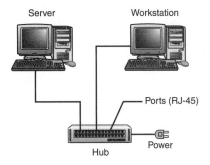

18

The way in which computers are put together to form a network and the kind of cabling it uses is referred to as the *topology* of the network. That is, topology is defined as the method in which a network is configured. Each computer, router, hub, or other device on the network is referred to as a *node*. Nodes on an Ethernet network are generally connected either by Bus or Point-to-Point topology:

- **Bus**—The bus method consists of the nodes connected to a coaxial or other cable in series by means of T-connectors. If the circuit breaks at any point, the entire network will be inoperable. You have to terminate the Bus (coaxial) network with terminators on each end. One of these must be grounded. It doesn't matter which one.

- **Point-to-Point**—This is the recommended and most widely used topology. The Point-to-Point topology connects exactly two nodes together. This is normally accomplished using a hub or switch.

A Local Area Network (LAN) is the type of network you would find in an office or business. It usually consists of two or more computers connected in an arrangement that allows them to communicate. If you have another office across town and you have your LAN connected to the LAN in the other office, you need a router to connect the two LANs so that they can communicate effectively. This is a Wide Area Network (WAN). A WAN is generally understood to be several LANs connected together.

As networks develop and expand, so do the protocols and acronyms. There are network protocols for schools, colleges, universities, hospitals, and even the Internet. Everything on a network must use the same type of protocol or one that can talk to other computers on other networks. Most networks today use the TCP/IP protocol. The TCP/IP protocol is native to UNIX/Linux; it was originally developed for it so it is natural that we use TCP/IP for our Linux network protocol. TCP/IP is a set of protocols developed to allow computers to share resources across a network. TCP/IP was developed by a community of researchers who wanted to allow the computers on the old ARPAnet to be able to communicate with each other and with other networks. This eventually led to the Web and the Internet.

Types of Cabling Used in Networks

There are four basic, general types of cables used in networks: thickwire, thin coax, twisted pair, and fiber optic. With the way things change in computers there are new types appearing every day, such as wireless, firewire, and USB.

Thickwire is nothing more than large diameter coaxial cable. It is referred to as 10BASE5 but is not used much anymore because it is bulky, hard to work with, and breaks easily. It is immune to electrical noise and may be used as a backbone for a Bus topology network.

Thin coax, also called 10BASE2, is of a smaller diameter, more flexible, and easier to use than thickwire. It is used to connect computers in a Bus topology where the nodes are connected directly to the cable using T-connectors (BNC). BNC stands for Bayonet Nut Connector. This type of topology is not used much any more because it is bulky, hard to run, breaks easily, and other cabling systems are much more efficient. One of the advantages of using this type of coaxial cabling system is that it resists electrical interference (EMF) and crosstalk. Crosstalk can be thought of interference between two signals that run adjacent or in close proximity to each other.

Twisted pair, also known as 10BASET, 100BaseT, UTP, or CAT-5 (Category 5), is similar to regular telephone cable. You may also know it as UTP (Unshielded Twisted Pair) or STP (Shielded Twisted Pair). This type of cable is used with Point-to-Point topology and is the most common type of network topology today.

Fiber optic is known as 10BASE-FL and is used the same way that you use twisted pair cables. It is easy to install, and insulates the network from lightning strikes and electrical interference. It is more expensive than twisted pair, but for some applications it is worth the initial investment.

Now you know what kind of cabling is used in networks and you have a better understanding of what to expect. You will be using a Point-to-Point topology to build your network so your job will be much easier than if you were using coaxial. Now that we have discussed the cabling, let's take a look at network interface cards and hubs, the two final components that will make up your simple network.

Network Cards and Hubs

Computers and other devices on a network are hooked together using network interface cards (NICs) that are installed in the computers. These cards allow a computer to communicate with other computers on the network. Network interface cards are either of the type for coaxial cable (BNC) or the unshielded twisted pair (RJ-45) variety.

One of the most important choices you can make when designing a network is to choose the right equipment. This choice includes such things as network interface cards and hubs. Network interface cards come in many brands and varieties. They are available in both ISA and PCI versions. Most newer computers have both types of slots but you should check your computer to make sure that your card will fit in it. If you have a PCI slot, you should use that because it is faster. The PCI cards are "plug-and-play," so they will be easier to install because the software will detect your card in most cases. The PCI bus will also automatically assign an IRQ to the card, which is helpful. If you end up using an ISA card, you will unfortunately have to do that yourself from the BIOS. How do you know if you have a PCI slot on your motherboard? Generally, PCI slots are white and ISA slots are black.

When you purchase your card, look at the speed of the card. Currently you have a choice of 10Mbps and 100Mbps cards. You probably should go ahead and purchase the 100Mbps cards because currently they are as cheap as the 10Mbps cards. Some cards will allow you to run both speeds. These are designated as 10/100 speed cards. You will find a variety of cards with a variety of different speeds including ones that can run faster than a gigabyte. You should purchase the fastest cards that you can afford, but if you're only setting up a small network in your home or office, the 100Mbps cards should be sufficient. You can generally get a good network card for anywhere from $10 on up. You probably can find a 100Mbps card for less than $30. Although a network of 10 computers will generally run well on 10Mbps cards, I would recommend that you purchase the 100Mbps units because they are much faster and if you decide to expand your system, you are already set up for it.

18

Another good thing to know about network cards is that they come with connectors for coaxial cables (BNC), for twisted pair cables (RJ-45), and for the older Attachment Unit Interface (AUI). You may see older cards with other types of connectors that you may not be familiar with. If you don't have the documentation for the card, do not use it because you may damage your equipment. You will be using the type for twisted pair (CAT5) with the RJ-45 connector.

If you will be using laptops, palmtops, or notebooks on your network, you will need a PCMCIA (Personal Computer Memory Card International Association) interface card. These are the small credit card size cards made specifically for laptops that plug into the PCMCIA port on your laptop. These cards usually come with enough documentation so that you can install them trouble-free. If you are using more than a few of the laptop type computers on your system, you should consider using "docking stations" because these units allow the user to remove the computer and take it with him. The docking stations also cut down on maintenance costs, and allow you to use a regular size monitor, mouse, and keyboard. The laptop simply slides into the docking station and can be just as easily removed. By using a docking station, you don't wear out or bend the pins on your connectors quite as fast.

Hubs, like network cards, come in many sizes, shapes, speeds, and with a variety of ports to choose from. A hub is simply a box that allows you to connect your computers and form a network. All of the computers hooked to one hub are basically known as a *segment*. That is, it forms a segment of the network. If you add another hub to the network, that is another segment. Large networks consist of many segments.

Hubs are generally 10Mbps or 100Mbps. You can buy dual-speed hubs that run both speeds. The computers hook into the hub with either BNC or RJ-45 connectors on the hubs called *ports*. A small home network can start with 4 or 5 ports and when it expands you can add more hubs. I would highly recommend that you buy at least an 8-port hub because the price is currently so low that you can hardly pass it up. You will need to purchase a 100Mbps hub if your cards are 100Mbps.

Hubs should be placed in a central location and your cables should be routed from your computers to the hub. One advantage of hubs over the coaxial (bus) system is that if the cable breaks on a bus you lose the entire network, but with a hub you only lose the one computer or node that is bad.

As your network grows you will need to add more hubs to compensate for the growth factor. You have to do this by plugging them together through an uplink port or with a crossover cable plugged into one of the standard ports.

Hub prices range from about $30 to more than $100. I recently purchased an 8-port hub for about $45. Hubs are something that you can expand on and extend your networking capabilities, so you should invest in a good one at the beginning of your networking adventure. You can purchase many networking kits, including NETGEAR and Linksys, for around a hundred dollars. These generally come with a hub, two cards, and enough cable to network your computers. You can expand your network by purchasing additional components or other kits. You should call or contact the manufacturer to see if they specifically support the Linux operating system. At the time of this writing, more manufacturers are in the process of supporting Linux.

Up until now we have discussed many of the issues surrounding building a network and have gotten acquainted with some of the common elements. Now we should be able to put the network together. Your network will consist of a couple of computers, two twisted pair (CAT-5) cables, a hub, and two network cards. It doesn't sound like much, but it allows you to extend your ability to do more work by sharing files, printers, modems, and other services that otherwise might not be available to you.

Planning the Network

One thing that I want you to remember if you become a network engineer is to plan your network to the last grueling detail before you start to set it up. This is not only good advice, it is plain common sense. You'd be surprised at how many people don't plan their networks and have to do it all over again in the end. I won't go into all that detail here but if you are interested, check out some of the resources on the Internet. One of the best books I have ever read is *Sams Teach Yourself Networking in 24 Hours*, which should be in your computer book stores about the same time you are reading this.

The first thing you will need to do is make up a simple parts list that records all of the hardware that you need to build the network. Here is an example:

- **Two Working Computers**—These machines should be running Linux or be capable of running Linux.

- **Two Network Cards (NICs)**—These can be any brand, but you should purchase some good 100Mbps cards. You will find 10Mbps cards that are cheaper but slower. The extra cost is worth it for the 100Mbps cards. At the time of this writing there is little difference between the cost of the two cards.

- **Unshielded Twisted Pair (UTP)** (often referred to as CAT-5 or Category 5 cable)—You will need one cable for each computer. You can buy these cables already assembled at a reasonable price at most computer stores. I suggest you purchase a cable of at least six feet, but if your computers are far away from each other you will need to purchase one that is sufficient for that distance.

- **Hub or Switch**—You will need either a hub or a switch to connect your computers to the network. You can connect two computers using a crossover cable, but it is not recommended because it is slow and limited to the two computers. A hub has

18

ports that allow you to connect several computers to the network using UTP cable. A switch is a more intelligent version of the hub that can remember such things as network addresses. NETGEAR makes a good selection of hubs and switches.

Task: Preparing to Install a Network Card

Now that we have done the brain work it is time to do some physical labor. Figure 18.2 shows a network interface card being installed.

FIGURE 18.2

A network interface card being inserted into a PCI slot.

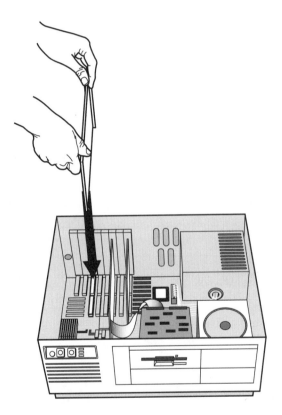

Before you actually install the network card, there are a few preparations and precautions you should consider. It is important to follow procedures such as these because it will save you time and money later. Here is a small list of things that I usually do before working on any computer:

1. Prepare a clean, quiet place to work that is free from dirt, water, and interruptions.

2. Unplug all equipment that you are going to work on. This includes any equipment such as printers that might be connected to a computer that you will be working with.

3. Use a static wrist strap or other protective equipment. Static electricity can destroy expensive computer chips. Always touch the back of the computer (on a metal surface) while it is plugged in. This will help to discharge most static electricity from your body, but you should still wear static discharge gear.

4. Do not remove any components such as NICs from static bags until you are ready to use them.

5. Do not use power tools such as screwdrivers. The magnetic fields can harm chips.

6. Mark all cables before removing them from the computer. You should disconnect all cables from the computer before working on it.

7. Make sure that you install the adapter card in the proper slot. Don't attempt to install a PCI card in an ISA slot.

8. Don't force adapter cards into slots. If it doesn't seem to want to go into the slot, take it out, check the slot for obstructions, and try again, gently.

9. Be sure you have all your documentation and tools before you begin the actual installation.

Task: Installing a Network Card in Your Computer

18

1. Following the instructions in your computer documentation (that came with your computer), remove the screws from the back of your computer and remove the cover or panels, exposing the motherboard. Be sure that you are statically correct.

2. Familiarize yourself with the interior of the computer. Note if you have an empty PCI slot. In some cases you may have to install your card in an ISA slot. This may be because you don't have a PCI slot or none are available. (You should have already checked this as per my previous instructions. This is mentioned here as a reminder).

3. Remove the network interface card from the static bag. Carefully handle it and try not to touch the components or circuits on the board. If you're not statically correct you may zap your card. This is a good time to read your documentation and record any information about your card and hub that you can. You will need it during the installation. Keep it handy.

4. Carefully insert the card into the PCI or ISA slot. Do not force it. Align the card with the slot and gently press down. If you cannot insert the card after using reasonable force, take the card out and inspect the slot to see if there are any obstructions, such as dirt or other mundane objects hiding in there. If so, remove them and try again.

5. Put the case back on and reconnect everything. You should leave the cover or case off until you have the computer hooked to the network. That way, if it isn't seated correctly you won't have to take the cover off again.

6. Now that you have installed the card, you have made great progress toward setting up your network. To install the card in the second computer follow the previous seven steps.

Remember that I said we were going to keep this as simple as possible? You'll soon learn that simplicity under Linux is happiness. In other words, the simpler it is the better it will work and the less trouble you will have with it. Here's an example of what I am talking about.

When purchasing network interface cards, you should purchase PCI cards because they are "plug-and-play," which makes them detectable by the system. Be sure to get cards with RJ-45 Jacks so they will work with your CAT-5 (twisted pair) cables.

I'm not promoting any single product, but one way you can find out about network components is to visit the NETGEAR Web site. There you will find not only descriptions of network cards, hubs, and other interesting devices, but there are also many pictures showing what they look like. NETGEAR sells quality networking components for the home user and small business user alike. I like the company because their products are priced competitively, their support is great, and they have a nice-looking Web site. Not only that but you will find lots of information on their site about home and small business networking. Just one visit there will help you to understand what I'm talking about. You can visit their Web site at `http://www.netgear.com/`. There also are many other networking systems manufacturers, such as Cisco Systems and Linksys.

If for some reason you are not using a PCI card or you are using an older card, you may have to set the IRQ and install a driver for the card. Please check the documentation that came with your card to find out how to do this.

You can purchase a 6-port hub and two network cards for about $100. The CAT-5 cable is the most expensive item if you don't watch what you are buying. One company that sells good products is AESP (Advanced Electronic Support Products) and they have a Web site at `http://www.aesp.com/`. I purchased a 10-foot section of CAT-5 cable for less than $10.

One way to safely clean a slot is to take a large paper clip, pull it apart until it is straight, and wrap a soft piece of cloth or static wipe (that has alcohol on it) over and around the end of it. Insert the item into the end of the slot and gently pull it through the slot. This should remove any obstructions and dirt in the slot.

Setting Up Your Network Hardware

Oh, did we forget something? Maybe you're looking hungrily at those nicely colored CAT-5 cables or the hub that you purchased. Go ahead and open the hub box and remove the hub. You will need to put this in a centralized place that is convenient to get to. Some people put them on the bench or table behind their computers or you can mount them on the wall. It doesn't matter as long as you can reach them.

Hubs normally come with a transformer (the black heavy thing with the power cord on it) that plugs into the back of your hub and the power cord to plug into an electrical outlet. These should be 115-120 VAC so you can insert them safely into any such outlet. If you plug your radio or TV into it, it is safe to plug your hub into it.

Now take your CAT-5 cable and plug one end of it into the RJ-45 plug of your network card in your first computer and then plug the other end into the first port (RJ-45 plug) of your hub. See the documentation that came with your hub to determine which port is safe to plug into. Some hubs have a port for crossover purposes or for connecting one hub to another one.

Go ahead and repeat the process for the other computer(s) on your network. Now comes the hard part: configuring your network card using linuxconf. Caught you by surprise, didn't I? You didn't expect a hard part but don't worry, we'll get through it together. I've done it many times and you will too before your Linux career gets too far underway.

18

We've blasted along at full speed like a rocket headed for Mars without considering that your computer might already have a network card installed. Some of the newer integrated boards include the card on the board. If this is the case, do not install another card in the computer. It won't damage your computer because some computers have several NICs, but you won't need it. Follow your motherboard's documentation to set up the card. In most cases, you will set it up using linuxconf. If you have problems with the onboard card, you will have to find out from the documentation how to disable it before installing a new one.

Task: Configuring Your Card Using linuxconf

If you haven't already installed Linux on your machines you will be prompted for the network card information when the machine is booting up after the install. Most newer plug-and-play machines will automatically detect your card and configure it for you. If your card is detected during the boot process you will be asked to press Enter to start the configuration. Following are some of the typical steps during the process. (If you are using an earlier version of Linux, this may be different than Red Hat Linux 7.0.)

You can use linuxconf to configure your network, make important changes to your network setup, change your users' passwords, and various other things. This can be done during installation or after you have set up and configured your network. Follow these steps to configure your network card:

1. Start your Linux installation and watch the screen for any sign that Linux has detected your card. You normally will be prompted to press Enter at some point to start the configuration.

2. The next dialog box should appear and you should see the brand name of your network card. Press Enter to continue with the configuration.

3. At this time you will get a prompt saying "Would You Like to Set Up Networking?" Select Yes and enter the information. If you need help with this, see the following steps where we use linuxconf to set up your card. If you are uncertain, enter No and we will go through what you have to do in the following steps.

   If you are successful, congratulations. Otherwise, we will go through the steps in detail in a few minutes.

4. You can access linuxconf from GNOME by clicking the Main Menu, System, LinuxConf. You can also start linuxconf from any shell or command prompt by entering `linuxconf`.

5. You will need to open Config, Networking, Client Tasks and finally, Basic Host Information.

6. Note the Host Name tab. Enter the hostname you have decided to give the computer. You will need to enter the hostname of the computer followed by a period and the domain name for the network. Your hostname can be anything, but I suggest something that means something to you. An example could be the name of your machine. If this is your first workstation, just call it WS1 or give it some other meaningful name. If your domain name were aes.com, you would enter WS1.aes.com here.

7. Now click the Adapter 1 tab where you will enter your Ethernet card settings. This is why I said to write down all the information about your card. You will need to get that now.

8. Look for the Enabled button and be sure it is pressed in. In the Linux screens it is sometimes difficult to tell if the buttons are in or out especially if your monitor is set up for high-resolution and everything is small.

9. Choose Manual if you don't have DHCP or BootP servers on your LAN. DHCP and BootP will automatically assign IP addresses to your clients, but if you don't have these continue on to the next step. If you do have them, choose DCHP or BootP and go to step 11.

10. Look under Primary Name + Domain and type the hostname of the computer followed by a dot. Enter the LAN's domain name. An example would be WS1.aes.com.

11. Under Aliases, enter the computer's hostname.

12. Under IP Address, type the IP address for the computer. You can use a number similar to 190.168.1.4 or any other number similar to this.

13. You are then asked for the Netmask, so type `255.255.255.0`.

14. Choose Eth0 under Net Device. This is the first network card on your network. The next computer would be Eth1 and so on.

15. The Kernel Module option is usually filled in automatically and it should contain the name of the driver for your Ethernet card. If you leave it blank, it should be filled in when linuxconf is exited.

16. Click Accept to end the process.

You must repeat this task for every computer on your network in order to set it up correctly. Make sure that you enter the information correctly and if you have problems getting the network to operate, check your steps once again. Once you have completed these steps, you have done all that is necessary to set up your network interface cards.

There are many more things that you must do to get your network operating, such as setting up your computer to share files, devices, and other things that make having a network useful. This is where you get to do some research. The best place to look for information is on the CD or on the Internet. The various Linux HOWTOs explain a lot of things that I don't have space or time to tell you about in this book. The list of HOWTOs alone would fill a couple of pages. For your convenience I have included the following list of HOWTOs that are relevant to this chapter. These HOWTOs are normally found on your Red Hat CD in the /RedHat/doc directory. You can also find them on various sites on the Internet.

18

Bridge-HOWTO	Mail-HOWTO
Ethernet-HOWTO	Networking-Overview-HOWTO
Config-HOWTO	News-HOWTO
DHCP-HOWTO	NFS-HOWTO
DNS-HOWTO	PCI-HOWTO
Ethernet-HOWTO	Plug-and-Play-HOWTO
IP-Alias-HOWTO	PPP-HOWTO
IPCHAINS-HOWTO	Security-HOWTO
IP-Masquerade-HOWTO	VPN-HOWTO

I know this looks like a lot of reading. There is so much information on Linux that it seems overwhelming at times, but if you take it one step at a time, it isn't so bad. Just search for the information that you need at the time. An example would be to read the Ethernet-HOWTO, which will explain a lot about Ethernet networks and other issues about your LAN. You can read other HOWTOs as you need to.

In the next part of the hour we will work on building a virtual private network (VPN), which allows you to have more control over who and what is able to use your LAN. I don't want to give away all my secrets, but it will help you to finish up configuring and setting up your network.

Virtual Private Networks (VPNs)

In this part of the hour we will define virtual private networks (VPNs) and what they mean to the security of your network or LAN. You will also be guided through the phases of setting up a virtual private network should you choose to do so.

One of the biggest issues with networks is security. A virtual private network can offer you added security for your system because it creates a virtual tunnel of security across a public network such as the Internet.

The basic concept of a virtual private network is to have a firewall set up on your LAN, which enables you to communicate with another LAN that is also protected by a firewall. This provides a virtual tunnel of protection between the two systems across a public network.

Virtual private networking is just a private network connection established over a public networking connection such as the Internet. This process involves encrypting the data at one end and decrypting it at the other end. This is the process that creates a virtual tunnel between the two networks. This means that the data is inaccessible to others while in the virtual tunnel created by the encryption. This is why it is called a *virtual* network. It is virtually inaccessible. Figure 18.3 shows how this basically works.

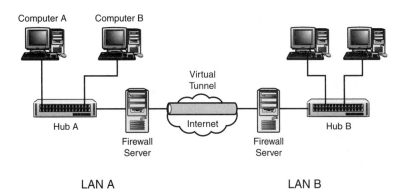

FIGURE 18.3
The virtual private network set up using the Internet.

Once you are connected in this manner, all the resources of the other network are at your command. This means printers, faxes, and other devices that the other LAN makes available to you. In effect, the resources of any such arrangement in the world is at your fingertips. In such an environment you could make all of your office resources available to other offices around the world, therefore creating a *global office* environment.

Setting Up a Virtual Private Network

The process of setting up a VPN is extensive and too involved to include in this book. I am going to simplify the process for you and show you where to get the information you will need to complete the setup. You can set up a virtual private network using the two computers you have on your present network. Additionally, the only piece of hardware that you will need will be for the firewall. You could set up the firewall on one of the existing computers, but that might allow someone to get directly into your system.

The best bet for setting up a VPN is to set up a proxy server that exists between your LAN and the external network or the Internet. We will discuss firewalls later in the hour. A firewall is a computer loaded with special software that can block messages and users that you don't want on your system. Figure 18.4 shows how the proxy server is set up to provide you with the firewall that you need to form your VPN.

FIGURE **18.4**

A proxy server set up to act as the firewall.

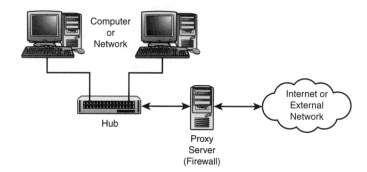

Both systems must have special, compatible software in order for this to work. The VPN software has encryption and decryption capabilities so that the data sent between the two (or more) systems is encrypted and protected at every stage. When you send an encrypted message from your LAN, the user on the other end must be running VPN client software such as the Linux PPTP VPN Client.

> Most of the VPN software solutions use an encrypted network protocol, usually PPP (Point-to-Point). When it is received by the server on the receiving end, it is un-encrypted again. This provides the secure VPN tunnel we were talking about.

Once you have your proxy server set up as a firewall, you are ready to use the Internet as the gateway to other virtual private networks.

It is important that you read the VPN HOWTO and other related HOWTOs before attempting to set up your VPN. You also have to take the encryption software (standards) into consideration. Most of these are mentioned in the VPN HOWTO. Once you have your VPN server set up you will need to follow the guidelines in the HOWTOs regarding disabling unneeded network protocols, user accounts, and other programs that may let someone into your system.

The VPN platform is growing rapidly and so is the information about it. To find out more search the Internet or read *Peter Norton's Network Security Fundamentals* (Sams), which outlines some of the more interesting features of the subject. In the next section we will take a look at a related topic, IP Masquerading.

IP Masquerading

IP Masquerading is also known as Address Translation and involves preventing crackers from accessing the system by making the legal internal (IP) address invisible to them. This technique simply hides the internal network addresses so that the users' IP addresses aren't apparent to outside prying eyes.

IP Masquerading works by connecting a computer to the Internet service provider (ISP) and assigning a legal Internet IP address to the computer. The legal IP address is then translated into internal network addresses that are not legal Internet addresses or known to the Internet. Anyone else on the Internet can only see the legal address, the rest of the addresses are invisible and unobtainable. A legal Internet address looks something like this: 200.50.66.30.

Every packet that is sent out by the machine doing the masquerading is relabeled with its own IP address. This makes it appear that all packets come from one machine. The masquerading machine will stamp all incoming packets with non-Internet legal addresses of machines on the internal network. The packets are then routed to the correct address or machine. This may sound confusing but if you read this over and absorb the information in the Linux VPN Masquerade HOWTO, it will become more apparent. You will find the Masquerade HOWTO on the Red Hat site at `http://www.redhat.com/`. Look under Support/Creating a Firewall. There is a lot of information there relating to creating VPNs, firewalls, and masquerading.

This subject is extensive and has several HOWTOs written on it already. You can check your Red Hat Linux 7.0 CD for the HOWTOs and search the Internet for related information. The Red Hat site has some information under Support that will help you to set up your Masquerade server. By using masquerading and firewalls, you can have a more secure virtual private network. In the next section we will look at firewalls a little more closely.

Setting Up a Firewall

A firewall is software that is installed on a computer to block unwanted traffic. You can download freeware firewall programs from the Internet for use on your computers. Most of these do a decent job, but the type of firewall you need to protect your LAN is a little more complicated.

A firewall essentially authenticates or verifies the logins of people who attempt to access your system. One method of making a firewall is to make the firewall part of a small, separate network that exists between the router and the internal network. These kinds of firewalls usually have two network cards. This is called a *sandbox*.

This network usually has a separate concentrator that routes packets from the router through the separate concentrator to the first card in the firewall. These packets are checked to see if they are legal and allowed to use the internal network. If they can't be authenticated, they are discarded. If authentication information is valid, they are routed through the second network card in the computer, which allows them access to the internal network.

That kind of firewall is well and good but a better way to do it is with a proxy server. If your network runs TCP/IP (and most do), each computer has a unique address. These addresses can allow crackers access to your internal network. How do you avoid this? Proxy servers are the answer because they make the IP numbers appear invisible to the outside world.

A proxy server exists between the internal network and the external network acting as a solicitor that edits all incoming and outgoing traffic. You must configure each computer's TCP/IP software to look for a proxy server at a specific IP address. When a user clicks on a link for a Web page, the data packets aren't sent out directly through the firewall and to the Web site. The proxy server intercepts the internal computer's request and takes note of the external computer's IP address and sends a request for the same resources that the user made. The trick here is that the request comes from the proxy server IP address and not from the internal computer. Anyone outside the internal network sees only the address of the proxy server and not any of the internal computer's IP numbers.

The proxy server intercepts or receives incoming packets, notes the IP address, and routes them to the user they are addressed to. There are many different types of firewalls and many software packages that implement them. This is growing by leaps and bounds. You can set up a complicated firewall on your single home computer or set up a proxy server to protect your entire LAN. The different types of configurations are enormous. It would be impossible to discuss all this information in this one single hour.

There are numerous HOWTOs and other information out there showing you specifically how to set up the particular type of firewall that you need. I suggest you check Red Hat's own Web site before anything else. Look under Support for the section on Firewalls. Another useful site is `http://www.linuxfirewall.org/`. This is the official site of the Linux Firewall Project, which has the latest information on firewalls.

Summary

In this hour you learned how to set up a simple network, installed and configured a network interface card (NIC), learned about virtual private networks (VPNs), and about securing your network using a firewall. By now you have the capability to purchase the components you need to set up a network, install the components, and configure the network. Just think how great it is that you can share printers, modems, and other hardware on your network.

Workshop

The Workshop contains quiz questions and exercises to help reinforce what you've learned in this hour.

Q&A

Q How do I expand my two-system network?

A When you are ready to expand your network or add more computers to it, you can do this by simply adding another hub and the appropriate CAT-5 cables. Depending on your hub or switch you will need a special port that allows you to connect the new hub to the existing one. Check the documentation that comes with the hub to see what kind of cable you will need. This port is normally the last one in the series, but it can be any one of the ports.

Q Can I use coaxial cable to set up my network?

A Yes you can. This kind of network is called a bus network and it is really much cheaper than using the CAT-5 cables, but it is bulky and the cable is easily damaged. The computers are hooked to the cable by means of T-shaped BNC connectors, which come loose at times and cause problems. You are much better off staying with a network using hubs and UTP.

Quiz

1. What does CAT-5 mean?
2. What is a firewall and how does it protect your system?
3. What is the graphical utility that you would use to configure your network, add users, and change passwords?
4. What is a firewall actually composed of?

Quiz Answers

1. What does CAT-5 mean?

    CAT-5 is terminology for Category 5, which is a standard rating for a class of conductors used to connect nodes on networks.

2. What is a firewall and how does it protect your system?

18

A firewall is basically made up of software that blocks incoming traffic and authenticates users.

3. What is the graphical utility that you would use to configure your network, add users, and change passwords?

   You can use linuxconf from GNOME or from the Linux command prompt to configure most of your network cards, user accounts, and so on.

4. What is a firewall actually composed of?

   The main part of a firewall is the software. That's what makes it work. It exists on a physical server, but it is the software that makes it so effective.

Exercise

You can do this just for fun and to gain some experience with firewalls. There are a number of firewalls on the Internet that you can get for free. There are a few for Linux. Use your Web browser to search for "firewalls" and download one to use on your system. If you are running Windows on your machine, try one called ZoneAlarm. It is probably the best freeware firewall on the Net. It doesn't support Linux yet, but by downloading it and installing ZoneAlarm you will get some experience in using firewalls. You can read some articles I wrote about ZoneAlarm at http://www.techrepublic.com. You can find out more about the product and download a copy free from http://www.zonelarm.com/.

PART IV

Advanced Topics

Hour

Hour **19**

Integrating Linux and Windows

The previous hours have pointed out all the great things you can do with Linux. Although Linux has an equivalent application for virtually everything now, you still may need to run Windows. You may need Microsoft Office for work or maybe some other operating system such as Solaris, BeOS, or HP-UX. Maybe you don't have an additional machine to dedicate to Linux or maybe you just don't want to switch over cold turkey.

In an ideal world, we would all have two top-of-the-line machines. One machine would be used for work and we could experiment with new things like Linux on the other one. Obviously, this is seldom the case. I always prefer one top-of-the-line machine to two mediocre machines. Besides, even if you have two machines, don't you want all of your important applications running on the fast machine? I know I always do! This hour is going to explore having Linux and Windows on a single machine and what the options are.

This may sound like a headache, but it is really not that difficult to do. It just requires a little patience, a little planning, and a little common sense. Pay attention to the warnings and always make boot disks while setting up two operating systems on one machine. It takes about two minutes to make a boot disk. It may take well over two hours to undo a mistake that a boot disk could have recovered from. You can do the math on that one—I can tell you from experience that the one time you don't make the boot disk will be the time you need it. Yes, Murphy's Law definitely applies to multi-OS systems.

I cannot possibly cover all the configuration ideas with boot loaders, WINE, VMware, samba, and so on. So in this hour I am going to try to show you what tools are available to you. We will identify what your needs are. From there you can choose what setup and tools suit you best and I will try to point out the resources available for them.

In this hour you will

- Analyze available resources and requirements
- Learn the installation consideration of a dual-boot system
- Install and configure VMware
- Install and configure WINE
- Set up a simple samba server
- Configure a samba client

Task: Preparing to Build Linux over Legacy Systems

Before diving right in to all the options available, you need to fill out a worksheet. Yes, I know this is supposed to be a fun book, not back to school. Trust me, this is *really* in your best interest. You need to figure out how much hard drive space you need, what resources you need to share, and what applications you need to run.

1. At the top of the sheet, write down how much space you have available on each hard drive. Take a minute to look at Figure 19.1 at the end of this section to get an idea of how it should look.

2. If you are willing to buy an additional hard drive, write down how big it would be. There are advantages to keeping the operating systems on separate drives. You don't have to worry about splitting partitions and it is just easier to deal with mentally. It really does not matter to Linux either way.

3. You now need to figure out how much space is needed to make things work. In one column, estimate the space needed by Windows and in the other estimate the space needed by Linux. Remember to count the base install and swap space. For most Windows 9x and NT installs, 150MB for the base and an additional 100MB minimum for swap space is a safe estimate. For Windows 2000 and ME, you will have to consult the available documentation for size information, but a safe bet would be close to 1000MB for the base install. The Red Hat 7.0 workstation install currently runs around 1000MB and, again, 100MB is a good initial estimate of swap space. Your actual swap needs will vary depending on what you do on the system. If you know your needs are different, use those numbers. A 1000MB install may sound excessive, but remember that Red Hat includes most of the odds and ends applications and libraries that you would find yourself adding to Windows later on. In the end it balances out.

4. List in each column what applications you think you will want to run and an estimate of their install sizes. It is better to guess high here and be safe than to run out of space later.

5. Applications are not the only things that will need space. You should list how much space you want for games and how much space you will need for your files. I usually double the estimate of space I need for personal files on Windows and I triple my space estimates for games on both sides. Modern games consume hard drive space at an alarming rate. Some new games consume upwards of a gigabyte of space each!

6. Decide how much space you want to set aside for future applications. Granted, you can't be extremely accurate with this number, but putting a little thought into it now can save you from major headaches down the road.

7. Now total both columns. Before you balance the budget, so to speak, you need to consider whether there are any services you want to share. If you are on a network, you may want or need to share partitions or printers with other Windows users. Jot those down now and if any shared partitions were not included in your drive space estimates, record their sizes now. Take a minute to total the numbers and look at the space you have available. Do you have enough space available for all this? If you have multiple hard drives, can you put Linux and Windows on separate drives? If you are short on space, take some time to rework the numbers.

19

After you have done this, gather the information on your hardware that you were told to at the beginning of this book for the initial install. You may need this to configure some of the tools we will discuss in a bit. Yes, this was time consuming, but now you have most of the information you need to make the decisions you will face in the rest of the hour.

FIGURE 19.1

The OS balancing worksheet can save a lot of time later.

Hard Drives
Ide: WD 10.1 gig   Scsi: none

Willing to buy: IBM 15 gig
Total: 25.1 gig

Windows: Linux:
Base install: 150 MB   Base install: 1000 MB
Swap: 100 MB   Swap: 100 MB
Microsoft Office: 300 MB   StarOffice: 150 MB
Photoshop: 200 MB   VMware: 10 MB
Code Warrior: 200 MB   Games: 500 MB x = 1500 MB
Games: 500 MB x 3 = 1500 MB   Personal Files: 50 MB
Personal Files: 200 MB
Windows Total: 2650 MB   Linux Total: 2810 MB

Shares
Cannon 600 printer
Shared partition: 500MB

Total space needs: 2650+2810+500 = 5960 one drive no problem
C: 5000 MB
/   4000 MB
swap 100 MB
/home 900 MB

System info:
Processor: 700mhz Athlon
Memory: 128 MB
Hard drive: 10.1 gig IDE
CD-ROM: 48x IDE
Video: ATI Rage Pro chipset

To Partition or Not to Partition

The next thing we need to discuss is setting up the partitions. If you plan to have Linux and Windows on two separate drives, you don't have to worry about most of this. If you want them to exist on the same drive, however, and you want to preserve an existing Windows install, you will probably have to look into splitting your partitions. Since the release of the FAT32 filesystem it is common for newer machines, even ones with huge hard drives, to have only a single partition. Although this is convenient for a single operating system machine, it creates more problems than it solves in a multiple operating system machine.

If you have the space requirements worked out, you can use tools like `fips`, which is included on the Red Hat CD, or commercial products like Partition Magic to split your partitions. There are quite a few choices available, so take a look around the Internet to learn about the tools available and choose the one you are most comfortable with. Once you select a tool, read the documentation! When you are altering partitions, it is very important you know exactly what to do. There are rarely second chances on this. In the `fips` documentation you will find a disclaimer that it is not responsible for any lost data. Don't rule it out because of this. Odds are you will find the same disclaimer on even the most expensive commercial product. So what does all this mean?

Most partition tools today are very reliable and very safe. But, problems do occur and data is lost. So when they say back up your important data first, that is not a suggestion to be taken lightly! Also, with a little common sense you can greatly reduce your risk of problems. Before you ever begin to split a partition, make sure the disk has been scanned for bad sectors and defragmented immediately before doing so! In Windows 9x, you will find the disk defragmenter under Accessories, System Tools, Disk Defragmenter. If you cannot find one with your current operating system, you should be able to find one in one of the many Internet shareware archives. Disk Defragmenter will move all of the data to one portion of the partition, so the remainder of the partition will be empty and can be split off without damaging anything. Many partition tools do this themselves, but it is better to be safe than sorry.

Once you have your space and partition problems solved, you can proceed with a normal install as discussed in the first few hours of the book. If you are installing both Windows and Linux from scratch, I highly recommend installing Windows first. During most Windows installs, the master boot record is overwritten one or more times. This will cause you to temporarily lose the ability to boot an existing Linux install without a boot disk. Granted, this can be fixed by using a Linux boot disk. Then you can configure LILO to also boot Windows, and rerun `lilo`. But, why go through all the hassle when all of this should be taken care of for you during the Red Hat install sequence? Remember, running Linux is supposed to be a fun learning experience, not Pain 101.

At this point you should be able to have a Linux and Windows install coexisting on your system, and you should be able to boot into either operating system with LILO. LILO's graphical front end is shown in Figure 19.2. If you are unhappy with LILO's capabilities you may want to explore alternatives. Maybe you want to run more operating systems. Then you might want to look into commercial boot loader programs like System Commander. They have additional features, such as managing installs and partitions, and most can run almost all known operating systems in some rather unusual setups. So if this hour does not come close to meeting your needs, reading about other boot loader tools is a great place to start.

19

FIGURE 19.2

*The graphical front end
to LILO is a nice touch.*

Now you can run Linux, Windows, and almost any other operating system on the same machine. So why did I have you jot down information on your hardware and stuff you wanted to share? Well, maybe you still want to do more. Maybe you want Linux and Windows running at the same time. Well, we will do that with VMware. How about running Windows programs in Linux? Thanks to the hard work of a lot of individuals, we will do that with WINE. Plus, maybe you need to share things with others on your network; that is why we are looking at samba. To set up these tools, you need all the information I asked you to find earlier. Let's start with VMware.

Installing and Configuring VMware

VMware may present an interesting alternative to porting code and trying to implement other operating system's calls. Instead of trying to emulate some form of Windows, the people at VMware, Inc. decided it would be better to create a virtual computer. You should be able to run any operating system on it you want. The VMware client only runs under Windows or Linux, however. It is a commercial product and at around $300 a copy it is not for everyone. However, the company does offer a 30-day free trial.

So if you are the tiniest bit interested, I recommend you give it a try. To obtain the software, you need to go to `http://www.vmware.com` and select to download. You will be asked for some information before proceeding. You need to fill this out to obtain a license for the trial period, which will be emailed to you. Then you will be offered a choice of format and ftp sites to download from. In RPM format, the package for version 2.0 is just under 6 Megs, which is very reasonable when you consider what it is capable of. After you start the download, I recommend taking some time to explore the site.

The VMware site has a lot of useful information to offer and the latest install instructions. It is in your best interest to read the install instructions, especially if you elect to install from a tarball. In this hour, we are only covering the RPM install. After completing the basic install, you will probably want to refer back to the Web site for help in troubleshooting the setup. Although VMware has drastically improved in a very short time, remember that the virtual computer they are creating has to interface properly with your very real hardware. Most hardware combinations will work, although some may need a little help. This is a good time to have the worksheet out that you created earlier in the hour. Let's get started installing VMware in Linux.

After you have the RPM downloaded, I recommend recording the license information that has been emailed to your account. Then as root, type the following to install the package:

```
# rpm -ivh VMware-*.rpm
```

If it installs successfully, you are ready to move on and configure the package. Otherwise, take some time to take care of any dependencies and then try installing again. After the package installs, you need to follow the directions in the email to install the license. This is usually just editing a text file, so it is not a big deal. Once the license is in place, you need to run the configuration script `vmware-config.pl` as superuser.

As the configuration script runs you will be prompted for various bits of information about your system. Most of the questions are about compilers, the kernel, and file locations. Answer the questions as best you can and consult the VMware documentation as needed. Generally, if you answer yes to most of the compiler questions and give the correct paths to everything else you should get a working profile. If during the install you find that it is complaining about missing paths or files, odds are you don't have all the kernel-related packages installed. I know it may seem like the packages should be dependencies, but there are so many kernel choices by so many package names that it would make things very cumbersome. To remedy this problem, get your installation CD-ROMs and verify that all of the kernel packages are installed.

To find the packages, mount the CD-ROM and go to the `RedHat/RPMS` directory. Then run the following command:

```
# ls kernel*.rpm
```

All kernel packages start with `kernel`. To make sure each package is installed type the following:

```
# rpm -Uvh <kernel package name>
```

Don't worry about conflicts. As long as one of each type of kernel package is installed you should be fine. If you have a multi CD-ROM set, you may need to do this for each disc. With all the necessary kernel packages installed, you should be able to run the `vmware-config.pl` script successfully. If you change kernels later on, you may need to rerun this script again.

19

To finish the setup and run VMware complete the following steps:

1. Start VMware by typing **vmware** in a terminal window. You should see something similar to Figure 19.3 after you do.

2. You will be prompted to choose a configuration. This is the first time the program has run, so you need to create a configuration. Choose Configuration Wizard to create a configuration.

3. Decide what OS you want the virtual computer to run and where it will be located. The Configuration Wizard will guide you through the rest of the process.

4. Once you have a configuration selected, click the Power On button to boot up the virtual computer. Windows or whatever operating system you chose should start in a few seconds.

Don't be discouraged if it doesn't succeed on the first try. There are a lot of possible configurations so the Configuration Wizard only covers the basics. Consult the documentation and make adjustments accordingly.

FIGURE 19.3

VMware is the cure for those who have to run more than one operating system at a time.

Although this may seem like a product only for an experienced user, with a little patience almost anyone should be able to set it up. There is a great deal of documentation available at http://www.vmware.com. The Web site will also point you toward other sources of information, such as newsgroups and books. Keep in mind that like many other problems encountered in Linux, odds are someone else has already had it and you can find out how they resolved it.

Installing and Configuring WINE

Instead of incurring the overhead of simulating a whole virtual computer, there may be a simpler alternative in some cases. WINE is an ongoing effort to implement Windows APIs for Unix- and Linux-based systems. It allows many Windows-based programs to run under Linux without any porting at all. To learn more about this you can go to the main Web site at `http://www.winehq.com`. If there is a copy included with your Red Hat distribution, you can install that. However, it would be a good idea to get the latest copy of WINE from the Web site. WINE evolves very rapidly, so even a copy that is only a month old could have drastically different capabilities than the latest version. This also means you need to consult the Web site for the latest news and configuration hints.

When you go to the Web site and look under Downloads you will see a variety of choices. Follow the link for the latest version of Red Hat that offers an RPM download. This should use the libraries included with your Red Hat distribution and, if it doesn't, it will tell you which libraries it has a problem with. Why figure out conflicts on your own when `rpm` will do it for you? You may be presented with the choice of several RPMs. You want to download the latest binary RPM. Don't worry about the source RPM, unless you are forced to manually compile WINE. After you download the file, `su` into the superuser account and change to the directory the RPM is in. Then type the following:

```
# rpm -Uvh wine-*.rpm
```

If there are no conflicts, you are ready to move on. If it complains about library dependencies, go back and see if there is a version better suited to the version of Red Hat you have. If no alternative package can be found, you may have to install from a tarball or build the source yourself. But, don't worry. We'll cover all you need to know to do that in later hours. If your install was successful you probably saw a message telling you to edit your `wine.conf` file and read the man page on `wine.conf`. So let's configure WINE together.

The best way I have found to do this is with one terminal displaying the man page, having `/etc/wine/wine.conf` open in another terminal in your favorite editor, and having a browser open to the WINE homepage. WINE has to be configured to your specific setup so I can't tell you exactly what to type in, but I can tell you what you will probably need to configure. Once you have all of that opened up, we are ready to begin.

The first thing you will see in `wine.conf` is a listing of MS-DOS drive entries of the form:

```
[Drive X]
Path=xxx
```

19

```
Type=xxx
Label=xxx
Serial=xxx
Filesystem=xxx
```

This is how WINE maps Linux to Windows drive letters. You need to go through and make sure the entries are correct for each drive. The possible choices are listed at the top of the file. Odds are you will only need to change the path for the C and D drives, but check the rest anyway. For D you need to put in the path for the CD-ROM. In most cases this is /mnt/cdrom for Red Hat Linux 7.0. The C drive needs to be your primary Windows partition. You need to change the path for the C drive to where you mount it under Linux. I usually create /mnt/c for this purpose, but it is entirely up to you.

At the end of the drives section, you will see a [wine] section. This is where the locations of important Windows folders and paths are listed. Unless you have an extremely custom Windows setup, odds are they will not need changing. If you have been following along in the man page, you probably have noticed that it parallels the configuration file setting for setting. Pretty convenient, huh?

The next two sections deal with dll locations and overrides. I would recommend you leave these as is until you are absolutely certain you need to change them. The other things you may need to change are the serial ports, parallel ports, and printer setting. As best you can, make sure they point to the correct devices. If you want to remove any of them, place a semicolon at the beginning of the line to comment the device out rather than deleting the line. I recommend reading through the remaining sections such as Spy, Tweak, Layout, Console, x11drv, and so on. You should not need to change any of them during the initial configuration, but it is a good idea to know what they are. It is always a good idea to get a few basic Windows programs working first and then try tweaking your configuration to suit the programs you want to run by using the information found on the Web site. Another good idea after you get a basic configuration working is to copy wine.conf to your home directory as .winerc and do all tweaking there. That way individual users can customize the setting to suit the programs they need.

After you are done with the configuration files, take a minute to read the man page for wine. It will give you a general idea on the command-line usage of wine. Once you feel comfortable with that, type in the following:

$ wine sol.exe

If your initial configuration was correct, Windows Solitaire should appear on the desktop after a few seconds and look something like Figure 19.4. After you kick the solitaire addiction, take a look at the terminal window you typed the command in. It probably is full of error messages complaining about font and path problems. That's the nice thing about WINE. If something doesn't work, it gives a lot of information on what failed. So with the online information and a little trial and error, most configurations are fairly easy to debug.

FIGURE 19.4

Switching to Linux doesn't mean you have to give up Windows games.

The fun doesn't end with basic Windows apps, though. A lot of major applications and games are supported. Go to the Web site and under Applications you will find a searchable database of supported applications. In addition to listing the applications, you will be able to find out how well they are supported and who you can contact if you do not have the same success. In fact, if you have been waiting for your favorite games to be ported to Linux, you definitely want to check WINE. Games such as Starcraft and Diablo are supported in addition to applications such as QuickBooks and mIrc. A word of caution though: WINE is an ongoing project, so they make no guarantees of what works properly. So just keep in mind that if you are running anything really important with WINE, you should make sure it is fully supported before risking valuable data.

19

Using Samba

Up until this moment we have explored fun ways to get Windows programs to run in Linux. But what if you are a network administrator and your users demand Windows? You can still use a Linux server and you don't have to spend a fortune on specialized software to make it work. Samba allows you to have a Linux machine share files and printers just like any other machine on a Windows network. Plus, newer versions of samba perform most of the other services NT servers perform on a network. So what exactly is samba? Samba is a suite of tools and daemons that use the SMB (Server Message Block) protocol to perform client-server networking tasks. Samba was started by Andrew Tridgell in 1991, and it has grown into a robust set of tools for networking. To find out more go to http://www.samba.org.

Before we dive in to the details of configuring samba, I would like to take a minute to clarify a few facts and myths about it. These are outlined in the following table.

Statement	*Fact/Fiction*
Samba acts as a file and printer server.	Fact
Samba is a one-stop shop for all networking needs.	Fiction
Samba can act as a Domain Controller, Master Browser, and WINS Server.	Fact
Samba is a very complex and robust package.	Fact
Samba is so complex no mere mortal can configure it.	Fiction
Samba has a setting for everything and then some.	Fact

Before I get carried away in the configuration, let's take a minute and make sure all the necessary files are installed on your system. For Red Hat 7.0, you need the following packages:

```
samba-2.0.7-17

samba-client-2.0.7-17

samba-common-2.0.7-17

xinetd-2.1.8
```

samba-client and samba-common are probably already installed, but it is easiest just to check them all. So mount your distribution CD and switch to the directory with the packages. This is usually RedHat/RPMS. Install the packages with **rpm -Uvh *<package name>*.** You may be wondering what xinetd has to do with samba at this point. It is not for samba—it is for the swat configuration tool that comes with samba. swat is a Web-based configuration tool for samba that can make life much easier. We will set it up in this hour.

Configuring every last detail of samba is quite a challenge. It would take an entire book to cover and is well beyond the scope of the current text. However, doing a basic setup for a home network is fairly simple and we will go through that. Don't worry about all the complex settings you will see in the next few minutes. If there is one thing samba has, it is a lot of good documentation. Remember, samba and all of its relevant files including smb.conf have useful man pages. There are also plenty of READMEs, text docs, and an entire book on samba! To see what is available, type in the following:

```
$ locate samba | less
```

You should have several screens worth of files listed that you can explore, but most of the documentation is in /usr/share/doc/samba-2.0.7 and /usr/share/swat. If you want to take a look at the book, open your favorite Web browser and type in the path /usr/share/swat/using_samba/index.html.

If everything installed correctly, you should have a samba directory under /etc. Go to /etc/samba/ and take a look at the configuration files there. The one we are interested in now is smb.conf. Make a backup of it and then open it in your favorite editor. You will probably want to open a second terminal window at this point so you can browse the man page for smb.conf while you view the file. There is a lot of commenting in the file so you can get a basic idea of the options. For now, the default file is fine. Just take a few minutes to become familiar with it.

You will notice the configuration file is really not all that complicated. It has only two sections: globals and shares. The globals section hold machine and network information such as workgroup name, NetBIOS name, and any server feature settings needed. Until you are a power user and need every last little feature of samba, you will probably only change the first few items. The shares section will appear much simpler. Each share's name is in brackets followed by a comment that tells what it is, the path of the share, and various options and permission settings. The share for a folder and a printer is very similar.

Now that you know about the basic configuration, it is time to look at the relevant commands involved with samba:

- nmbd—NetBIOS name server program.
- smbadduser—Used to update the smbpasswd and smbusers files.
- smbclient—A simple SMB client that allows access to SMB shares. It is very handy for testing a setup.
- smbd—The server responsible for providing SMB/CIFS services.
- smbmount—Similar to mount, just used to mount samba shares.
- smbmnt—Tool used by smbmount to do actual mounting.
- smbpasswd—Tool used to maintain passwords and related files.
- smbprint—Tool used to send print jobs to shared printers.

19

- `smbtar`—Script used to help backup shared drives to tape drives.
- `smbumount`—Used to umount SMB shares.
- `swat`—Web-based configuration utility for samba.
- `testparm`—Used to check the current configuration for errors.

After becoming familiar with the configuration file, it is time to set up `smbd` and `nmbd` as daemons and `swat` as a service. During the install, an `smb` script should have been placed in `/etc/rc.d/init.d/`. If it is present, you can configure the rest in linuxconf so start that now by typing **linuxconf-auth**. If for some reason the `smb` script is not there, you can find an example of it in the samba book that is in the documentation. Once in linuxconf, select the Control tab and select Control Service Activity. You want to edit `smb` and `xinetd`. Both should be set to automatic as shown in Figure 19.5. Then click on the Run Levels tab and assign the run levels. I recommend assigning levels 3, 4, and 5. Then start both of the services, quit out of linuxconf, and choose to accept the changes.

FIGURE 19.5

Set the daemons to start automatically.

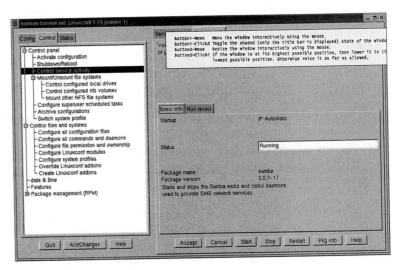

At this point samba should be running. You can confirm this by running the following command:

```
$ smbclient -U% -L localhost
```

As long as you do not see "connection failed," the server is running. The rest is just a matter of configuration details. Now that `xinetd` is running, you can set up `swat` to listen to respond to a port. To do this you need to edit the `/etc/services` and add the following line:

```
swat            901/tcp    swat
```

Now look in the /etc/xinetd.d directory. There should be a swat file in there. It does not need editing, but it is worth looking at to see how service configuration files work. At this point you need to make sure all configuration changes have taken effect and the easiest way to assure that is to reboot the system and take a coffee break. After you reboot and log back in, open a Web browser and enter **http://localhost:901**. You should be prompted to log in. Log in as root and you should see the screen shown in Figure 19.6.

FIGURE 19.6

swat—the user-friendly way to configure samba.

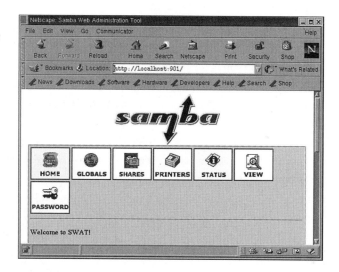

Task: Configuring a Small Home Network Using Samba

19

From this point on, the examples show how to configure a small home network of Windows 9x machines and a Linux system. This assumes you have an existing small network and a basic understanding of networking. If any of this is confusing, consult Hour 18, "Setting Up a Simple Network." Keep in mind that this is just a simple demonstration and should be updated as your understanding of samba grows. It would be ideal to have both machines close by so settings can be quickly compared. Under ideal conditions, you would create a special account and set up DNS and WINS servers, but to see what is going on this will do.

1. On the swat screen choose Globals. Under Base Options choose a name for the workgroup, choose a unique NetBIOS name for the system, and add a descriptive server string. Good choices for the NetBIOS name are server or whatever you chose for the hostname during the installation, as long as it is not localhost.

2. Next for the guest account, choose a user account on the system you control and enter its login. Creating an additional account for this might be a good idea later on. The account is used to determine access and for login purposes.

3. Finally, you need to add the IP address of the Windows machines you are connecting with to the hosts allow list. After doing this, scroll back to the top and choose to Commit Changes. Click on the Status tab and choose to restart both smbd and nmbd.

4. On the Windows machines, open the Control Panel and double-click on Network. Select the Identification tab and make sure a name is entered in Computer Name and that Workgroup is the same as the one entered in swat.

5. Click back to the Configuration tab and choose Client for Microsoft Networks as the primary login. Also click on File and Print Sharing and make sure it is enabled. Click OK to accept changes and reboot the system.

6. After the system reboots, you will be prompted to log in. Use the login and password of the Linux account you specified in swat. Once at the desktop, double-click on Network Neighborhood.

7. At this point, you should see the Windows machine and the Linux system listed as the names you just assigned them as shown in Figure 19.7. Double-click on the Linux machine to open it. It may prompt for a password, and if it does, enter the password for the Linux account you specified to swat.

You may or may not see any folders or printers listed at this time. The important thing is that the machine granted you access. At this point, you know the server settings and the network settings are okay and you can proceed to set up shares.

FIGURE **19.7**

Browsing a samba server in Network Neighborhood.

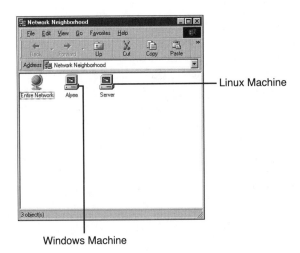

To set up a share, click on Shares, enter the name of a new share (for this example use **home**), and click on Create Share. You should see something similar to Figure 19.8. Under Base Options, enter a meaningful comment and enter the path of the home directory for the account you entered earlier. It should be of the form /home/<login>. Scroll down to Security Options and change Guest OK to yes. For a simple share, this should be all that is necessary. Choose to Commit Changes, go to Status, and restart the smbd daemon. The share should be visible on the Windows machine now when you double-click on the Linux machine. If it is not, try refreshing the window by pressing F5.

FIGURE 19.8

Setting up a share.

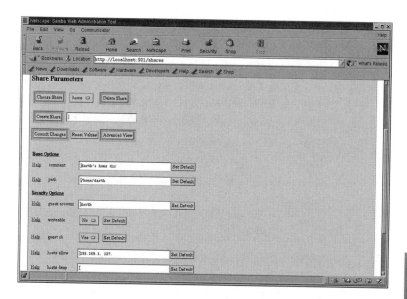

If you encounter problems getting samba to work, remember all of the resources available. There is an entire book installed with samba, plus there is the Web site at http://www.samba.org. It may seem like there are way too many things to configure in samba, but the fact is there is no such thing as a one-size-fits-all network. In the real world, samba needs all of its options to be robust enough to interact with all the networks it is needed in. If things do not work in the first few tries, don't worry—setting up a network takes time and patience.

Summary

In this hour you learned how to make Linux and Windows coexist. You can run both operating systems on the same machine. With VMware they can even run at the same time. Plus, you learned how to use WINE to run your favorite Windows programs under

Linux, and with samba you learned how to make a Linux system interact with a Windows-based network. With knowledge of these tools it is easy to integrate a Linux system into a Windows environment and to retain the benefits of a Windows system in Linux.

Workshop

The Workshop contains quiz questions and exercises to help reinforce what you've learned in this hour.

Q&A

Q Can I put Linux and Windows on the same hard drive?

A Yes, putting Linux and Windows on separate drives is just a suggestion to make things easier. If you put them on the same drive, you will probably need to split a partition and you have to be careful about what happens to each resulting partition.

Q Why can't I get Microsoft Office to run in WINE?

A WINEnce you feel comfortable with that, type in the following: is an ongoing effort to implement the Windows API for Unix systems and is not complete yet. Although the progress of WINE is very impressive, there are still more APIs to implement and as such it is still somewhat experimental.

Q Why does VMware run really slow sometimes?

A VMware is simulating an entire computer so it takes more resources than running a real version of the system. If you look at its requirements you'll see that they are much higher than most software for Linux. About the only thing to do is upgrade your system and wait for future releases of VMware. Efforts are being made to improve its performance.

Q If samba is so complex to configure, why is it so popular?

A Samba is a pretty efficient server. If you optimize a Linux server with samba and shut down unnecessary daemons, it will often outperform a Windows NT server with the same hardware. This can be a considerable cost savings for an IT department.

Quiz

1. What should you do before splitting any partition?
2. Why is WINE faster than VMware?
3. Where is the samba book?

Quiz Answers

1. What should you do before splitting any partition?

   Back up all data, scan the hard drive for bad sectors, and defragment the hard drive.

2. Why is WINE faster than VMware?

   WINE implements the Windows API, whereas VMware simulates an entire computer running Windows. WINE does not suffer from the overhead that VMware does. Of course, in return WINE has to address a lot of Windows-to-UNIX differences that VMware does not have to deal with.

3. Where is the samba book?

   `/usr/share/swat/using_samba/index.html`

Exercises

1. Visit the WINE Web site and search the applications database for your favorite Windows applications. You may be surprised at what is supported.

2. Read the samba book on your system and refine the initial setup we performed in this book.

19

Hour 20

What Every User Should Know About Security

Security issues should be at the top of your agenda whether you have only one computer or you are the systems administrator in charge of a large LAN. Just one vicious attack from someone can leave your system useless. Your data could be stolen or your system could have other damage that impairs your performance. It could even cost you your job if you have been negligent in your security duties. But don't despair because there are proven ways and means to protect yourself and your computer system.

In this hour you will

- Learn why you should be concerned about security issues on your system
- Understand security measures you can take to protect your system
- Discover Shadow Passwords
- Restrict network access from potential threats
- Learn how to tell if your security has been compromised
- Take action after you've been violated

Why Worry About Security?

There is nothing in this world more frustrating than having your home broken into or your property stolen or damaged and feeling helpless to do anything about it.

If you don't take a proactive approach in securing your system, someone will get into your system and do some major damage. If you are responsible for someone else's network, it is your job to protect their data and their property. With the recent attacks on computer systems of all kinds it is imperative that you take adequate action to protect not only your personal computers, but any other systems that you might be responsible for.

From a legal perspective you have to worry about liability in regard to your computers. If someone steals data that belongs to one of your clients, you could be sued or suffer other losses, including a damaged reputation. It is a crazy world and you have to protect yourself from it in as many ways as you can.

In the next part of the hour you will learn about the many different ways you can protect your system. You may not have thought about some of them because they are so simple. So let's fix up your system so you don't have to worry so much about it any more.

Taking Security Measures

Some people don't think about security until it is too late. But, just what is security anyway? We all have seen security officers at malls and other places protecting property, but how does security relate to your computers? There are two kinds of security protection in regard to computers: physical security, which covers the environment such as the structure the computers are housed in; and software security, which relates to the software and data that is stored on your physical computers.

Let's talk about physical security first. This is an area that many people ignore or don't think about when designing computer security systems. It is actually one of the most effective ways to protect your equipment. If a burglar breaks into your home or place of business the first thing they will go for is your computer equipment, especially if you have something that they can sell and make a few dollars from.

Protect the outer perimeter of your property. If a burglar or other people can get in, you will suffer some major losses. One way you can protect your property is to keep it well lighted on the outside and on the inside. Lighting is fairly cost effective and it is easy to install. This in itself will deter most people out to do some mischief.

You can also install burglar alarms, closed-circuit television (CCTV) systems, card access systems, and good locks on all the doors. But taking these measures will not ensure your safety and the security of your property. You have to use some common sense along with this. You should be aware of who is in your place of business and what they are doing there. Some people can walk into a computer department pretending to be someone else and walk out with a laptop or a computer disk with your important data on it. I call these internal threats. You should also carefully check out any employees that work for you or people that you let into your place of business. These measures apply to your home environment too, to some extent.

I can't emphasize enough the importance of making regular backups and storing the backup media in a very safe place. If your system were attacked tomorrow, would you have the backup tapes to restore your entire network and all your data? I hope so because sometimes that is the only option that you have. Some viruses can destroy your system to where you have to replace most of the equipment and start all over again if you can't safely remove the virus from the system. This usually involves viruses that render hard drives useless, thus removing your access to them. So be safe and backup. If possible, have your computer equipment in a room or area that can be locked. This is one of the simplest and most cost-effective measures that you can take. In the next section you will learn some things that you can do to protect your data and software. The bottom line here is to do everything you can to keep out the unwanted elements.

Computer security has been one of the hottest issues in the news for the last several years. Unless you have been underground or never listen to radio, watch television, or read the papers you couldn't have missed it. These stories are usually about people making vicious attacks on Internet sites or personal computers in homes, offices, and businesses.

One form of attack is to install a special computer program on a remote computer, perhaps at a university or college and then use that program existing on someone else's computer system to mount attacks on other computer systems. This type of attack usually involves sending so much email or other types of files that the system is overloaded and crashes. Most of these attacks have been on the larger Internet service providers (ISP) such as AOL. That's not to say that everyone else has been left alone—there have been enough attacks to go around; some of them have closed down entire organizations.

20

You may have heard of the viruses and other dangerous programs that are attached to email. When you open the email, the virus is transferred to your computer system. There are also macro viruses that are attached to word-processing files as well as other documents.

How do you protect yourself from these types of attacks? The solution is not simple, but you normally shouldn't open email if you do not know where or who it came from. You should not download programs without using a virus scanner and never download or open documents that you are unfamiliar with. To be double sure, download or purchase a good virus scanner such as those from McAfee and use them. You can never fully protect yourself because crackers are always inventing something new, but you can make your life a little easier.

In the next section we will talk a little about using passwords and other methods to protect yourself and your equipment.

A *cracker* is a person who breaks into a computer system to do mischief, whereas a *hacker* is a person who attempts to crack computer code or break into a system to test the vulnerability of the programs or systems.

Using Shadow Passwords

When you first installed Red Hat Linux 7.0 you were given the option to set the Shadow Passwords (see Figure 20.1). You may not remember this because most people elect not to use them, especially if they aren't using Linux on a network.

FIGURE 20.1

The Authentication Configuration screen with the Use Shadow Passwords option.

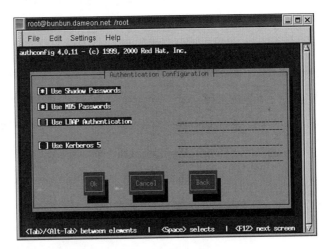

Task: Viewing the Authentication Configuration Dialog

In this Task you will learn how the select Shadow Passwords options. You can choose to enable them or not.

1. Login as root.

2. At the command prompt (#) or in a terminal screen, enter `authconfig`.

3. The Authentication Configuration dialog should pop up showing you the Shadow Passwords options. You can elect to use them or not. You have two options: OK to enable them or Cancel to exit the dialog.

4. In this case, just press Cancel to exit the dialog since we won't set them at this time.

You have the option to enable Shadow Passwords or MD5 Passwords. If you choose not to select these options, all your user passwords will be stored in the `/etc/passwd` file. The `/etc/passwd` file is not protected with extensive encryption so anyone can look at it. The password is encoded so that the average person will not know what it is. You won't see anything but garbage if you look at it with a text editor, but someone with the right computer knowledge can crack it. By doing this they will be able to get your password and other information. If you elect to use the Shadow Password option, the passwords will be encrypted. Any person with the right knowledge can "crack" an encoded password file and log into your system using a user's password with all the rights and privileges of that user.

If you decide that using Shadow Passwords (and you should) will help to secure your system, you can use the steps outlined in the preceding task to install them. I would recommend this, especially if you are running Red Hat Linux 7.0 on a network or you have access to the Internet.

If you are interested in learning more about Shadow Passwords, you can find more information at `http://www.redhat.com/mirrors/LDP/HOWTO/Shadow-Password-HOWTO.html`. There is also a HOWTO on your CD called Shadow-Password-HOWTO. Probably every book that Macmillan publishes mentions this topic, so you can check them out at `http://www.mcp.com`.

With the confidence that your computer is now protected a little bit better by using Shadow Passwords, we'll now move on and you will learn about how to restrict access to your network.

20

How do you select the right password? Even though it is an extensive subject there is some logic to selecting a good password. You should use a password that has both alpha and numerical characters. For example, if your name is Elizabeth Laker and your social security number is 402-39-3196, you can use your first initial, your last name, and about four random numbers from your social security number. You can also use parts of your telephone number.

Restricting Network Access

Security should start with the users whether you are on a single PC or on a network. You can set up your user accounts in linuxconf to give users the privileges that they need to get the job done while restricting them from areas that they don't need access to. Refer to Chapter 17, "Using linuxconf and Graphical Administration Tools," to find out more about setting up your user accounts where security is an issue.

There are many other steps that you can take to protect your system from intrusions. Some of these can be as simple as educating your users as to how to properly select a password. Have you ever noticed people in companies and offices that have their password written on a sticky note and stuck on their computer screen for everyone to see? These are the types of things that you need to look for as a network administrator. All a cracker needs is one password to get into your system.

You can also control what your users can do by controlling permissions that you grant them when you create their accounts. You will normally use linuxconf to set up these accounts as discussed previously. You should never give a user more rights and privileges than he actually needs to do the job.

linuxconf is a valuable tool that you can use to control your user accounts and therefore enhance security on your system. You should check the linuxconf log file on a regular basis to see any strange activity that might be occurring. You currently have two log files: Boot messages and LinuxConf log under the Logs option.

A few years ago when the Internet was relatively new, almost every company gave each of their users access to the Internet. With the recent attacks on various Web sites and networks, companies have wisely chosen to restrict this access to only those people who actually need it. This is a good idea because it prevents problems on both ends (especially if it is through an intranet, which is just a way of connecting your network to the Internet). It may get some complaints, but that is better than you having to deal with a lot of problems caused by unauthorized access to your system.

Crackers and others can sometimes gain access to your network by searching for an open port on your system. Most networks have many open ports or places where someone can get in and you as the systems administrator may not know it. You can think of ports as the different ports on the back of your computer, an open doorway into your system. If you want to use your modem, you access a serial port (usually). You access the printer port (usually LPT1 or LPT2) to use your printer. If you want to access the Web you access port 80, which is the HTTP protocol port.

You can find ports that the computer is aware of but may not be using by looking in the /etc/services file. So now that you know people are scanning your ports looking for an open gateway, how do you protect yourself? The answer is simple: You adopt the same methods they use. Crackers use a tool called a port scanner that scans a computer's ports to find a way in. There are many of these programs out there, but two of the better ones are NMAP and PortSentry. NMAP can scan an entire network by issuing a single command.

PortSentry can be downloaded, easily installed, and can be protecting your network in no time. The reason that I like PortSentry is that it can detect and actively block port scanning programs and prevent them from accessing your system. Although I dearly love talking about PortSentry and all that it can do there just isn't enough time (there never is) to tell you all about it here. You can download it free and learn more about it. You can get it at http://www.psionic.com/download/. Please be aware that this is distributed as source code and you will have to install it and do a little configuration before you can run it. But, when the hard work is over you will know that it is all worth it because your system will be more secure.

Of course one of the best ways to protect your system is with a firewall installed on a proxy server. We discussed this in Hour 18, "Setting Up a Simple Network." For more information on firewalls, please see your HOWTOs on the CD or search the Internet.

The more software you have running on your system the more you are making yourself available to outside crackers. Crackers can get into your system, install a program or gain access through an existing program, and you'll probably never know they are there. You should never let users bring in software from home or download software and install it. This is asking for big trouble. You should never download shareware or freeware without checking it out. Some freeware programs will install other programs on your system and let crackers know things about your system or even give them access to it. So be careful.

Another way to enhance security is to limit the services that load when you boot your machine. There probably isn't any reason to load every service available to you. If you aren't connecting your machine to Windows-based systems, don't load samba. If you don't play games, don't load games. One way to limit services is to tell Linux which services you want to start and which you don't want to start. You can do this using a utility called `ntsysv` (see Figure 20.2).

Task: Starting `ntsysv`

1. Click on the Red Hat Linux 7.0 Main menu and open a terminal window. You can use GNOME Terminal if you like or work from the command prompt. To access GNOME Terminal click the Linux Main menu, Utilities and you're there.

2. Type **ntsysv** at the command prompt (#).

20

3. The dialog will give you the option of selecting which services you want to start on boot up and which ones you don't want to run.

4. Make your choices and select either OK or Cancel.

That's as simple as it can get and it gives you great security.

FIGURE 20.2

The ntsysv *dialog allows you to select services to run at boot up.*

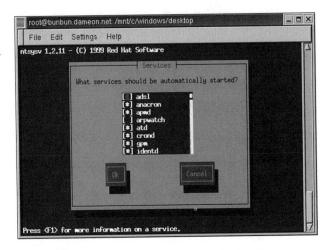

In this part of the hour we have discussed a few of the many ways you can protect your network from intruders. If you want to know more, search the Internet by using the term "security" and you will find many interesting sites to visit. There are many books out there on computer-related security, such as *Peter Norton's Network Security Fundamentals*, published by Sams. This is one of the better books that I have read on the subject.

You have done some things to make your network more secure, so now let's see what we can do about using a shell that was actually designed to be secure. It is called the secure shell (SSH) and it is available for you to use.

Using the Secure Shell

Linux has many shells, which were discussed in Hour 15, "Working with Shells." The default shell is normally bash, but another kind of shell that can be used to protect your system is called SSH (secure shell). You should not confuse this with sh or some of the other shells such as ksh. I will explain exactly what it means and how it works.

SSH is a protocol that lets you log in on another machine on a network, transfer files, and execute commands. What is so different about this? Well, networks that use FTP

(File Transfer Protocol) and Telnet are open to security problems because those protocols are weak in the authentication areas, which makes them insecure. Since most networks use these protocols, SSH was developed to provide a more secure protocol for accessing other computers on a network.

SSH is an excellent alternative to FTP and Telnet because it provides secure shell or file access to your computers. Currently, it can replace Telnet, FTP, rlogin, rsh, and rcp. There are two versions available at the time of this writing: SSH 1 and SSH 2. Here is basically how SSH works in a nutshell:

- RSA is a public/private key for authentication. SSH uses this type of authentication to identify users.

- When you set up an SSH server, it creates two keys: public and private. The private key is used locally while the public key is shared with those who log in to the server.

- A client logs in to the SSH server and has the host's private key, which it received either from a trusted source or directly from the SSH server (host).

- The client needs to verify that it is communicating with the right host so it sends a random message to the SSH server. The message is encrypted with the public key. If the message contains the same key that the host has, they will be able to communicate. The host will read the message if the key is correct and send it back to the client. The client then knows that it is talking to the correct host.

Because SSH involves encrypted authentication it is illegal in some countries, so be careful that you don't upload or send it to a friend in another country.

SSH is available for just about every operating system including Windows, Beos, Unix, Linux, and a multitude of others.

If you want to install this program on your Red Hat Linux machine, you can get it from the Secure Shell Community Site. The SSH 1 and SSH 2 versions can be downloaded from ftp://ftp.ssh.com/pub/ssh. You can also get it from http://www.cs.hut.fi/ssh. Don't look for it on your Red Hat Linux CD because it doesn't come installed. The current version of SSH is 2.

20

The ssh command can be used to log on to a remote computer or server and execute a command. The correct syntax for executing ssh is ssh [options] host [options] [command].

When you download the SSH package you should also receive documentation that will instruct you how to install and configure it. The installation and configuration is too extensive to cover here. You won't have any problems if you follow the instructions and read the documentation. One of the better sources I found for SSH was *Special Edition: Using Red Hat Linux 6.2* (Que), a book by Alan Simpson.

In the next section you will learn about using the secure remote password.

Using the Secure Remote Password

Secure Remote Password (SRP) is a protocol that provides a method to secure your password through authentication. It virtually solves the problem of securely authenticating clients to servers. It plays the role of being a drop-in replacement for insufficient password authentication. SRP is just a technique to accept a password from a user and produce a secure authentication and key-exchange as its result. SRP provides secure Telnet and FTP connections.

SRP is part of the Stanford University SRP Authentication Project and is available under open-source licensing terms. It was first proposed in 1997 and the variant in use today, SRP-3, was first published in 1998 after lengthy discussion and refinement. The SRP is the core technology behind the Stanford SRP Authentication Project. The project's main objective is to improve network security from the ground up by integrating secure password authentication into most protocols in use today. The Stanford project site serves as the semi-official home of the SRP distribution.

The Stanford project also offers more secure versions of Telnet and FTP. These enhanced versions offer encrypted authentication and cryptographic key exchange to establish a secure connection. You can find out more information and download a free copy of the Telnet/FTP programs from `http://srp.stanford.edu/srp/`. The documentation on the site informs you how to install the program and how to configure it to protect your system.

You can download the most recent version (Version 1.5.2 as of August, 2000) at the following sites:

`ftp://srp.stanford.ed/pub/srp/` (Palo Alto, CA)

`ftp://labrea.stanford.edu/pub/srp/` (Palo Alto, CA)

`http://srp.stanford.edu/srp`

SRP has been designed to protect passwords against passive and active network attacks. Because both Telnet and FTP have some security issues involved, this is a good way to further protect your network from aggressive intrusion. You should check out the

Stanford Project site for more information. Now that we have covered a lot of ground concerning network security, it is time to find out what to do when you really are attacked.

How to Tell If You've Been Violated

If you have taken all the precautions that you can to protect your system you may think that you are safe. These precautions include such things as controlling user activity, instructing users in proper password procedures, setting up a firewall, and monitoring your network on a daily basis. Things seem to be going smoothly, no problems and nothing that looks to be out of the ordinary. But how do you actually know that someone hasn't gained access to your system?

Fortunately for you, the UNIX/Linux systems create all kinds of activity logs letting you know what the system is doing. These logs are stored in /var/log. You should be looking through these on a daily basis, checking for strange or unusual activity such as port scanners. One file that usually tells you if your ports are being scanned is the message file in /var/log/messages. If you check this each morning you can tell if someone is scanning your ports. You can see some of the directories in the /var/log directory in Figure 20.3.

FIGURE 20.3

The /var/log directory contains many kinds of system log files.

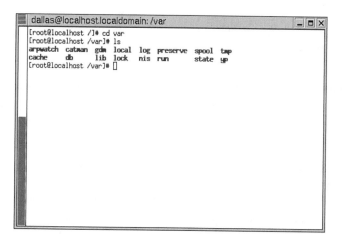

While you are inspecting the /var/log/messages file, look for any failed attempts from unknown or unfamiliar sources. These failed attempts (if they are pretty close together in time) can represent a failed attempt by a port scanner.

Although monitoring and auditing your system on a daily basis can go a long way toward protecting your system and detecting intruders, you still need to pay attention to other areas. When a user has left the company or has been terminated, always make sure that he is immediately removed from the system. You should keep a list of past passwords and never let anyone use them. You might even write a script file that will compare new passwords with old ones and reject any matches.

I mentioned earlier that physical security was extremely important too. Be sure your users are trained in how to handle their machines and their passwords. Be sure they turn off the machines (shutdown) at the end of each shift and that they don't leave passwords taped to their computers.

If you see a lot of violations, you can expect some kind of an attack and you should be on guard for it to eventually happen. In this section you learned what to watch for in order to determine if your system has been violated, but it is up to you to constantly monitor your system and make sure that users are doing their part for security. In the next section you will spend some time taking action once you have discovered a break-in.

What to Do After a Break-In

The action that you take after a confirmed break-in is determined by what kind of break-in occurred. If it was a virus attack, you should shut down all of the computers on the network until you can determine what kind of virus was used. Sometimes you can use virus software to safely remove the virus and restore your system.

Some types of viruses are much more destructive and you may have to replace CPUs, hard drives, or even entire systems. In this event you will probably have to replace most equipment and restore your system from backup tapes or other media. You should make sure your programs are running and the virus is securely removed before restoring your data. You can save yourself a lot of work.

If a cracker has succeeded in getting in through an open port, you should make copies of all your log files. This serves as evidence in case the cracker is caught and you have to go to court. You should also document everything that you can. In most situations these log files can help you to track the person(s) who got into your system (if they haven't messed with the log files and covered their trail). Your documentation and copies of your log files can be the only evidence in helping to track down the culprit and putting them where they need to be.

Only after you are sure that everything is documented should you delete your log files that have been tampered with. You should back up the entire system, especially files that show tampering was involved, before deleting files or closing ports.

It is never too late to close open ports that you missed or take other actions that you might not have thought about to protect your system. You have to have an inventive mind and always be on the alert for new ways of doing things. There are a few things that you can do to prevent future attacks.

You should have a good intrusion detection system installed, such as Tripwire. If you haven't already done so you should make sure your log files are written to a safe, secured server where they aren't accessible to others. Always disable unneeded services, as we discussed earlier. Implement good user access levels and try to install the same software across the entire network platform.

If you want to use Tripwire, it is not hard to find. Just search for Tripwire with your favorite Web browser or go to the site at http://www.tripwire.com/.

You should remember to keep your users informed about the system, but only tell them what they need to know. You will need to inform the company executives or others directly responsible for the network. They should be told everything because you may end up in court if the intruder is caught. The reason for being honest with them up front is that you will need their support and their money should they decide to press charges against the person(s) who broke into the system.

There is a wealth of information about network security on the Internet. Here are a few sites that you can visit for more updates and news releases as well as other important information:

CERT (Computer Emergency Response Team) at http://www.cert.org/

CERIAS (Center for Education and Research in Information and Security) at http://www.cerias.purdue.edu/programs.html

COAST (Computers Operations, Audit and Security Technology) at http://www.cs.purdue.edu/coast/

20

There are various newsgroups, hacker newsgroups, and Web sites devoted to the subject. The hacker newsgroups can have some good, valid information but you have to be careful because some of these people aren't as informed as you may be led to believe. But then again, some are. So, the secret to maintaining some kind of sanity here is to keep auditing and monitoring your system, make sure your virus software is up to date, and most important of all, keep informed.

Summary

In this hour you learned many aspects of securing your computer and your network against many kinds of threats. Some other topics included Shadow Passwords, which you learned how to set up; and the SSH, secure shell utility, which enables you to communicate with other computers on a network and assure that your communications are private. You took a look at what to do to prevent your system from being compromised, what to do if you suspect it has been violated, and what to do after you are sure it has been violated.

Workshop

The Workshop contains quiz questions and exercises to help reinforce what you've learned in this hour.

Q&A

Q How do I manage a user account if I can't get GNOME to run?

A This is a common problem if your network or computer has problems with the X server. All you have to do is log in as root and issue the linuxconf command from the command prompt (#). You can take care of many of your maintenance tasks from linuxconf.

Q I typed in LinuxConf at the command prompt but it doesn't run. What happened?

A Linux is case sensitive. To run linuxconf from the command prompt or shell you have to type it in all lowercase: **# linuxconf**. Of course, if you have GNOME running you can access it as root from Linux Main Menu, System.

Q I tried to run the ntsysv utility to restrict some services on my computer, but it won't run. What happened?

A You must run it as root. If you aren't running as root and you're at the system prompt, type **su**, enter your root password, and then enter **ntsysv** at the prompt (#).

Quiz

1. What is the name of the utility that you can use to set the Shadow Password and what directory does it store the passwd file in?

2. This is a thinking question so put on your thinking cap. What do you personally feel is the most destructive type of break-in?

3. What is probably the most cost-effective way of protecting your property?

4. What program or utility could you use to change user accounts, add user accounts, and manage privileges?

Quiz Answers

1. What is the name of the utility that you can use to set the Shadow Password and what directory does it store the passwd file in?

   You would run the `authconfig` utility to set the Shadow Password and the `passwd` file is in the `/etc` directory.

2. This is a thinking question so put on your thinking cap. What do you personally feel is the most destructive type of break-in?

   There can be several answers here but the most important thing is that you're thinking about them. Probably the most destructive type is a "denial of service" attack because it can put a company out of business for long periods of time, especially if they depend on the Internet for business reasons. This could be anything from "spamming" to a serious, dangerous virus that destroys your data.

3. What is probably the most cost-effective way of protecting your property?

   One of the simplest and most cost-effective is having plenty of lights. This deters burglars and others and helps to protect your property to a certain extent but it should be backed up with other forms of supported security measures and procedures.

4. What program or utility could you use to change user accounts, add user accounts, and manage privileges?

   linuxconf will allow you to change your user accounts as well as other things.

Exercises

1. You have absorbed a lot of information and done a lot of hard work in this hour, so how about doing a simple little exercise to help you to understand your personal concept of network security. For this task all you need is a piece of paper and a pencil. You don't even have to look at the computer if you don't want to. Write down all of the ways you can think of to break into the largest computer system in your town. This can be the bank, library, or general store down the street.

   Now I'm hiring you as a computer security consultant to protect my establishment, the one you have planned to break into. How would you go about protecting it? Obviously you know all the ways to get into my system, so write down all the ways you can think of to protect it from outside intruders and internal threats. Remember those two words, internal and external. Those are where the threats come from.

20

HOUR **21**

Automating Tasks with Shell Scripting

In previous hours you learned to set up and use your Linux system. You also learned the basics of shell scripting. In this hour you will see the value of shell scripting and which tool to use for which job. There are quite a few scripting languages to choose from and some are better choices for specific tasks than others.

You are probably asking why you need scripting at this point. There are so many graphical tools for system maintenance already. Plus, most distributions come extremely preconfigured. But, it is unlikely that there will ever be a preexisting script or tool to suit every user's needs, considering it is unlikely that any two Linux users have exactly the same needs and preferences. Most Linux users do have repetitive tasks to perform. If you have repetitive tasks to perform and want to free up some time, then it will be worth your while to learn the basics of shell scripting.

In this hour you will

- Learn how shell scripts work
- Understand how to write a shell script
- Learn the advantages of various scripting languages

How Shell Scripts Work

The scripting languages discussed in this hour are all interpreted languages. This means that they are not compiled and stored in machine code form. Every time the script is run, the shell or interpreter parses the file into commands it recognizes. It then executes the recognized commands. This is fine for simple tasks, but it is not how you would write a 3D-render engine program. Running an interpreted script has a significant amount of overhead. If you have any programming background it is easy to visualize why. Imagine trying to run the program while you are compiling it with the compiler. In addition to the resources required by the program, you have to provide all of the resources the compiler needs. Granted, most interpreters are friendlier on resources than a compiler, but the program will still run slower.

Shell scripts are simple text files that usually begin with a bash-bang statement that specifies which interpreter to read the script with. The format of the bash-bang statement is

```
#!<path of interpreter>
```

An example would be

```
#!/bin/bash
```

The appropriate interpreter is started and the rest of the script is read by the interpreter. The interpreter then translates the scripts into a sequence of commands that it can execute. It will then execute the script. Depending on the implementation of the interpreter, the whole script may be translated at once, or only the piece currently executing may be translated.

Writing Shell Scripts

Writing a shell script does not have to be a difficult task. Shell scripts are supposed to make life easier, not make you pull your hair out. Just because writing a script is not as complex as coding a software package does not mean you can do it without any planning. If you are writing a very simple script you can just go ahead and dive into an editor, but if it is anything more substantial than a few lines you should take a few minutes to plan.

The first thing to do is jot down exactly what you want the script to do. You should always be clear on what you want the script to do before you begin. If you cannot write it down, you are not ready to start writing the script. The next step is to sketch a very simple flowchart of the steps you want it to take. Again this is for your benefit, so take the time to make sure you know what actions need to occur in the script. At this point you could begin writing the script, but I advise one more step. Take a minute and figure out how you want to lay out the script. Just briefly jot where you want the variables, maybe what their names are, where you want any functions, and the general flow of the script. If you don't understand this now, don't worry. It will be explained later in this chapter and in many other programming texts. There are few things more frustrating than having to edit a 1000-line script that someone just haphazardly threw together. Plus, when you have variables assigned all over the place or values repeated hard coded, it just makes things worse. Hard coding occurs when you have a constant such as the path to a file directly entered into the script instead of assigned to a variable and using the variable throughout the script. Instead of having to change the variable you assigned the path to, you would have to go through and change every single instance of that path in the script.

A general rule of thumb is if you are dealing with a file path or any value that is used repeatedly, make it a variable and place it at the top of the file. That way you have to change only one value in one obvious place later on. Also, I cannot emphasize this enough: *Comment your code!* You may understand the code today or tomorrow, but three months down the road when you need to modify the script again, odds are you won't. Even though you have the script before you it will take nearly as long to understand it as it would to write the whole thing from scratch. This is another lesson I admit I have learned the hard way.

> When you write scripts, give them meaningful names. If the script searches for core dumps, call it something like `find_core`, not `foo`. Silly names like `foo` are used in the examples because the examples have little real use. They are just used to demonstrate certain concepts of a language.

gawk

gawk (GNU awk) is one of the newest implementations of the awk programming language. awk was developed by Alfred V. Aho, Peter J. Weinberger, and Brian W. Kernighan in 1977. The name of the language comes from the initials of their last names. There are plenty of other versions of the awk language available too, such as awk, nawk, and POSIX awk. There are usually multiple implementations of each version of the language.

21

gawk typically resides under /bin and under /usr/bin. In Red Hat 7.0, gawk is under /bin and there is a symlink under /usr/bin. Although gawk does have a man page, odds are you will need more information for it to be useful. You can find quite a bit of useful documentation under /usr/share/doc/gawk-3.0.5. There is also an ample supply of online resources and books available. A good place to start online is http://www.gnu.org/manual/gawk/index.html.

The awk language is best described as a pattern-matching tool. It is great for processing text files, extracting data, gathering statistics, and generating reports. awk scripts are often easy to write since awk handles most of the processing details on its own. You may find the actual syntax very similar to C, which makes sense considering the background of the people involved in creating it. However, you will also find the actual programming much easier. Strings and arrays are dynamic in awk and file I/O has been greatly simplified.

awk can be used directly on the command line or run from a script file. Although all awk scripts technically could be run from the command line, it is a good idea to place any multiline awk programs in a file. As you will see in the following examples, an awk program is simply declaring the source of the data, what to search for, then what to do when you find a match. This pattern may not be apparent in very large scripts, but it is still there. Let's start with the simplest program possible. This program will count words per line and you can run it on a file called foo.txt that looks like this:

```
My fellow Linux users
A great day is at hand
The day you will learn the power of awk.
```

Run

```
$ gawk '{print NF ": " $0}' < foo.txt
```

The output will look like this:

```
4: My fellow Linux user
6: A great day is at hand
9: The day you will learn the power of awk.
```

The backticks (``) are used to prevent the shell from trying to process the contents of the awk program. This is to appease the shell and is not part of awk. After looking at this program you can probably guess that awk has a lot of predefined variables. Let's take a look at what just happened. This awk program does not have any pattern specified, so it matches anything and then performs the specified action. NF is a predefined variable that contains the number of fields per record and $0 contains the entire record. The fields in a record are accessed by $1, $2, ... $n. To see the fields accessed, run the preceding program again and change $0 to $1.

At this point you are probably wondering what a record is and what a field is. A *record* is a line in a text file and a *field* is a word or number separated by a space. Thus the 4, 6, and 9 in the output of the preceding example are the number of fields per record, which you can see is the number of words per line. This also is part of the reason awk can only be used on text files. Binary files would appear to contain a lot of special characters and greatly confuse awk. The new line character and the field separator character can be redefined, but for the time being assume that words are fields and lines are records. The actual syntax of the gawk command is

```
$ gawk 'program' <input files>
```

You can list as many files to process as you want, and it will sequentially go through and process each. All of the usual piping and redirection applies to gawk I/O as well. If you have the program in a file, you can use the following syntax to run it:

```
$ gawk -f <program name> <input files>
```

Earlier I mentioned that awk handles patterns. Where syntax is concerned there are three types of patterns. The special BEGIN block pattern is executed before any records are processed. The special END block pattern is executed after record processing has finished, and the regular patterns are specified between a pair of slashes (/ /) before the actions. If no pattern is specified, awk automatically assumes true and the action is executed.

Actions are specified between braces ({ }) and can contain as many commands as necessary. The default action if none is specified is to print $0, which prints the contents of the record. What really makes all of this useful is awk's ability to match regular expressions. Regular expressions are special patterns of characters used to specify and match strings. Support for regular expressions allows extremely complex search sequences without an extreme amount of scripting. A regular expression consists of normal characters (such as a, B, and 1) that match themselves, and metacharacters that specify special actions. Think of the metacharacters as commands and not as characters. A listing of the supported metacharacters is shown in Table 21.1.

TABLE 21.1   Metacharacters Supported by gawk

Metacharacter	Meaning
\	Escape sequence (signifies next character has special meaning, or if it precedes a metacharacter, the metacharacter will match like a regular character).
^	Start matching at the beginning of a string.
$	Match at the end of a string.
/^$/	Match a blank line.

21

TABLE 21.1 continued

Metacharacter	Meaning
.	Match any single character.
[ABC]	Match A, B, or C.
[A-Ca-c]	Match by ranges; that is, A, B, C, a, b, or c.
foo|bar	Match foo or bar.
[ABC][DEF]	Match an A, B, or C. Then match a D, E, or F.
*	[ABC]* means match zero or more occurrences of A, B, or C.
+	[ABC]+ means match one or more occurrences of A, B, or C.
?	[ABC]? means match zero or one occurrence of A, B, or C.
()	Combine regular expressions. For example, (Blue|Black)berry would match Blueberry or Blackberry.

In addition to regular expressions, awk also supports all of the C comparison operators and compound pattern operators. Going through all the details of these operators is beyond the scope of this book, but you can find a great deal of information on this in the documentation. awk also supports C's flow control and looping constructs. It supports multidimensional arrays, internal and user-defined functions, and many other features. So now let's see what we can do. Try the following to see how a normal awk program works. This program is a simple pattern matching program that will run on the foo.txt file from earlier. The script looks like this:

```
BEGIN {x="My"; print "ready to run"}
$1 == x {print "Found my"}
/awk/ {print NR ": matched awk"}
END {print "Done reading " NR " records"}
```

To run it type

$ gawk -f test.awk foo.txt

and the output will look like

```
ready to run
Found my
3: matched awk
Done reading 3 records
```

In this example you can see BEGIN is executed first, setting the variable x equal to "My". Variable types do not need to be declared in awk. The script then prints the message "ready to run". Now each record is read in and tested against each pattern. The first record starts with "My" so the first pattern matches and prints "Found My". It is then tested against the second pattern, but nothing matches since the first line in foo.txt does not contain "awk". The second record is read and fails both pattern tests. Then the third record is read and fails the first test, but the line contains "awk" so the second pattern matches and the record number along with "matched awk" is printed. This is the end of the records, so the END block is executed. The END block just prints out the number of records read.

awk is an easy and powerful pattern-matching tool that anyone with C programming experience should be able to learn to use with ease. If you want to know if you should use awk for a script, ask yourself this question: Am I only trying to extract and format text data from a command or a text file without special processing needs? If you can answer yes, then awk will be a very good choice. If you need a nice interface or if you need really complex processing capabilities, you may want to look at another language. awk is far too complex to cover in a single chapter and if you find a lot of use for it I recommend looking into a good book on the subject. A lot of offerings have popped up in the last few years and you should be able to find one to your liking.

Tcl and Tk

The tcl (Tool Command Language) scripting language and the tk toolkit provide an environment to create graphical user interfaces for the X Window system. The language is fairly easy to learn, and it allows much more rapid development of GUIs than conventional programming. Tcl/tk was developed by John K. Ousterhout while he was a professor at the University of California at Berkley. It is used in a wide range of software products today. The official Web site for tcl/tk is `http://dev.ajubasolutions.com`. The site is hosted by Ajuba Solutions, which supports commercial and open source tcl/tk efforts.

The power of tcl/tk is in its ability to hide the unpleasant interface details you would normally have to deal with in C or a similar programming language. In the actual scripts you only have to specify what the interface should look like and what actions it should take. You are not responsible for determining when something has been clicked, when to refresh the screen, or any other common GUI problems.

Before diving into tcl/tk programming, check and make sure the proper packages are installed. To do this type the following:

```
# rpm -q tcl
# rpm -q tclx
```

If the packages are installed, their names should have been displayed after you ran the command. If they are not installed currently, please get your Red Hat CD-ROMs and install them, or download the latest versions from `http://dev.ajubasolutions.com`.

21

The important binaries for tcl/tk are tcl, tclsh, wish, and tclhelp. There are man pages available, but you will find the tclhelp command much more useful. Try all of these commands to see if everything is ready. If they all gave you a response, then it is time to begin examining tcl/tk.

The shell interpreters you will use to interact with tcl/tk are tclsh and wish. The difference between tclsh and wish shells is that tclsh supports only tcl, whereas wish supports tcl and the tk window features. The shell can run interactively or in script form. To create a simple tcl script, save the following as hello.tcl:

```
#!/usr/bin/tclsh
puts "Hello World"
```

Exit the editor and use chmod +x hello.tcl to make it executable. Now when you run hello.tcl, it will print "Hello World". Unlike most other scripting languages, the tclsh interpreter may be in different locations on different Linux distributions. In that case the script would have to be edited, or you would have to use special tricks to figure out where the shell is.

Commands in tcl are very simple. They follow the form

<command name> <arguments>

Commands should be terminated with a semicolon, although it is not required as long as they are entered one command per line. A comment in tcl is any line that begins with #. Variables in tcl can have almost any name and they do not have declared types. tcl determines if a variable is a string or a number by its usage. All of the ANSI C supported numeric types are understood by tcl. I recommend opening a tclsh shell at this point by typing tclsh in a terminal window and trying the examples that follow. It is really the best way to understand tcl. Don't be afraid to experiment here. You would really have to try hard to hurt something.

```
$ tclsh
% set foo 5
4

% set baz 13;
13

% set fruitcake "has a half life of 1 million years" ;
has a half life of 1 million years

% # comments are ignored
% set foo 4; set baz 12; # multiple commands are allowed
12
```

To use the value of one expression inside of another, you enclose the expression in brackets.

```
% puts [ expr 50 / 2 ] ;
25
```

To access the value of a variable you would precede its name with a $. Thus to print out the value of fruitcake you would:

```
% puts $fruitcake ;
has a half life of 1 million years
```

tcl supports single and multi-dimensional arrays and its indexing is string based. To see what this means take a look at the following:

```
% set simple(0) 1;
1
```

```
% set array(1, 1, 1) 3;
3
```

```
% set schedule(lunch) "12:00";
12:00
```

```
% set schedule(meeting) "3:00";
3:00
```

```
% puts $schedule(lunch);
12:00
```

tcl also offers several array commands to aid in searching, and to find out the size of an array try the following:

```
% array size schedule;
2
```

String manipulation is very easy to perform in tcl using the append command. When more advanced string features are needed you can use the string command.

```
% set str "Lunch is at "; append str $schedule(lunch);
Lunch is at 12:00
```

Tcl flow control and looping constructs are very similar to ANSI C and would take a while to explore. If you want to learn more about them consult the documentation. There is also support for file I/O and procedures (the tcl version of a function). Right now we must move on to the GUI portion of tcl.

The tk toolkit provides support for graphical components known as widgets. Widgets can be of the following types:

- **canvas**—Used for drawing objects
- **entry**—Used for entry of a single line of text
- **frame**—Used to hold other widgets
- **listbox**—Displays strings and allows one to be selected

21

- **menu**—Displays a menu bar and menu items
- **text**—Displays multiple lines of text
- **label**—Displays a single line of static text
- **button**—A clickable button widget
- **checkbutton**—Displays a check box
- **radiobutton**—Displays multiple mutually exclusive check boxes
- **scale**—Displays a slider-like widget

You can create widgets interactively with the wish shell, which is handy for experimenting. Once you figure out what you want to do you can put it in a script, and then your interface will be ready for testing. All of the widgets follow a hierarchy from the root window known as ".". The details of the hierarchy are beyond the scope of the book, but it is not difficult to learn and with a little time it will become very intuitive. To see an example of widgets, save Listing 21.1 as `mywidget.tcl`.

LISTING 21.1   Simple Widget Example using `wish`

```
#!/usr/bin/wish

foreach i {raised sunken flat groove ridge} {
        label .$i -relief $i -text $i;
        pack .$i
}
```

Use `chmod` to make the file executable and run it. If everything is entered correctly, you should see the window shown in Figure 21.1. The program creates five types of labels. The `pack` command places them on the window in the default location.

FIGURE 21.1

A simple GUI using wish.

Tcl/tk is a great tool for rapidly developing simple GUI interfaces. You should consider using tcl/tk if you like csh- or C-style syntax or you need to develop a GUI quickly and the application does not require extreme performance or exotic buttons, menus, and so on. Tcl/tk offers a lot of nice features, but it is not a replacement for conventional GUI development in C or C++. If you want to develop a full-scale application, you are still probably better off writing it in C or C++ using a set of X Window libraries. You will learn more about this in Hour 24, "Introduction to Linux Programming."

Perl

If there is one scripting language you heard of before trying Linux, odds are it's Perl. Perl stands for *practical extraction and report language*. It was developed in the mid-1980s by Larry Wall. Perl gained great popularity as a choice language for CGI programming on the Web. It may be an interpreted language, but it has immense capabilities that allow many tasks to be greatly simplified. It has gained popularity in most areas of software and network administration. There are even interpreters available for Windows-based systems.

The important thing to understand about Perl is that it is probably the closest thing to an all-powerful language currently available. It takes care of most of the annoying language details other languages leave to the users, such as declaring variable types and handling memory allocation. It has absorbed the best features of most of the major programming languages. With such an eclectic variety of features there is more than one way to do just about anything in Perl. A common joke is that you can do anything with three lines of Perl code. While this is an exaggeration, once you learn Perl you will realize that it is only a minor exaggeration. Unfortunately, while a language wielding this much power makes it is easy to do any task, it is just as easy to shoot yourself in the foot and make things ridiculously hard.

If you decide Perl is for you, I highly recommend investing in a few good books on it and consulting the resources online. The main Web site is `http://www.perl.com` and from there you can access many other helpful Perl sites. You can also download the latest source code and Perl packages. Before going any further, though, find out what version you have. The easiest way to do this is to type `perl -v`. The version shipping with Red Hat 7.0 is 5.6. It is very important to know which version of Perl you have because there are no guarantees of compatibility between versions. If something fails when you move a Perl script from one system to another, that is the first thing to check.

Perl supports almost every flow control and looping construct possible. It can also access any shell, which makes it popular with many network administrators. Another advantage of using Perl is the ability to process binary files. This is a weakness that stops many Linux commands including `sed` and `awk`. To see an example of Perl accessing the shell, try Listing 21.2.

LISTING 21.2 Accessing the Shell with Perl

21

```
#!/usr/bin/perl
# test.pl lists the contents of a directory
$ curr_dir = `pwd`;
@listing = `ls -al`;
print "Listing for $curr_dir\n";
```

LISTING 21.2   continued

```
foreach $file (@listing) {
        print "$file";
}
```

Save this as test.pl and use chmod to make it executable. When you run it, it should show the contents of the current directory with details. Although it would be easier to type in the commands manually in this case, think about what is possible. Almost any system administration task could be reduced to a single Perl script. This would not only save time, but it would also reduce errors. Think about having to generate 500 user accounts and having to set the permissions on each one. You could do this through linux-conf, but what are the odds they would all be entered correctly? A single Perl script could generate all the accounts, set permissions, and generate home directories.

If you need a script capable of virtually anything, you probably want to write it in Perl. Perl really has only three drawbacks: The syntax is a little confusing while learning the language; there is no guarantee of compatibility between versions, though this is usually only a minor issue; and Perl is an interpreted language, so if the program is not fast enough you will still have to code it in C, C++, or some other compiled language. If you are okay with those three limitations, I recommend reading up on Perl. Here are some good books to start with:

Sams Teach Yourself Perl in 21 Days by Laura Lemay

Perl: The Complete Reference by Martin Brown

Programming Perl by Larry Wall, Tom Christiansen, and Jon Orwant

Python

Python is really the new kid on the block as far as scripting languages go. It was developed in 1990 by Guido van Rossum and is named in honor of the Monty Python troop. Python is public domain and object-oriented language, so it is useful as both a scripting language and a rapid prototyping tool. Python can be viewed as an effort to bridge the gap between scripting languages such as Perl and compiled languages such as C++. Python code is also very easy to read, as opposed to some of the cryptic syntax of other scripting languages. Python has been ported to run on virtually any operating system.

Although you are not required to use the object-oriented features, they allow very sophisticated code that can be expanded. The object-oriented features support inheritance and encapsulation of data, making Python almost C++ without the need to declare variables, worry about memory details, and many of the other aggravations. To see how readable Python code is, try Listing 21.3.

LISTING 21.3   List Arguments

```
#!/usr/bin/python

import sys
print "Args are: ", sys.argv
print "The number of the counting shall be, ", len(sys.argv),
print "and ", len(sys.argv), " shall be the number of the counting."
print "Program name is ", sys.argv[0]
print "The last arg is ", sys.argv[len(sys.argv)-1]
```

Save this as `test.py` and use `chmod` to make it executable. When you run the script, type in some additional arguments after its name. The first line prints the list of arguments. Notice that the first one is `test.py`. The command is an argument too. The next line tells how many arguments there were including the command. The third line prints the program name and the last line prints the last argument you typed in. Of course, you probably figured all of this out from reading the listing and it makes sense if you have any programming background in C or C++.

If you want a lot of capabilities, easy-to-read code, and object-oriented support, then you want to try Python. There is no real downside to using Python aside from devoting the time to learn the language initially. If you want to learn more, start at `http://www.python.org`. You can obtain the latest versions of Python and learn about many great Python resources. If you prefer books, here are a few choices:

Learning Python by Mark Lutz and David Ascher

Python: Essential Reference by David Beazley

Sams Teach Yourself Python in 24 Hours by Ivan Van Laningham

Summary

In this hour you learned about several of the advanced scripting languages available. You learned how to go about writing a script and you know how to decide what language to write it in. You know where to find additional information on each of the scripting languages. Remember, in Linux there are many ways to do things and you have just been shown some of the choices. You do not have to learn the intricate details of every tool and every language, but you should try to learn the advantages and disadvantages of as many tools and languages as possible. Above all, use the tools you are more comfortable with. Even if one language has an advantage over another for performing a certain task, if you are not comfortable with it, use the language you are comfortable with. If you follow these guidelines, scripting will always be an enjoyable experience.

21

Workshop

The Workshop contains quiz questions and exercises to help reinforce what you've learned in this hour.

Q&A

Q I heard the tcl\tk stuff was on the Scriptics site. What happened?

A Scriptics changed names to Ajuba Solutions. You can find its Web site at `http://www.ajubasolutions.com`.

Q I installed a copy of Python from `http://www.python.org`. Why do I keep getting errors when I try to run any scripts?

A If you install Python manually, quite a few options have to be set. Consult the Python documentation and make sure all paths are set correctly.

Quiz

1. You need to scan binary files for information. Should you use awk?
2. Can you use widgets in tclsh?
3. What makes Python such a good prototyping tool?

Quiz Answers

1. You need to scan binary files for information. Should you use awk?

   No, awk cannot process binary files. If you have to process binary files, use Perl.

2. Can you use widgets in tclsh?

   No, tclsh only understands tcl. It does not understand the tk toolkit that the widgets are a part of. If you want to use widgets, you have to use wish.

3. What makes Python such a good prototyping tool?

   Python can mimic the object-oriented behavior of languages like C++ and the code is very easy to read. This allows the prototype to be very thorough and easy to translate into compiled code.

Exercises

1. Write an awk to scan system logs for a particular type of entry or for the events from a particular user and display the results.
2. If you are interested inPperl, study the sample scripts that are available from `http://www.perl.com`. Try to understand a new script every day. With patience you will master Perl.

HOUR 22

Troubleshooting and Getting Help

Although you will learn the basics of how to run a Linux system from this book, inevitably you will encounter a problem or question that this book does not cover. Everybody's system is different, so it is impossible to cover everything that could possibly go wrong in 400 pages (or 800). One of the most important skills you should acquire to be a successful user and administrator of your Linux system is good problem-solving skills. In fact, you will most likely develop those skills as you become more advanced. This hour, you will learn how to approach a problem or new topic, and where to go for help.

In this hour you will

- Learn a simple, general approach to solving problems and getting help
- Discover more resources for help other than this book
- Report a bug to Red Hat using Bugzilla
- Use Bug Buddy to create a bug report

One of the greatest strengths of Linux is the amount and quality of help that is available. There is no tech support line staffed by the lowest rung of the tech ladder. You don't have to hire a consultant or local guru to help you through a problem (though they are available if you need a guru on retainer), or take a class (although that helps).

As we have stressed repeatedly throughout this book, Linux is all about understanding as much as possible about the system, and having nothing about the system hidden. It's all available for everyone to study and learn. This is a beautiful thing for two reasons:

1. You can become a Linux guru yourself. All it takes is practice, time, experience, and desire.

2. There are thousands of people out there who have a lot of knowledge and experience who are happy to help others with problems.

Because everything is out in the open and available for anyone who wants to become familiar with the innermost workings of the system, Linux users as a whole tend to be a group of very knowledgeable people. This makes it quite a simple matter to get help when you have a problem—probably more help than you actually wanted. Quite possibly help from the person who created or maintains the very piece of software with which you are having a problem.

The following list is a general strategy you can use when solving a problem or learning a new topic. After the list are some more specific guidelines to using the resources mentioned in the list.

The Smart User's Guide to Troubleshooting

The first thing you should do when you encounter a problem is to sit back and take a deep breath. It's easy to become frustrated and angry when you can't do something you want to do, or when your computer responds in a way other than you expected, but if you are going to solve the problem (and eventually, given enough time and effort, you will solve the problem), you must be in a calm state of mind. If you are reading this book and are operating a Linux system, chances are that you are curious and a bit of a tinkerer/do-it-yourselfer. Problems are an excellent opportunity to learn. Not only do you learn a lot by solving the problem, but you also learn a lot about how the part of the system works, and you might be pointed to other interesting topics that you might not have been exposed to or thought about before. The following are a few tips that can handle the most common problems:

- If you get an error message, read it carefully. An error message is your first clue to how to solve the problem. If you get a segmentation fault or a page fault, or if the

22

application crashes and you see a core file in the directory, the problem is almost certainly a bug. Make a bug report using Bug Buddy.

- Make sure you have the most up-to-date, stable version of the software. Many problems are fixed in newer versions, so if you don't have the latest version, upgrading might fix it.

- Read the relevant man and info pages, as well as documentation that comes with the application in /usr/share/doc. These documents might also refer you to other documents that could help.

- See if there is information on the problem in the Red Hat guides, in a HOWTO, mini-HOWTO, newbie-ized HOWTO, or guide at linuxdocs.org or linuxnewbie.org. The Linux Resources Page is a great collection of links about all things Linux, just about every Linux resource on the Net. The site is maintained by SSC, which publishes the Linux Journal. You can find it at http://www.luv.asn.au/linuxresources.html.

- Search for information on the problem in the Red Hat archives, and on the Web and Usenet.

- If there is no information on the specific problem, start doing some background reading on the subject. Learn as much as you can about the subject, so that you can pinpoint what the error message means or at least report the problem intelligently.

- Keep a log of how you have gone about trying to solve the problem. Take a separate sheet of paper and write down a possible cause and solution on each sheet. Then write down what you have tried for each possibility on the appropriate sheet of paper. Try to make your notes as detailed as possible so that you don't get confused, and also so that you can later help others who have the same problem. Troubleshooting can be like following a maze—after you have gone up several blind alleys, if you haven't kept track of where you have been, you might forget to try certain steps that would lead to a quick solution.

- Try posting to the mailing list or Usenet group that seems to be the closest in subject to your problem. Also, try IRC to get an answer or some clues right away, particularly the #linux and #linuxhelp channels.

- Try the mailing list for your local Linux Users Group (LUG). You might even be able to bring your computer to the next LUG meeting and get help right there.

- If you are seriously pressed for time, consider hiring a Linux consultant in your area.

The Linux Documentation Project

It is important to remember that the Linux Documentation Project (LDP) is made up of volunteers. The guides, HOWTOs, and other documentation that you will find at the linuxdocs Web site exists because someone thought that the piece of documentation would be useful. There isn't anyone in charge of what gets written, although there are guidelines on how to write and there are people in charge of what gets posted. For this reason, there isn't much consistency in the level of detail, the assumed audience, the amount of theory and background, the writing quality, or the general usefulness of the guides and HOWTOs. Some are extraordinarily useful references, and you will find yourself referring to them again and again. Others give a rich amount of background information, which can enable you to solve problems on your own, because the guide or HOWTO taught you how a concept works. Some HOWTOs, particularly the mini-HOWTOs, are simply step-by-step instructions or advice on how to solve a particular problem or approach a task.

If you find yourself wishing that there was a HOWTO on a particular topic, consider writing one yourself. Remember, there is no central authority at the LDP who assigns writing projects. All you have to do is get on the mailing list, announce yourself, announce the document you will write, read the LDP HOWTO, and start writing.

Mailing Lists

Mailing lists are slowly becoming as important, if not more important, to maintaining the Linux community, solving problems, and getting help. Red Hat sponsors a number of mailing lists, which can be a great resource. The level of complexity and knowledge of the users varies widely, from the newest newbie to kernel hackers, so don't be put off if you have a hard time understanding most of the posts. A great way to learn is to scan the posts that you don't understand, just to get a feel for the vocabulary. Eventually, you will find yourself understanding more and more, particularly when you come across terms you saw in the mailing lists, HOWTOs, guides, and books.

Man and Info Pages and Source Code Comments

The man and info pages provide a wealth of information about almost every part of the system. If you're not sure which term to use to look up a man or info page, you can use the GNOME Help Browser to browse through listings of every entry (the lists are long!) Finally, do not be afraid to look at the source code for an application. If you installed your Red Hat system via the installation program on the CD-ROM, then you might not have the source code on your hard drive, but there should be a CD-ROM that contains source code. You can also find source code for programs at the Red Hat Download site at `http://www.redhat.com/apps/download`. Even if you don't know anything about C or C++ code, you can often get a feel for the program and an answer to your questions from the programmer's comments.

> If you have a problem or question, chances are that someone else has already had the same problem. You can search Usenet for keywords about your problem with Deja, Google, or AltaVista.

Reporting Bugs to Bugzilla

One of the most useful ways for new members of the Linux community to help the project is to report bugs. Anybody can report bugs, even if you just started using Linux yesterday. As a Red Hat user, you can report all bugs to the central bug repository at Red Hat, which is called Bugzilla.

Red Hat's Bugzilla page is at `http://bugzilla.redhat.com/bugzilla/`.

Bugzilla is a bug reporting system that was created by Mozilla.org (you learned about the Mozilla Web browser in Hour 11, "Linux Applications"). You can learn more about how Bugzilla works by reading the Bugzilla Fact Sheet at `http://www.mozilla.org/bugs/`. Red Hat has taken the Bugzilla software and applied it to its own bug reporting system, also called Bugzilla. Bugzilla is a database of bugs and a system for reporting and fixing bugs, as well as for requesting software enhancements.

To look at bugs or to report a bug, you must have a Bugzilla account. You can create a Bugzilla account on the Web page. To learn more about Red Hat Bugzilla, read the FAQ at `http://bugzilla.redhat.com/bugzilla/redhat-faq.cgi`.

Reporting Bugs Using Bug Buddy

An easy way to report bugs is to use the brilliant bug-reporting program called Bug Buddy. Bug Buddy, created by Jacob Berkman, makes reporting a bug as simple as entering some basic information and clicking a few buttons.

The purpose of Bug Buddy is to make it easy for the user to send a bug report, while automatically collecting the information that is useful for the developer. Bug Buddy can also help you determine whether a program crashed because of something wrong with your system or because of a true bug in the program.

Before Bug Buddy, if your application crashed you had to start gdb and then try to re-create the conditions that caused the crash. You had to know about stack traces and how to run gdb (not an easy prospect), as well as enough about programming to be able to read the results of the trace. With Bug Buddy, anyone can submit useful bug reports to Bugzilla or the individual project's bug tracking system.

> Although you can submit bugs to Red Hat for any application that is part of the Red Hat Linux distribution, a more direct way to report a bug is to send your Bug Buddy email to the maintainer of the application or the bug tracking system of the project the application is part of. X-based applications usually have an About menu entry that lists the maintainer. Non–X-based applications virtually always list the maintainer in a README file or in the man page for the application.

The more ways users discover to crash Linux applications and the more bug reports that are submitted, the better Linux will become in the future for everybody. Don't be shy about submitting a bug report because you think that it's probably a common problem that has already been reported. You might actually be the first person to have experienced that exact problem, or you might give a particular insight on your bug report that nobody thought of before. At any rate, the more bug reports you submit, the better you will get at writing them.

Features and Requirements of Bug Buddy

For such a small utility, Bug Buddy has some extraordinarily useful features:

- It automatically finds and includes the components on your system; there's no need to hunt through /proc files for them yourself.
- It gathers a stack trace automatically, either from a crashed application or from the core file.
- It can be started by double-clicking a core file in GNOME File Manager or from the crash error message dialog box.

You must have the following packages installed to use Bug Buddy:

- gnome-libs
- libglade
- gdb

Task: Submit a Bug Report with Bug Buddy

1. When you get an error message such as the one shown in Figure 22.1, click Submit Bug Report. Bug Buddy starts. You can also enter the command bug-buddy at a shell prompt.

FIGURE 22.1

The segfault message contains a button for you to start Bug Buddy directly.

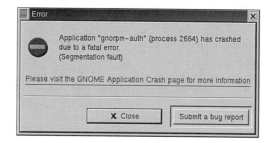

2. The first time you use Bug Buddy, you must enter your contact information, including your name, email address, and the full path of your sendmail command, as shown in Figure 22.2. Bug Buddy searches for this path when it is installed, so the default pathname is most likely correct.

FIGURE 22.2

After you enter your contact information the first time, it will be retained in a configuration file.

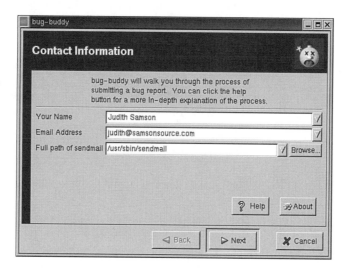

3. In the Report Information box, shown in Figure 22.3, the software that crashed will automatically appear in the window. Enter the version of the software that is on your system manually.

FIGURE 22.3

The report information gives basic information about the type of bug and the application involved. Don't forget to enter the application version number!

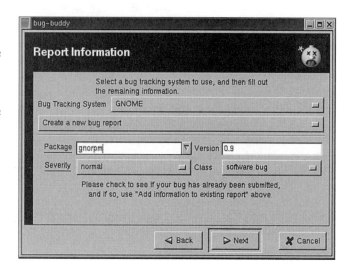

4. In the Description dialog's Short Subject for the Bug Report field, shown in Figure 22.4, enter a bug report title (this will be the subject of the email you send). then in the Full Description of the Bug field, enter all the information you can think of about the bug. You might have to go through all the steps again as you describe them to make sure you don't miss anything.

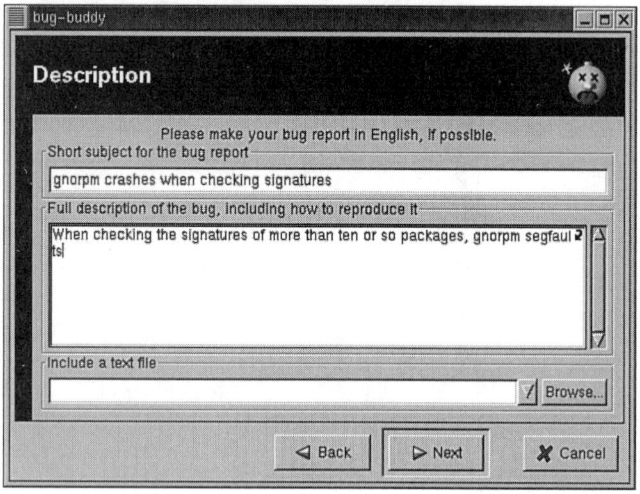

FIGURE 22.4

In the Description dialog, enter exactly what happened before, during, and after the problem occurred.

5. The Debugging Information dialog box, which is shown in Figure 22.5, is particularly important. Here is where Bug Buddy displays the debugging information that is essential to fixing the bug. Check the box that is pertinent to the bug:

   • If the application crashed, check Attach to a Crashed Application.

   • If there was a core dump, check Read from a Core File.

   • If there was some other problem for which there is no record, you can check Skip this Step.

6. Bug Buddy will probably have checked the correct box for you, but verify to make sure. Bug Buddy should also have entered the correct application and Process ID number automatically, in the case of a crashed application, or the core file pathname in the case of a core dump. This is the most important step in the process, so do not check Skip this Step unless you are reporting a documentation bug or making a feature request.

FIGURE 22.5

Bug Buddy collects the debugging information automatically after a core dump or crashed application.

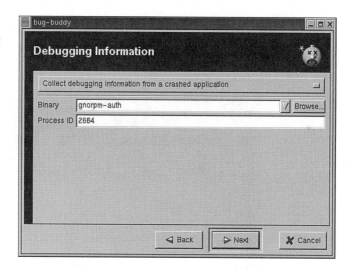

7. In the next step, Bug Buddy displays the debugging information. An example is shown in Figure 22.6.

FIGURE 22.6

*The debugging infor-
mation might not mean
much to you, but it can
mean a lot to the devel-
oper of the application.*

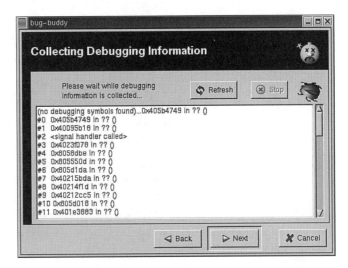

8. The next window contains the system information that Bug Buddy automatically detects, shown in Figure 22.7. Look over the information to make sure that it is correct.

FIGURE 22.7

*Bug Buddy checks your
system's configuration
automatically.*

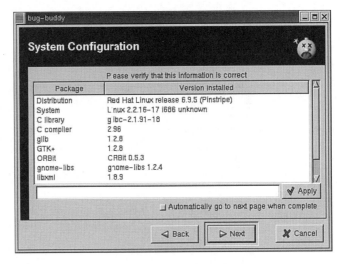

9. When Bug Buddy is done, click Next. In the Submit Report dialog box, you can select Submit Bug Report to the Bug Tracking System, in which your bug report will be emailed to the address you specify. You can also send the report to yourself only if you want to double-check it before sending it to the bug tracking database, or you can save the bug report to a file to send later.

22

10. The last dialog box is a synopsis of your email information. Click Finish to submit the bug report.

> Do not close the crashed application until you have filled in all the Bug Buddy dialog boxes. Otherwise, the process will be killed before Bug Buddy can read the results or send a bug report.

Other Books on Linux

Once you start to get more proficient in Linux and have digested the information that books like this one can give you, it's time to move on to the next level. There are many books out there that will enable you to continue your Linux education beyond the introductory level. Some particularly good ones are

Red Hat Linux 7 Unleashed, by Bill Ball, et.al., Sams Publishing, 2000.

Running Linux, by Matt Welsh, et. al., O'Reilly, 1999

Essential System Administration, by Aileen Frisch, O'Reilly, 1995

The Linux Reading List HOWTO, listed in the HOWTOs as Reading-List HOWTO, lists many more books that are recommended for a complete Linux education.

Summary

In this hour you learned how to solve problems with your system and get help. You learned a general method for solving Linux problems, and a hierarchy for finding resources to answer questions. You learned how to report bugs to Bugzilla and how to use Bug Buddy to develop a bug report.

Workshop

The Workshop contains quiz questions and exercises to help reinforce what you've learned in this hour.

Q&A

Q Can't I just reinstall to fix a problem?

A Probably, but once you have customized your system, (which you should do), and added new applications, it would be more time-consuming to reinstall than to investigate and fix a problem. It is also very bad administration practice, and you never learn anything that way.

Q Where can I find my local Linux User's Group?

A There is a central listing of all the LUGs at http://www.linux.org. There is also a HOWTO on creating your own LUG, called User-Group HOWTO, at http://www.linuxdoc.org.

Quiz

1. True/False: The LDP assigns authors to write documents.

2. If you get a segmentation fault or a page fault, what should you do?

3. Name two IRC channels that are useful for getting help and asking questions.

Quiz Answers

1. True/False: The LDP assigns authors to write documents.

   False. Anybody can write a document for the Linux Documentation Project, although you should announce yourself to the LDP and read the HOWTO-HOWTO.

2. If you get a segmentation fault or a page fault, what should you do?

   Submit a bug report to the maintainer of the application that faulted.

3. Name two IRC channels that are useful for getting help and asking questions.

   #linux and #linuxhelp

Exercises

1. Open the source code for an application in a text editor. Look at the comments. Can you make sense of them? Comments in C are encased in a slash, followed by an asterisk. For example: /* This is a C comment. */.

2. Subscribe to the Red Hat 7.0 mailing list.

3. Go to http://bugzilla.redhat.com/bugzilla and read a bug report.

Exercise Answers

1. Open the source code for an application in a text editor. Look at the comments. Can you make sense of them? Comments in C are encased in a slash, followed by an asterisk. For example: /* This is a C comment. */.

   Mount the Red Hat source code CD-ROM, and run an rpm -Uvh on a SRPM file. The source code tar file should be copied to /usr/src/redhat/RPMS/SOURCES. Untar the tarball with the command tar zxvf [filename]. The source files should be in a subdirectory of the source directory that the tar command creates. The source subdirectory is usually called src. Open a file in emacs, vi, gedit, or another text editor.

2. Subscribe to the Red Hat 7.0 mailing list.

    Go to `http://www.redhat.com/mailing-lists/` and subscribe to `redhat-list`, or another list that interests you. Note: `redhat-list` is very high volume.

3. Go to `http://bugzilla.redhat.com/bugzilla` and read a bug report.

    Click Query Existing Bug Reports and select a bug report that interests you.

Hour 23

Compiling and Installing Applications from Source Code

Up until now everything you have installed on your system has been in an RPM (Red Hat Package Manager) package. RPM packages are a great way to distribute and install software and they are extremely popular. However, not every piece of software you want may be available in RPM format. Maybe you want to try the latest version of a program that no one has built a recent package for or an early beta of a new program that has never been made into a package. Perhaps the RPM install failed or you need more control over the install.

If any of the above is true you will have to install the software from a tarball. This chapter will discuss every step in a tarball install. However, every tarball install is slightly different, so this chapter will concentrate on the general procedures and answer as many "what if" questions as possible. Before diving into the tarball install, let me emphasize one thing: *You must read the directions!* This is not the neat, fully automated procedure that an RPM install is.

In this hour you will

- Learn exactly what a tarball is
- Understand the steps in the install process
- Extract files from a tarball
- Configure a Makefile
- Compile and install source code
- Clean up after the install
- Uninstall a tarball installation

A Tarball Is Not a Ball of Black Goo

What is a tarball? It is not made of tar, it is not a ball, and it is definitely not gooey. The tar comes from the `tar` (tape archive) tool that is used to create a tarball. As for the ball, think of putting all of the files for a program on pieces of paper. When you have to move them from one place to another, would you really want to deal with every single piece individually? Odds are you wouldn't. It would be easier to put all the pieces in an envelope or, in this case, roll it up into one big ball. Instead of dealing with all of the files independently, you just have to move the ball. This is why it has been so popular since the early days of the Internet. Package the program in a ball and throw (ftp) it to anyone who wants it.

The only difference between a tarball and a ball of paper is when you extract the files. Obviously when you extract a file from the paper ball it will come out crumpled, whereas extracting a file from the tarball will give you a perfect copy of the file and you can extract it as many times as you want. You can recognize a tarball by its `.tar` extension. But, at this point, we are only looking at an archive. Nothing has been compressed, so the tarball is actually a little larger than the size of the files it contains. This is not desirable from a storage standpoint and it is certainly undesirable for Internet distribution purposes. Nobody wants to download a 50MB archive over a dial-up connection.

The answer, of course, is to compress the archives. You can do this with the `gzip` command on a tar archive, which creates a file with a `.tar.gz` ending, or you can compress the files using `tar`'s options when the archive is created, which typically has a `.tgz` ending. If you come from a Windows background, you are probably familiar with zip, rar, or arj files. They are based on the same idea. In fact, the Windows utilities `pkzip` and `Winzip` can process `.tar` files. With a little searching I am certain you can find other utilities with similar capabilities.

The Tools of the Trade

The next thing to look at is the tools required to install a tarball. Technically an install could require virtually everything, but typically if it is extremely unusual it will be included in the tarball or it will be pointed out very clearly in the documentation. Generally you will need gcc, autoconf, make, tar, and gzip, and a working knowledge of each program. So let's take a look at these tools.

gcc is the GNU Compiler Collection. Given enough time it will eventually be able to compile anything. Currently it supports C, C++, Objective C, Chill, Fortran, and Java. It is the standard for Linux systems. I will not dive into the details of it here, because to support so many languages and be able to optimize the code, the package has to be extremely complex. In fact, there is more than enough documentation on it to warrant a book. To find out more, go to the gcc homepage at gcc.gnu.org.

autoconf is a tool used to generate configuration scripts for software source packages. Once the scripts are generated, autoconf is no longer needed. Ideally this tool allows the developer to generate a script typically called configure. A user who wants to install the software from source code should have to run only the configure script before compiling. It will generate all of the Makefiles, installation scripts, and other scripts that would normally need to be edited before a compile and an install could proceed. So although you may not need autoconf installed, now you know what is going on if you use a configure script. The actual details of how autoconf works and what is involved in creating a configure script is beyond the scope of this book, but you can find a lot of information online. Two good places to start are sources.redhat.com/autoconf/ and http://www.amath.washington.edu/~lf/tutorials/autoconf/.

make is a tool used to generate programs and related files. It also often handles the task of installation, clean up, and sometimes even running test sequences. make gets all of its information from a Makefile. make allows users to compile and install complicated pieces of software without manually typing lengthy compiler commands and without knowledge of source code. It also can keep track of which files are up to date so you don't spend time compiling anything unnecessary. We will explore the details of a Makefile later in this hour. If you want to learn more about make, go to http://www.gnu.ai.mit.edu/software/make/make.html.

tar (tape archive) is the program used to place files into an archive file and extract the files from an archive. It was originally created to back filesystems up on tape, but has since grown into a very versatile archiving tool. It has an extensive list of options, but you will find you only need a few common ones in most cases. The untar options will be explored in a bit. To learn more, consult the man page and http://www.gnu.org/manual/tar/html_chapter/tar_1.html.

gzip is a GNU compression tool. Its usage is very simple and it usually achieves very good compression. You can find out more about its usage on a man page, and you may find the online documentation interesting. It can be found at http://www.gnu.org/manual/gzip-1.2.4/gzip.html.

The Installation Process

The installation process may vary from program to program so this section cannot cover every possibility. The best way to learn is by working through an example. Most programs at least use autoconf, so the example we cover will use that. Everything that needs to be done in a non–autoconf-based install cannot be predicted. The general patterns in configuration files will be explored, though. In this hour we will install Bombermaze, which is a GNOME-based Bomberman clone. If you have spent as much time as I have playing this game, I apologize ahead of time for bringing all productivity to a halt.

To begin with, go to http://www.gnome.org/applist/ and follow the Browse the Software Map by Category link. You can follow the link to find many other GNOME applications, but today you are just looking for Bombermaze, so follow the Entertainment link. There you will find a link for Bombermaze, which gives you more information about the program. You will also find a link to the Bombermaze home page at bombermaze.sourceforge.net. Go to the home page and take a few minutes to read about the program. It is always good to have some idea of what you are installing. Take a look at the requirements section and look at all the libraries required. In an RPM install, all of that would be checked for you. Now aren't you glad you don't have to do that all of the time?

After you are through examining the Bombermaze site, go to the download page and download the bombermaze-0.6.2.tar.gz. RPMs are available for this program, but we want to learn how to do a manual install. You should save this file in your home directory or in /tmp. Many of the steps can be performed in a user account, but odds are the actual installation of the files will have to be done in the root account. So if you are not in the superuser account while performing the following steps and you encounter problems, odds are that is why.

Untar the Tarballs

Like most things in Linux, there are several ways to uncompress and extract tarballs. Two examples will be examined in this section. The first uses gzip to get the tarball and then uses tar to extract the files. To do this, switch to the directory of bomberman-0.6.2.tar.gz and type the following:

```
# gunzip bombermaze-0.6.2.tar.gz
# ls
...
bombermaze-0.6.2.tar
```

gunzip has decompressed the archive so now only the uncompressed tarball remains. To extract the files from the tarball, enter the following:

```
# tar xvf bombermaze-0.6.2.tar
```

A long listing of files should follow the command similar to the list shown in Figure 23.1 and if you list the contents of the directory now you should find a bombermaze-0.6.2 subdirectory. Generally, any tarball you download will usually extract into a subdirectory of its own. The tar options used here were x for extract files, v for verbose output, and f to specify the file, which was bombermaze-0.6.2.tar. The alternate method uses another switch of tar. If you want to try the other method, use gzip to compress the tarball again. Then type the following:

```
# tar xvzf bombermaze-0.6.2.tar.gz
```

FIGURE 23.1

All of the files are extracted into the bombermaze-0.6.2 *subdirectory.*

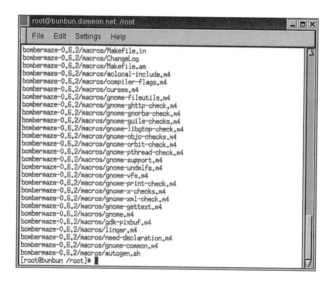

The z option tells tar to run the archive though gzip before extracting the files. Aside from saving keystrokes, this leaves the file in compressed form, whereas the previous method leaves the uncompressed tarball. In this example it does not make a lot of difference, but on a 30MB or greater gzipped file, this can make quite a bit of difference. If you encounter any problems with tar, I recommend starting by checking the man page. It is rather lengthy, but it is also thorough.

Configure the Makefile

This program's Makefiles and install scripts are set up by autoconf so this will be a piece of cake. But, you should still take some time to look through the files generated by the configure script. If autoconf had not been used, odds are you would have some manual editing to do. If you ever encounter this, do not worry. There will be a text file in the tarball that will tell you what you need to edit. It is up to you, however, to determine the correct information to enter.

Whether autoconf was used or not, the first step is always to read the included text files. Change to the bombermaze-0.6.2 directory and read the text files you find there. Usually, the names of the text files are in all capital letters and typically you will find at least a README and an INSTALL text file. Depending on the program you may find various other text files. After you are comfortable with the directions, configure all the files and run all the scripts in the sequence you are told. In this case, just run the configure script by typing the following:

```
# ./configure
```

You will see several screens of text displayed reporting all the things configure is checking and doing. At the end of the output listing you will see a list of files created, as shown here:

```
Creating Makefile
Creating src/Makefile
Creating src/maps/Makefile
Creating src/themes/Makefile
Creating src/themes/default/Makefile
Creating doc/Makefile
Creating doc/C/Makefile
Creating intl/Makefile
Creating po/Makefile.in
Creating macros/Makefile
Creating bombermaze.spec
Creating config.h
```

I recommend taking a few minutes to briefly look through all of these. You do not need to understand every detail of what is going on, but you should have a basic idea what they mean. Start with the Makefile in the current directory. This is the Makefile you will call make on to build the entire project. If this were not generated by autoconf, you would probably have to edit a few of the variables at the top of the file to correct the locations of files and the compiler information to properly compile. You would have to do this in the remaining Makefiles, and some programs come with an `install` or an `install.sh` script to handle the installation. Once all of the config and Makefiles are ready, it is time to compile.

Compile and Install

All of the real compile instructions are in the Makefiles, so really the compile is just running `make`. Before you compile the files though, it is often a good idea to remove all partially compiled files and existing compiled programs. This is an easy way to be certain that everything is freshly built. You do this by passing `make` an option like so:

```
# make clean
```

In the actual Makefile there will be a section labeled `clean:`. All of the commands in that section will be executed. If you looked through the Makefile earlier you probably saw many more options. It is fairly common for a Makefile to have `all`, `clean`, and `install` as options. Many other options may exist also, but these are the most common and usually the only ones needed.

To compile the actual code all you should have to do is type

```
# make
```

It should build all of the necessary files from this point and you should see screens and screens of text scrolling across your terminal window as shown in Figure 23.2. Another thing to keep an eye out for while reading the included text files is `make` options. You may need to use special options to compile the program with other language support, special graphics support, or with debugging information. Using a Makefile, all of these separate options had to be entered only once. At this point you should have an executable program and all of the necessary files, unless you had problems during the compile. I had problems with the Makefile in the `src/` subdirectory. It wanted to link a library known as `db1` that apparently does not exist on my system. If you encounter a problem like this, consult the Red Hat Web site and the site of the compiler. Someone may have encountered this problem before and have the solution posted. After reading a few sites, I began to suspect the program might not need that library, so I simply deleted all instances of `-ldb1` from the Makefile in `src/`.

23

FIGURE 23.2

Some of the output from running make.

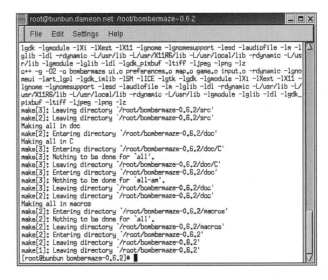

My next attempt to build the software appeared to have been successful and the program appeared to work fine later. This is not the ideal solution though. Always try to provide the software with any libraries it requests rather than trying to get it to do without. This is not a big deal for a game, but when it causes a corporate server to crash, you can bet someone will be very angry.

Now that all the source code has been compiled, it is time to install. Most of the work was done while configuring the scripts. If everything is right, you should only have to type the following:

```
# make install
```

This tells make to run the install option in the Makefile, which logically copies all of the files to the installation directory. In this case, all of the files should be installed under /usr/local/share. At this point you are ready to run most programs, unless the program has additional configuration files you must edit. Consult the documentation for this. Not every program is installed with make, however. It is common to see an install or an install-sh script to perform the task. This will vary from package to package. You will probably see a config.in script too, but that is for autoconf, not for performing the install. So are we ready to play yet? No, not just yet. This has left a little mess on the hard drive that should be cleaned up. Type in **bombermaze** and see if it works first, before you start cleaning up. Then exit the program.

Clean Up

It is always important to clean up after you build and install a program. Of course it is always a good idea to make sure the program runs before cleaning up; otherwise you may be making more work for yourself. At this point you have a bunch of partially compiled files lying around and an extra copy of the program. While these would save compile time later, they also eat quite a bit of hard drive space. There are two ways to clean up. You could run make clean to delete all of these files and leave only the source code, scripts, and documentation behind, or if you are certain you don't need the source code you can just delete all of it. Remember, you still have a copy of the tarball lying around too. If you don't see any need for it and you want to free up some space, delete it too.

Now there is only one important step left: to play Bombermaze. If everything worked correctly, you should be able to type **bombermaze** at the command line and it will run. You should see something resembling Figure 23.3. Just take a minute to set your preferences and you are off playing another extremely addictive GNOME game.

23

FIGURE 23.3
*Bombermaze is pure
counterproductive fun.*

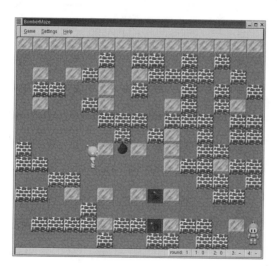

Uninstalling the Application

After playing with a piece of software for a while, you may decide that you do not like it, do not want it, or in this case, lose way too much time to it. Well you need to know how to uninstall the program. Since this is not an RPM-based install it is not a simple matter of running rpm -e. To begin, consult the documentation that came in the tarball. It may have been quite a while since you installed the program, so it is important to remember all of the details. Some packages provide an uninstall script or an option in a

Makefile. Other smaller packages just tell you to delete the program's executable. In the case of Bombermaze you use a Makefile option. To uninstall, type the following in the Bombermaze source directory:

```
# make uninstall
```

This should remove all Bombermaze-related files. But, the documentation warns it may miss the user settings files. So run a search for .gnome/bombermaze files in the user's home directories. If you do not trust make, it is also possible to manually delete all of the files. Although this can be a pain, there should be a list of all the files in the documentation, which can be used to locate and delete them.

Summary

In this hour you learned the general procedure to install packages from tarballs. You learned how to deal with problems when they occur and what to consult for information. Tarball installs just require time and patience. I encourage you to try more, but if you get frustrated, take a break. Tarball installs can be destructive if not handled properly. Now you can be proud that you have another game on your system and that you know how to install almost anything. You also know how to uninstall anything you do not like. The only thing left to do now is to explore the world of Linux and try any program you find interesting.

Workshop

The Workshop contains quiz questions and exercises to help reinforce what you've learned in this hour.

Q&A

Q Why do I need autoconf?

A Odds are you do not, unless you are creating a program to install. But, you do need a little knowledge of autoconf to know what is going on when you install tarballs that used it.

Q Will every source tarball build with gcc?

A No, there is no rule requiring programs to be built with gcc. However, gcc is immensely popular and most source tarballs will be built with it.

Q **The `configure` script failed. What do I do?**

A The `configure` script checks to see if everything necessary is available to build a program. Something probably was not available. Check the output of the script to find out what. Then locate the appropriate files, install them, and try again.

Quiz

1. If the `configure` script runs successfully, is there any need to watch for missing dependencies or programs?

2. Will there always be a `make install` option?

3. Why isn't there an RPM available for this program?

Quiz Answers

1. If the `configure` script runs successfully, is there any need to watch for missing dependencies or programs?

    `configure` is good for catching a lot of potential problems, but it is far from fool-proof. As you saw in the example in this chapter, the script ran successfully, but a problem was still encountered with a library.

2. Will there always be a `make install` option?

    There is no requirement for `make` to have an install option. Although it is quite common, it is also possible to a have an `install` or an `install-sh` script instead.

3. Why isn't there an RPM available for this program?

    The latest development version of any program will be available in tarball. It does not make sense to keep rebuilding RPMs if the package is changing every 3 or 4 days. Generally, RPMs are only made once a package is fairly stable and most of the development is done.

Exercises

1. When you have some free time, explore the program listings on GNOME site further. Pick one or two additional programs and try installing them from a tarball.

2. If you are building anything from a tarball, it is almost guaranteed you will be using `make`. So take some time to read the online documentation on `make`. A good place to start is `http://www.gnu.org/manual/manual.html`.

23

HOUR 24

Introduction to Linux Programming

In previous hours you learned where common applications are, where to locate additional applications, and how to install them. This is all fine if what you want already exists, but what happens when the application you want does not exist yet? You can't very well install an application that does not exist. That is why this hour is devoted to learning the basics of programming in Linux. Now that you know how to use Linux, why not take it to next logical step and start programming for it?

Obviously I cannot teach you all there is to know about programming for Linux in this hour, considering that it is a topic that takes up several books for each language. What I can do is point out the benefits of learning to program with Linux and the easier ways to do so. We will also look at the Linux development model. The remainder of the hour will be devoted to introducing common programming languages and the resources available for working with them.

In this hour you will

- Discover the value of Linux programming
- Understand the Open-Source Development Model
- Examine development tools such as GTK+
- Write, compile, and run simple C programs
- Write, compile, and run simple C++ programs

What Learning to Program in Linux Can Do for You

At this point you may still be wondering why learning to program for Linux is important. Programming for Linux may sound like a burden, or perhaps you just want to have a Linux server on your network. Maybe you just need to run a few applications under Linux, or maybe you have Linux running to feed a Quake addiction. The last thing on your mind is developing new software. Well, there are still plenty of good reasons to learn to program with Linux.

If you want to understand how your programs are working, you need to have a basic understanding of programming. Think about it—if you understand programming, you can download the source to any open-source Linux package and after reading through it you will understand how it works. Plus, a knowledge of Linux programming can greatly enhance your professional skills. It is also a great way to give back to the Linux community.

If you don't think it is worth your while, go on some job search sites such as http://www.monster.com and http://www.dice.com and search for Unix and Linux programming jobs. It's a safe bet that the pay and benefits will not be something to laugh at. Many companies are embracing developing products for Linux now and it is an excellent career opportunity. Also if you are a network administrator, you can customize the networking packages and write tools to aid in network maintenance. This is an age where you can get ahead by working smarter instead of harder.

The first thing that we must do, though, is get past one of the last Linux phobias: programming for Linux. For some reason many people (and many programmers, for that matter) have the impression that programming for Linux is a horrible, painful task. Actually, nothing could be further from the truth. Linux was developed by programmers fed up with existing tools, so they made a system that is easier to develop for, easier to fix, and easier to debug. The other benefit is the variety of free tools to aid in the development process. If you have ever priced Microsoft's Visual Studios or any Borland products, it is clear what a great deal these free tools are.

Understanding the Open-Source Development Model

Now that you know why learning to program with Linux is a good idea, you need to know how software is developed for Linux. A good understanding of the development model is critical if you ever want to contribute to any of the Linux development projects or develop commercial software for Linux. Even if this is only for personal use, it may still prove helpful.

Almost all noncommercial Linux software is developed under the Open-Source Development Model. This model is radically different than most existing software development processes and not only defines how to develop software, but also redefines how to think about software development. To begin with, the software license cannot restrict the redistribution of the software or the bundling of it as part of a software package. You can get as many copies for free as you want. Plus, the source code must be made available in addition to the executable program, and the source code can be modified and redistributed by anyone. Of course they are also required to make the source code available for any changes.

There are also provisions to prevent discrimination. There cannot be any restriction against specific people, uses of the product, or by software distribution. For example, a tool can not be open-source if it is only free to users of Red Hat or Debian, but no other distributions. Also, the license cannot place requirements on any other software it is distributed with.

So why is this so different? Well, suddenly software is free and you have access to the source code. You can build it, run it, or modify it as you please. Everyone interested in an open-source project has access to all code and information. Many developers would like to see this become the new standard. It has been proven to generate code with fewer bugs, and the bugs that do exist are fixed much more rapidly. However, open-source has been plagued with problems in gaining industry acceptance.

Think of trying to present this idea to the heads of a major software corporation: Give away your software for free, allow others to distribute it, and give everyone access to the code you developed. Most companies fear this would put them out of business. The current mentality is that money is made by selling the program. An open-source company would make money by providing service and support. In coming years this may cause radical changes in the software industry. To learn more about the open-source movement, visit http://www.opensource.org.

24

Linux Application Development with GTK+

Another common misconception about programming for Linux is that everything has to be built from scratch. If you are designing an application with a GUI (graphical user interface), coding buttons, windows, and other GUI items that have already been invented may seem boring and pointless. Many prefer easy drag-and-drop development environments such as Visual Basic where you only have to code the actual functionality. Although there is not a Visual Basic port available for Linux, Linux GUI development is far from developing from scratch. A plentiful supply of tools and libraries exist to aid in software development. In this hour we will look at only the GTK+ (Gimp Toolkit) development library, but there are plenty of others available. If you prefer KDE there are the QT libraries and there are still the original libraries for X11.

GTK+ provides objects and widgets that provide commonly used functionality. To get an idea of what GTK+ offers, take a look at the GNOME desktop. GNOME is an extension of GTK+. Widgets are the objects that you generally interact with in a GUI, such as buttons, scrollbars, text boxes, and so on. By using these widgets, programmers do not need to spend a great deal of time developing the actual GUI and can concentrate on the functionality of the program. Widgets provide easy access to all the commonly used graphical information. To get an idea of how much work this saves, look at the simple application in Figure 24.1.

FIGURE 24.1

A simple graphical application.

Creating a Simple Application

This application is just a window with a single button. It may seem rather trivial, but once you try to code it without using widgets, it will become apparent just how important they are. To create this simple application, you would have to follow the sequential steps that are listed below. I am not expecting you to do this task, but I wanted to show you all that is involved in creating an application.

1. Sketch an initial diagram of the window and the button, including how the button will look when up or while pressed.

2. Assign dimensions to the windows and buttons in pixels and research the low level X11 drawing routines.

3. Develop software routines to draw a button in each state and the window. You would also need a routine to draw text on the button.

4. Next, enhance the drawing routines to be able to draw at an arbitrary location on the screen and add error checking. After all, you should not be able to draw the button outside the screen.

5. Develop software routines to read system events including mouse clicks.

6. Use that code to develop code capable of processing events and determining when the mouse has been clicked while over a button drawn by the draw routines.

7. Join all the previous code in an object-oriented manner so that the button realizes it has been clicked.

8. Write a program that will create one of these windows and place a functional button on it.

9. Write the code to respond to a button click.

Not such a simple little application anymore is it? All of this would have to be done just to write an application that has a single button on the window. The following task will show you a simpler method.

Task: Creating an Application with a Widget

Since this is an interactive graphical program, most of the processing is based on events. An event is exactly what it sounds like. When something happens on the system, such as a mouse click, an event is generated. It is then processed by an event handler. With widgets, you would only be responsible for the event handler, but in the preceding example you would have to code everything. Thus, the first seven steps in the preceding list would be extremely time consuming. Most GUI software is not developed this way. Try creating this using widgets:

1. Open a new source code file and include the GTK+ libraries.

2. Create a window widget and a button widget.

3. Initialize GTK+, create the objects, and tell GTK+ to show the objects.

4. Tell GTK+ to start processing events.

5. Code the application's response to the button being clicked.

6. Go have a cup of coffee and rejoice in your programming brilliance.

Clearly this is far more practical than the first method. To see how simple this is, we will write this program. To start, open your favorite text editor and type in the code in Listing 24.1.

LISTING 24.1   A Simple Program Using GTK+ Widgets

```
/* hello world */
#include <gtk/gtk.h>

/* event handler to close window */
gint eventDestroy(GtkWidget *widget, GdkEvent *event, gpointer data)
{
  gtk_main_quit();
  return(FALSE);
}

int main(int argc, char *argv[])
{
  /* declare some widgets */
  GtkWidget *window, *button;

  /* initialize gtk+ */
  gtk_init(&argc, &argv);

  /* create widgets */
  window = gtk_window_new(GTK_WINDOW_TOPLEVEL);
  button = gtk_button_new_with_label("Hello World!");

  /* assign event handlers */
  gtk_signal_connect(GTK_OBJECT(window), "destroy",
              GTK_SIGNAL_FUNC(eventDestroy), NULL);

  /* place button on window and format window*/
  gtk_container_add(GTK_CONTAINER(window), button);
  gtk_container_set_border_width(GTK_CONTAINER(window), 20);

  /* display everything */
  gtk_widget_show(window);
  gtk_widget_show(button);

  /* begin processing events */
  gtk_main();
  return 0;
}
```

Save this file as ghello.c. Now take a minute to study the code in Listing 24.1. The #include statement will add all of the necessary GTK+ header files when you compile. Next you see an event handler declared. This is just a function that has a special format. The format for an event handler is always defined by whatever library is used for event processing. In this case the library is GTK+. All this handler does is stop the processing loop so the program can end. In the main function of the program we first see pointers to the widgets declared. Then GTK+ is initialized with a call to gtk_init(). There are quite a few things that can be done during initialization, but they are beyond the scope of this book.

After initializing GTK+, we create the window and the button widget. The event handler is then assigned to the window allowing it to be closed when the program runs. Before everything can be displayed, though, the button has to be placed on a window. Thus, the window is the button's container. Generally if a widget cannot be a container, it must be placed in a container. In most cases you will also need to configure the container, but for simplicity we are merely setting a border on the window so the button will not occupy the entire window. Once the widgets are in the widget container and the containers are configured, they can be displayed with a call to `gtk_widget_show()`. At this point all that is left is to start processing events. That begins with a call to `gtk_main()` and will be stopped when the handler calls `gtk_main_quit()`.

Compiling Complex Programs

Now that you know the basics of what is happening, it is time to compile this example and run it. You can do this using a really long `gcc` command or by using a Makefile. A fact of life you will quickly come to realize is that the more complicated and the cooler a program, the more complicated the sequence of compile commands necessary to build it. Instead of typing in the entire sequence every time, the compile commands can be placed in a Makefile and then all you have to type is **make** to build the program.

`make` is a tool that processes the specially formatted Makefiles. Although `make` is capable of doing more than compiling software, that is its primary use. So open your favorite editor and type in the Makefile given in Listing 24.2.

> `make` is very picky about tab characters. If something in the example is indented, use a tab to indent it. Otherwise, when you run `make` you will encounter some rather odd errors.

LISTING 24.2   Makefile for `ghello.c`

```
CC=gcc
LIBS=`gtk-config --libs`
FLAGS=-Wall -g `gtk-config --cflags`

ghello: ghello.o
        $(CC) $(LIBS) ghello.o -o ghello

ghello.o: ghello.c
        $(CC) $(FLAGS) -c ghello.c
```

Save this as `Makefile` in the same directory as `ghello.c`. If you take a quick look at the listing you can see that variables are declared at the top of a Makefile and the rest of the file contains a set of rules. The exact details of how all this works is well beyond the scope of this book, but if you want to learn more you can find more information on Web sites such as `http://www.cslab.vt.edu/manuals/make/make_toc.html`.

Now you are ready to build the program. At the prompt, type

```
$ make
```

If everything is correct, the program should compile successfully and you can type **ghello** on the command line to start the program. Look, it's the little application from Figure 24.1. You can play with it and resize it and so on. Granted, the button does not do anything currently, but that can be fixed by adding another event handler. It was just omitted to keep the example as simple as possible. To learn more about GTK+ go to `http://www.gtk.org`. Following is a list of a few good books out on GTK+ programming that might be of interest:

> *GNOME/GTK+ Programming Bible* by Arthur Griffith
>
> *GTK+/GNOME Application Development* by Havoc Pennington
>
> *Sams Teach Yourself GTK+ Programming in 21 Days* by Donna S. Martin

C

Now that you know about some of the tools that are available to aid in development, it is time to move onto the actual programming. And where better to begin the discussion of Linux programming than with the C language? C truly is the language of Unix. Most of the original varieties of Unix and Linux were written in C. C was originally developed by Dennis Ritchie as a successor to the B language.

Unlike the scripting languages introduced earlier in this book, C is a compiled language. That means that the code you write is parsed, analyzed, and translated into an executable machine form before execution. This is handled by a compiler such as gcc.

C programs are composed of functions. A function is a logical grouping of operations to perform a task. This could be computing an equation, printing information to the screen, or any other imaginable task. A function receives data in the form of arguments, manipulates the data, and then returns the result. When you invoke a function, it is known as *calling* the function. In addition to being called, functions can also call other functions or they can call themselves. When one function calls another, it is known as nesting. *Nesting* means that one function was executing and has paused and now another function is running inside of it. To begin, try the traditional Hello World program in Listing 24.3. Type it in with your favorite editor and save it as hello.c.

LISTING 24.3   Hello World

```
#include <stdio.h>

int main()
{
  printf("Hello World!\n");
  return 0;
}
```

Compile and execute it with the following commands:

```
$ gcc hello.c
$ ./a.out
Hello World!
$
```

24

The source code begins with a `#include` statement. This statement is used to include other source and header files when compiling. By using `#include` statements, all the code does not have to exist in a single file. The next thing in the file is `int main()`, which is the declaration of the function called `main` that returns an integer. The `main` function is a special function that every C program is required to have. It is the first function executed when a program starts. Since there is nothing between the `()`, the `main` function does not have any arguments at present. In the body of the function there is a call to `printf`, another function which tells the system to print `Hello World!` to the screen. The `\n` is a formatting character that tells `printf` to end the current line. `return 0` simply causes the function to return a value of zero. As you can see, all expressions have to be terminated with a semicolon. In this case an expression is any variable declaration, any mathematical expression, or any function call.

Hello World may prove amusing, but odds are that in order to do anything productive there will be data. So there must be a way to store that data. All data in C is stored in variables. Since C is a strongly typed language, you must declare what type of data you want to store in each variable. Some of the default variable types are short, integer, long, float, double, and char. You can also define additional data types. To declare a variable, you use the following syntax:

```
<variable type> <variable name>;
```

The variable name can be any combination of alphanumeric characters and underscores, but it cannot begin with a number. The rule of thumb is to always choose meaningful variable names. Variables can be declared in three general ways:

- `Int aNumber;`—Declares an integer variable
- `Int *aNumber;`—Declares a pointer to an integer variable
- `Int aLotOfNumbers[10];`—Declares an array of integers

Regular variables are fairly self-explanatory. Just use them in place of the desired number or letter. Pointers are a rather complicated matter and I recommend consulting a book on C programming to learn about them. Arrays are groups of data of a common type. In real life a lot of data is organized into arrays, such as student's grades and the temperatures during a week.

Now that you know how to create variables, it is time to manipulate them. All the standard operators apply and are shown in Table 24.1.

TABLE 24.1 Operators

Operator	Function
Mathematical Operators	
+	Addition
-	Subtraction
*	Multiplication
/	Division
%	Integer remainder
Comparison Operators	
<	Less than
>	Greater than
==	Equal to
<=	Less than or equal to
>=	Greater than or equal to
||	Logical OR
&&	Logical AND
!	Logical NOT
Bit Operators	
&	Bitwise AND
|	Bitwise OR
-	Negation
<<	Bit shift left
>>	Bit shift right
Assignment Operators	
=	Assign Value

At this point you can create variables and manipulate them in any way desired. But, this is still too limited to be useful. It only allows you to create code that runs straight through. Although this is fine for number crunching, it will not do for interactive programs. Odds are you want a program to do multiple tasks and you want to offer the ability to choose which task it will perform at runtime. That is why there are flow control statements. *Flow control* statements evaluate an expression and, depending on the results, decide what the program will do next. The two types of flow control statements are branching and looping. *Branching* consists of if and switch statements. The syntax of the if statement is as follows:

```
if ( expression )
        statement 1;
else
        statement 2;
```

If the expression is true, the first statement is executed; if it is false, the second statement is executed. There is no condition where both statements will be run. If you want to respond to a menu selection, a switch statement may be a better choice. The switch statement examines the expression and executes the code of whatever case matches the value of the expression. The syntax is

24

```
switch ( expression ) {
    case 1:
      statements;
    break;
    case 2:
      statements;
    break;
    default:
      statements;
    break;
}
```

This is fine if you want to execute only one piece of code or another, but if you want to repeatedly execute one segment of code you need to use looping constructs. Two of the common types of loops are the for and the while loops. A while loop repeatedly executes the block of code below it as long as the expression is true. The syntax for the while loop is as follows:v

```
while ( expression ) {
        statements;
        …
}
```

The for loop is just a special version of a while loop and it is useful when a task needs to be executed a certain number of times. It just handles counter expressions in a more convenient manner. Here is the syntax for the for loop:

```
for ( expression1; expression2; expression3 ) {
        statements;
        ...
}
```

The first expression is used to assign an initial value to a counter variable. The second expression ends the execution of the loop when it evaluates to false. The third expression is used to update the counter. To see how this works, try the example in Listing 24.4. Save it as foo.c.

LISTING 24.4   Using a for Loop

```
#include <stdio.h>

int main()
{
  int counter;

  for ( counter = 0; counter < 10; counter++ )
  {
    printf("%d ", counter);
  }
}
```

Compile and execute it with the following commands:

```
$ gcc -Wall foo.c
$ ./a.out
0 1 2 3 4 5 6 7 8 9 $
```

The program in Listing 24.4 declares an integer variable called counter and the first expression assigns counter a value of 0. Then each time through the loop it checks to see if counter is still less than 10. If it is, the loop executes and the value of counter is printed to the terminal window. After the loop statements execute, the third expression is executed, which updates the counter. This continues until counter is not less than 10 and then the loop exits.

Now you know the basic concepts of C programming, but there is still a great deal more to learn about C. If you want to learn more I recommend buying a book on C programming. There are plenty of choices available, but here are a few:

C for Dummies by Dan Gookin

The C Programming Language by Brian W. Kernighan and Dennis M. Ritchie

Sams Teach Yourself C in 21 Days by Peter Aitken and Bradley Jones

C++

It may be true that the core of Linux and most versions of Unix are written in C, but most current software development is done in C++. C++ was developed by Dr. Bjarne Stroustrup at AT&T's Bell Laboratories. C was a good choice for developing software, but its object-oriented capabilities were severely limited. As the complexity of the code grew, it became increasingly difficult to organize and track the code. At that time C code was just a collection of data variables and procedures. It was not in a form that a developer could easily relate to.

By making code object-oriented it is easier for programmers to understand. Object-oriented code organizes the procedures and variables into logical objects. Think about trying to write code to simulate a car. In C you would have a collection of variables representing the attributes of the car along with variables for the functions, and a collection of functions to simulate the various behaviors of a car. In C++ you can create a car object that stores its attributes in member variables, and all of the car's behavior is represented by member methods. In C++ it is clear what the car is and what it can do.

C++ offered support for object-oriented design and is an extension of the C language, so it is no surprise that it gained immense popularity. C++ objects are defined as classes. An object is an instance of whatever class it was declared as. To see an example of a class, look at Listing 24.5.

LISTING 24.5   A sample C++ Class

```
class Car {
public:
        char color[];
        int weight;
        int horsepower;
        void run();
        int start();
        int stop();
};
```

The example declaration of the class Car has the member's color, weight, and horsepower. It also has the methods run(), start(), and stop(). The methods are defined like regular functions and can be defined inside or outside the class declaration. Methods must be declared inside the class, however. To define a method outside a class you must use the following format:

```
<class>::<method name> ( <arguments> ) {}
```

When you want to create an instance of a class, it is declared just like any other variable. The declaration for a Car would be

```
Car myCar;
```

To access the members of a class, you use the dot operator. To "start" the car you would call

```
myCar.start();
```

You can use the g++ command to compile C++ programs. To learn more about it, read the man page. You will find it is very similar to gcc in many respects. There is a great deal more to learn about C++ and classes; however, it is beyond the scope of this book. There are many excellent books on C++ and I highly recommend that you invest in one. Here are a few good choices to begin with:

Sams Teach Yourself C++ for Linux in 21 Days by Jesse Liberty and David Horvath

Sams Teach Yourself C++ in 21 Days by Jesse Liberty

The C++ Programming Language by Bjarne Stroustrup

Other Programming Languages

Although C and C++ comprise most of the code used in Linux, they are by no means the limit of languages available. Odds are you can find a Linux compiler for almost any major programming language. For Fortran there is the g77 compiler, which should be included with the distribution. If you want support for the latest version of Java, you can go to http://www.blackdown.org/java-linux.html for the latest port of the Java SDK. If you want support for any other language, start by searching the Red Hat documentation and the Internet for the available compilers.

Summary

In this hour you learned why you should learn more about programming. You now know the basics of C and C++ and where to learn more. You also know about GTK+ and how graphical libraries can help you develop software. Obviously, this chapter will not turn you into a software developer, but you can walk away with the knowledge of where to find out more.

Workshop

The Workshop contains quiz questions and exercises to help reinforce what you've learned in this hour.

Q&A

Q Where is more information on gcc?

A Start by reading the gcc man pages, then look through other documentation. gcc is a very complicated compiler and the best thing to do is read the most current documentation available on it when you have a task to perform.

Q Do C and C++ have any standards?

A Yes, both C and C++ have an ANSI (American National Standards Institute) standard that defines the language. This is another good Web search to do on a rainy day.

Q Why am I getting strange errors when I run `make`?

A Make sure all indents are done with tabs. `make` is very picky about formatting, so make sure you follow the format.

Quiz

1. What tools should you use if you have a very complex compile to perform?
2. Where are examples of GTK+ programs?

Quiz Answers

1. What tools should you use if you have a very complex compile to perform?

   The `make` tool will handle even the most complex compiles involving hundreds of source files.

2. Where are examples of GTK+ programs?

   GNOME is derived from GTK+, so take a look at your favorite GNOME applications to learn more about GTK+ programming. You can also go to `http://www.gtk.org`.

Exercises

1. After you have read a little more on GTK+, try adding an event handler for the button in the simple widget program we made earlier. Also, experiment with adding GTK+ widgets. It is always nice to have a little sample program to study new widgets on.

2. Find a simple GNOME game you like. Download the source code for it and read through the source. You don't have to understand everything, but it is a good thing to do as you learn to program. As your programming skills improve, try making small changes to the program.

24

INDEX

Other Related Titles

Red Hat Linux 7 Unleashed
William Ball
ISBN: 0-672-31985-3
$49.99 USA/$74.95 CAN

Sams Teach Yourself Linux in 24 Hours, Third Edition
Craig and Coletta Witherspoon
0-672-31993-4
$24.99 USA/$37.95 CAN

Installing SuSE Linux
John Scroggins
0-672-31832-6
$24.99 USA/$37.95 CAN

Sams Teach Yourself WordPerfect Office 2000 for Linux in 24 Hours
Alan Golub and Judith Samson
0-672-31911-X
$24.99 USA/$37.95 CAN

Sams Teach Yourself GNOME in 24 Hours
Judith Samson
0-672-31714-1
$24.99 USA/$37.95 CAN

Linux Hardware Handbook
Roderick Smith
ISBN: 0-672-31918-7
$39.99 USA/$59.95 CAN

Maximum Linux Security
Anonymous
ISBN: 0-672-31670-6
$39.99 USA/$59.95 CAN

SAMS
www.samspublishing.com

All prices are subject to change.

What's on the Discs

The companion CD-ROMs contain Red Hat Linux 7, Publisher's Edition.

Installing Red Hat Linux from the CD-ROM

1. Insert the installation disc (Disc 1) in the CD drive.
2. Restart your computer.
3. You may need to change your BIOS settings to boot from the CD-ROM. Typically, you enter your BIOS setup program with the F2 or DEL keys during the boot sequence.
4. Make your changes (if any) and exit the BIOS setup utility.
5. If your CD drive is capable of booting from CD-ROMs, you will boot into the Red Hat Linux setup program.
6. Follow the onscreen prompts to complete the installation.

Installing Red Hat Linux from Boot floppies

1. Using DOS or Windows, format one 1.44MB floppy disk.
2. Navigate to the DOSUTILS directory on the installation disc (Disc 2).
3. Double-click on RAWRITE.EXE or type RAWRITE from a DOS Prompt.
4. When prompted to do so, type in the name ..\IMAGES\BOOT.IMG and press <ENTER>.
5. When prompted to do so, type in the drive letter of the disk(s) you are going to prepare and press <ENTER>. Since you are going to be booting from this disk, it's typically A:.
6. If you don't already have the boot floppy in your disk drive, insert it now.
7. Restart your computer.
8. You may need to change your BIOS settings to boot from the floppy drive. Typically, you enter your BIOS setup program with the F2 or DEL keys during the boot sequence.
9. Make your changes (if any) and exit the BIOS setup utility.
10. If your computer is set up properly, you will boot into the Red Hat Linux setup program.
11. Follow the onscreen prompts to complete the installation.